HOW TO BE
SUCCESSFUL
IN THE
ANTIQUE
BUSINESS

HOW TO BE SUCCESSFUL IN THE

ANTIQUE BUSINESS

REVISED EDITION

A COMPLETE GUIDE TO OPENING AND RUNNING YOUR OWN ANTIQUE SHOP

Ronald S. Barlow

CHARLES SCRIBNER'S SONS
New York

Copyright © 1979, 1980, 1981 by Ronald S. Barlow

Library of Congress Cataloging in Publication Data

Barlow, Ronald S.
  How to be successful in the antique business.

  Bibliography: p.
  Includes index.
    1. Secondhand trade—United States—Handbooks, manuals, etc.   2. Sell-
ing—Antiques—Handbooks, manuals, etc.   I. Title
HF5482.B37   1981   745.1'068'8   81–4672
ISBN 0–684–16985–1   AACR2

1 3 5 7 9 11 13 15 17 19 Y/C 20 18 16 14 12 10 8 6 4 2

Printed in the United States of America

*Jacket photographs courtesy of Fred and Joanne Cadarette, Country Antiques,
Pittsfield, N.H.*

*All photographs and illustrations not otherwise credited are from the author's col-
lection.*

CONTENTS

INTRODUCTION

Although this book is written primarily for the American collector who dreams of opening an antique shop, it will be an important reference for anyone who purchases antiques. Where and how the dealer buys—the tips, traps, and pitfalls—are all gleaned from insiders in the trade.

The antique business is not nearly as sophisticated or sedate as you might assume from the image projected in some magazines. Those few dealers who look down their noses at customers are most likely to be comfortably covered by a bundle of inherited wealth or some other secure situation. The commercial dealer whose income depends solely on his or her business really has to hustle! This book addresses that reality.

Currently some 35,000 auctioneers, promoters, and full-time antique dealers share a market pie estimated at over $12 billion a year. Add to these statistics the myriad of part-time dealers who operate from stalls and spaces in over 1,000 weekend flea markets, and you have a fair idea of the competition one might be facing.

On the bright side is the phenomenal growth of the marketplace at large. It is the consensus among veteran observers that the whole world has entered into the first stages of an unprecedented collecting boom. *Time, Newsweek, Barron's, Business Week,* and the *Wall Street Journal* are but a few of the "smart money" publications whose coverage attests to the burgeoning popularity of antiques among many sophisticated investors.

Just where you might fit into the spectrum of opportunity is a question that perhaps this book can answer. Strong aptitude and financial backing are important, but an inclination toward hard work and serious study can also be one's ticket to independence.

Are you really the horse trader you think you are?

Chapter 1

TO THINE OWN SELF BE TRUE

Are You Really a Horse Trader?

Einstein once said, "Ordinary life in an ordinary place on an ordinary day in the modern world is a dreary business. I mean DREARY! People will do anything to escape this dreariness!" The antique business attracts its share of people who are bored with the ordinary life. I won't take up a lot of space to tell you how "happy" and "well adjusted" most antique dealers are, but it is safe to say that those who survive are rarely tempted to enter any other field of endeavor. Retired antique dealers are as rare as hen's teeth. They not only find it difficult to amass enough capital on which to retire, but they frequently find it emotionally impossible to quit the trade. As long as a gold miner has a grubstake, he keeps on searching. So it is in this fascinating quest for above-ground treasure. I recently interviewed a ninety-year-old "retired" dealer (at a swap meet) and he suggested that I would be wasting my time writing this book. "Nobody on the outside would ever believe that you could buy something in the morning for $5 and sell it that afternoon for $500," he lamented. Well, this doesn't happen every morning, but it does happen often enough to keep the adrenaline flowing.

Before you give your employer two weeks' notice and rush out to buy a gold pan, take a moment to think about your reasons for wanting to open an antique shop. The necessary personal qualifications for entering the antique business are basically no different than those for starting any other retail business venture. The motivations are sundry; but for most potential entrepreneurs self-employment becomes a necessity—they are driven to it! I read recently that twenty-five million Americans change jobs every year. Four out of five workers are unhappy in their employment situations, and most men change professions three or four times in a lifetime. With today's options, nobody should feel chained to a job.

If you are apprehensive about making the big leap, go to a professional psychologist and ask for a business aptitude test. Above all, be honest with yourself. Were you the boy or girl on your block with the most comic books, movie star cards, bottle caps, and other juvenile trading commodities? Did you acquire your adult collection by way of hard bargaining and advantageous trading, or were you content to pay the going price to get what you wanted? If you're not a shrewd bargainer, keep on collecting, but leave full-time antique dealing to others.

Antique dealers are a diverse group of highly individual operators. Some keep regular hours, while others are rarely to be found in their shops. Some have elaborate store fronts, while others have never found time to put up a sign. Ask any ten dealers what they were doing for a living prior to entering the trade and you will get ten different answers. The only generalization which I would venture to make of the entire group is that most of them would rather be out buying antiques than eating or sleeping. Buying is the emotional high! Selling is something you have to do to get more money with which to buy. Exhaustive knowledge of antiques is not nearly so important as an inborn aptitude for shrewd buying.

We interviewed hundreds of dealers from coast to coast, looking for a common denominator. Several neophyte traders were men in their late fifties who had suffered heart attacks (or felt that they were heading for one). Many were the wives of disabled wage earners. The men seemed to be the finders, or pickers, while the women generally were found in the shops—often running them in conjunction with a household. A number of dealers were college dropouts who found hustling for a living at swap meets and shows more fun than a dull office job (or standing in unemployment lines). Most of the auctioneers we met had worked for another auction house before striking out on their own. Generally, the antique dealers we interviewed had no previous experience in the trade. Surprisingly enough, they all seemed to have fallen into the business. (When you stop to think about it, how many kids do you know who say, "I am going to be an antique dealer when I grow up"?)

It would be reassuring to many readers if we could list some hard and fast personal qualifications necessary for success in the antique business, but the only authoritative statements we plan to make are in the areas of retail business administration and sources of merchandise. Obviously, a background in the arts is going to be an aid in decorating the shop and choosing tasteful merchandise, but not everyone is going to appreciate *your taste.* Mechanics and craftsmen are going to have an advantage over the "all thumbs" crowd, but then again, they may waste a lot of time fixing when they should be out finding. Bright, sensitive, intelligent individuals from all walks of life will naturally succeed, you say? Not necessarily true in the small business world! We have seen plodding pedestrian types grow rich where aggressive, creative, confident people have failed.

Chapter 2
GETTING A "DEGREE" IN ANTIQUES

Where to Study in Your Own Hometown

The University of Delaware recently announced a doctorate program in the history of American civilization, with a special emphasis on American material life (antiques). Other colleges and universities have experimented with programs related to the antique trade. A Valuation Science degree is offered by a network of schools including Hofstra University, Loretto Heights College, Pepperdine University, Skidmore College, and South West Texas University. This program is sponsored by the American Society of Appraisers, and information regarding classes that might be offered in your area can be obtained by writing the A.S.A. at Dulles International Airport, P. O. Box 17265, Washington, DC 20041. Business schools, trade magazines, and dealer associations also conduct seminars, forums, and retreats for collectors and investors from coast to coast.

Sotheby Parke Bernet Auction Galleries in London has, in the recent past, offered a two-year apprenticeship program in England that included actual behind-the-scenes working experience in many phases of its fine art and antique business. Not many of us can afford a substantial tuition fee plus two years' room and board in London, but we can study the actual sale catalogs of this worldwide auction firm. They are obtainable by annual paid subscription (or priced individually) from Sotheby's offices in London, New York, or Los Angeles (see page 9 for the New York address).

Chances are that a college or adult school in your area offers some courses in Antique Appreciation or Art History. These are worthwhile subjects, but this type of study is likely to remain largely academic in its approach to the antique business. After all, how many successful dealers are going to step up to the rostrum and shout their hard-earned knowledge to the world? It's kind of like telling everybody in town where your favorite fishing hole is located and just what kind of bait to use for best results. When it gets down to the wire, experience is the best teacher! The shortest road to broad realistic experience in the actual buying and selling of antiques is auction sale attendance. Looking at antique shop inventories and frequenting shows is profitable, but the real "Quick Market Value" of most art and antiques is ultimately determined by auction. There are no museums or dealer showrooms where one can personally examine as many antiques or have the opportunity to speak with as many experts as in the nation's auction halls. The "retail" antique market is also governed, to a very great degree, by the fall of the auctioneer's hammer. Almost every antique tabloid or price guide on the market today is filled with the latest auction prices realized. News in the trade travels quickly. Each important new auction high (or low) can preclude a rush to reprice, or snap up, existing merchandise in shops throughout the land. Auctions have long been a primary stock source for antique dealers everywhere. Some auctioneers limit their direct mail advertising to dealers only, knowing that they will have plenty of active bidding if only a handful of serious buyers are present.

Many beginners are unaware that regular auctions are conducted several days, or nights, each week in most cities or counties throughout the land. You don't have to rush off across the country looking for antiques to resell. They are to be found at local events. Look in the Yellow Pages of both city and outlying county area phone books for the names and addresses of auctioneers. Write to them and request that your name be placed on their mailing lists for all future sales. Also, write or phone county officials for information regarding Sheriff's or Public Administrator's Auction Sales. Watch the classified section of local and out-of-town newspapers for weekend announcements of upcoming auction sales (don't overlook household, farm, or factory sales as sources for old furniture, antiques, and collectibles).

Sotheby Parke Bernet and Christie's—Newsmaking Auction Prices. The world's two leading auction firms often generate spectacular auction prices through their important sales. Both of these famous houses were founded in England in the middle

1700s and have found their way to our shores in more recent times. They have major showrooms in London and New York, as well as a chain of representatives and smaller salesrooms throughout the world. Many foreign sellers continue to favor the London salesrooms for consigning their finest properties, but the New York market is catching up rapidly.

A list of Christie's catalogs may be obtained from 502 Park Avenue, New York, NY 10022. Below is a listing of a few of those available by yearly subscription at the time of this writing.

19th Century Continental and Topographical Paintings—$45

Old Master, Modern, and Contemporary Prints—$45

Jewelry—$70

American Paintings, Drawings, and Sculpture (to circa 1945)—$30

Impressionist and Modern Paintings, Drawings, and Sculpture—$70

Silver—$35

Books, Manuscripts, and Autograph Letters—$40

Chinese Ceramics, Bronzes, Works of Art, and Archaic Jades—$45

French and Continental Furniture, Objects of Art, and
 Tapestries—$30
Continental Porcelain—$20
Art Nouveau and Art Deco—$55
Ethnographica, Primitive, and Tribal Art—$20
Eastern and European Rugs, Carpets, and Textiles—$20
Miniatures, Gold Boxes, Russian Works of Art, and Objects
 of Vertu—$25
Photographic Images—$20

Sotheby's (at 980 Madison Avenue, New York, NY 10021) recently published a list of their catalogs that included *postsale
prices* and a bimonthly newsletter (as well as major relevant sale
catalogs from Los Angeles). Some of the titles were:

European Impressionist and Modern Paintings, Drawings,
 and Sculpture—$95
European Old Master Paintings and Drawings—$35
American Furniture and Decorative Arts—$75
Jewelry—$95
American Representational Paintings, Drawings, and
 Sculpture—$50
European and American Prints—$60
19th and 20th Century Photographs and Photographic
 Material—$25
Stamps—$25
Books, Manuscripts, and Autographs—$40
Early Chinese Works of Art—$55
European Ceramics—$40
Pre-Columbian Art—$20
Early European Furniture and Works of Art—$25
Art Nouveau, Art Deco, and Other Modern Furniture and
 Decorative Arts—$40
(catalogs for individual sales are not as expensive)

You don't have to be a bonafide buyer to attend an auction,
but it helps you to learn faster if you are prepared to risk a dollar
or two in the quest of knowledge. It is very important that you
attend the "preview showing," which is usually held the day or

hour before the actual auction. With pencil in hand, walk down the aisles examining each piece carefully. You are looking for damage or irregularities which can only be detected by an unhurried scrutiny at all available angles! Most sophisticated dealers carry a flashlight, magnifying glass, penknife, and magnet to these events.

After a careful examination of each item, write down in the auction catalog, or a notebook, *the retail price* that you would expect to pay in an antique shop for a similar item (if you don't know, guess). As the auction proceeds, write down the actual prices realized next to your presale estimates. Over a period of months, you will develop an invaluable price guide to antiques in your immediate area. This record will also help you to "buy right" privately. Why pay the local picker $35 for a stoneware crock that goes consistently at auction for $20? On the other hand, you might be only too happy to give him $100 for a good primitive portrait, knowing that it is unavailable for three times that price at auction.

AUCTION BUYING TIPS FROM A PROFESSIONAL PICKER

- *Do not exceed your predetermined maximum bid* (a little less than half of retail on all but the most desirable items).
- *Do not bid on any item that you have not personally examined* (otherwise you are buying blindfolded).
- *Don't believe anything anyone says at an auction* (they have their own interests at heart).
- *Don't believe the auctioneer* (he might own the merchandise).
- *Don't pay any attention to what known dealers are willing to bid* (they may not be buying for resale)!
- *Get in on the bidding early.* The auctioneer appreciates prompt opening bids and you also will have gained his attention. Late bidders are often overlooked or ignored.
- *Don't be afraid to buy a lot of stuff if the price is right!* There are haulers at most auctions or trailer rental firms nearby, and some auction houses will temporarily store your purchases.

American Antiques.   If you are interested in primarily American antiques, Garths Auctions at 2690 Stratford Road, Delaware,

OH 43015, offers its season's catalogs at $25 per year, with postsale prices. If autographs are of interest to you, Charles Hamilton Galleries at 25 East 77th Street, New York, NY 10021, offers a season's ten catalogs for $34. California Book Auction Galleries at 358 Golden Gate, San Francisco, CA 94102, is the West Coast's oldest auction house specializing in books, prints, posters, photographs, and Western Americana. It offers a set of twelve catalogs for $35, including postsale prices. If you are an advanced doll collector, you will be interested in the fine catalogs produced by Theriault Auctions, Box 174, Waverly, PA 18471. Many dealers who become full-time appraisers subscribe to dozens of auction catalogs a year in order to keep abreast of the booming market for art and Americana. Public libraries in most major cities subscribe to a worldwide selection of auction catalogs; they usually are kept under lock and key. Ask your librarian for available information.

Last, but Not Least, Are the "Catalogs of Catalogs." These yearly auction record books are huge volumes of prices realized in the worldwide auction market for specific categories of antiques. One of the largest-selling price guides of this type is *Lyle's Review* (at Glenmayne, Galashiels, Selkirkshire TD13PT, Scotland), which is very popular in America as well as in Great Britain. Apollo Books, of Poughkeepsie, NY 12601, markets it in the United States at about $16. *The Lyle Review of Antiques* for 1980 contained more than 670 pages and 6,000 illustrated entries covering 250 categories of collecting. Its *Arts Review* for the same year contained 478 pages with more than 5,000 prices of paintings, drawings, watercolors, and prints. Illustrated were 2,000 of the works sold at more than 50 worldwide auction houses during the year.

For $125 you can own the *Art Sales Index.* This excellent two-volume set offers the most complete record of paintings sold throughout the United States and the world. Included are the results from over 1,300 international art auctions. United States auctions covered are: Butterfield & Butterfield of San Francisco; both Christie's and Sotheby's of New York; Weschler in Washington, DC; Morton's in New Orleans; Freeman's of Philadelphia; and Eldred's, Skinner's, and Bourne of Massachusetts. About 20,000 important artists are listed along with 66,000 prices. The publisher, Richard Hislop, an English computer accountant, also offers a printout service (much like Standard & Poor's stock market charts) on the sales history of any given artist's works. Hislop currently keeps tabs on more than 40,000 artists of merit. You can write to him for information about his computer service at: Art Sales Indep. Ltd., Pond House, Weybridge, Surrey, England. (His yearbook is also sold in the United States by Apollo Book Co.)

Before we leave the subject of authoritative price guides we should mention the *Benezit Dictionary of Artists*. This ten-volume set (French text) is *the criterion* for establishing an artist's worth in the marketplace. Not that you are going to buy a set ($400), but you should know that most large libraries and art galleries own one. The latest edition contains 7,800 pages, lists 300,000 names (as well as photos of some signatures), and indicates the actual prices at which the artist's works have changed hands. The more lengthy the biographical material, the more valuable a listed artist's works are likely to be.

These price guides are not infallible, but if you find the "average" works of a particular artist, in a specific medium such as oil painting, selling in a narrow price range at several auctions, you might feel reasonably assured that his comparable works would be worth as much if offered to a similar audience under similar conditions. The exception is that if one or two wealthy collectors or museum buyers drop out of the market for a given artist's work, it can plummet drastically, never again to return to its previous high!

Before you spend your entire "educational" budget on auction catalogs, we urge you to subscribe to at least a half dozen of the inexpensive periodicals privy to the antique and collector trade. The quickest way to learn the sources of any retail business is to subscribe to its trade publications.

News about British Antiques. In England, there are several newspapers and magazines that are primarily aimed at the antique trade. These weekly or monthly tabloids carry advertisements and announcements from dealers, auction firms, show promoters, shipping and packing specialists, exporters, importers, and reproduction manufacturers. They are a gold mine of information for any prospective dealer who plans to buy or sell

Courtesy Tom Warren

antiques in Great Britain. The *Antiques Trade Gazette* is published weekly by Metropress Ltd., Langley House, 116 Long Acre, London WC2E 9PA, England (send $1 postage for a sample copy). *Antiques & Art Weekly* is another trade-oriented publication from England; 57 percent of its readership earns a living from art and antiques. A six-month subscription is about $20 from Independent Magazines Limited, Bridge House, 181 Queen Victoria Street, London EC4V 4DD, England.

News about American Antiques. The most widely read trade weekly in the United States is the *Antique Trader Weekly*. This general-interest collector tabloid is filled with thousands of buy-and-sell advertisements for everything from stuffed aardvarks to zithers. There are more sophisticated publications in the field, but the *Antique Trader Weekly* is the Bible of the general-line antique business! Almost every company even remotely interested in popular antiques or collectibles advertises in the pages of this 100,000-plus circulation newspaper. Fifty-two issues are $19 per year. Write for a 75-cent sample copy to: *Antique Trader Weekly,* P. O. Box 1050, Dubuque, IA 52001.

At the other end of the spectrum is the fifty-year-old *Magazine Antiques.* Prices are rarely quoted in this prestigious publication (the connotation being that if you have to ask, you probably can't afford). Editorial content is unsurpassed, and only the finest in American furniture and art are featured in every museum-quality issue. Address inquiries to: *Magazine Antiques*, 551 Fifth Avenue, New York, NY 10017. Two other monthlies aimed at the upper-income collector are: *Antiques World*, 122 East 42nd Street, New York, NY 10017, and *Art & Antiques*, 1515 Broadway, New York, NY 10036. These three magazines reach a combined circulation of about 200,000 well-heeled investors every thirty days.

Don't be misled by the regional sounding title of the *Maine Antique Digest*. These people are really on top of the nationwide market for Americana! Every important auction, show, or sale gets in-depth exposure and a pragmatic "dollars-and-cents analysis" by the enthusiastic editor and his staff. The photographs and dealer advertisements here are of the highest quality, and priced captions are rarely missing. Each issue is an armchair journey into the exciting active market for authentic American antiques. Send $1 for a sample copy to: *Maine Antique Digest*, Box 358, Waldoboro, ME 04572.

If fine furniture, Americana, museum news, auction results, and wide coverage of antique-oriented social events are your primary interests, we heartily recommend the sophisticated newspaper *Antique Monthly*. Within its colorful pages you will find advertisements from the nation's most prestigious auction firms and furniture and carpet dealers. A paid circulation of more than 80,000 subscribers attests to the active market for fine antiques in America today. For a sample copy send $1 to: *Antique Monthly*, P. O. Box 2274, Birmingham, AL 35201.

A timely, fact-filled weekly that focuses on the auctions, shows, and flea markets of New England and the Middle Atlantic states is *Antiques and the Arts Weekly*, a veritable bulletin board of the trade. (Hundreds of photos and prices abound in every issue.) Send 35 cents plus postage for a hefty 100-page sample to: Bee Publishing Co., Newtown, CT 06470.

Covering the collectibles' market in the Far West is a very colorful tabloid called the *American Collector*. Many of the offbeat or "pop" collectibles, overlooked by traditional antique publications, are featured in depth in this monthly, which is written with a decidedly "human interest" slant. Sample copies are available for $1 from: *American Collector*, Drawer C, Kermit, TX 79745.

Midwestern dealers and investors keep tabs on the auction market for better quality items through the pages of *Antique & Collectors Mart,* emanating from 15100 West Kellogg Street, Wichita, KS 67235 (sample copy $1.25).

The *Ohio Antique Review* does not limit its excellent reporting to shows and exhibits in Ohio—also covered are the states of Pennsylvania, New York, Michigan, Illinois, West Virginia, and Indiana. You will find the show coverage, written from a decidedly dealer slant, stimulating. Send $1 for a sample of this monthly to: *Ohio Antique Review,* P. O. Box 538, Worthington, OH 43085.

Another interesting monthly newspaper covers the national market for all sorts of collectibles. *Collectors News* is just what the title indicates; if it's being bought, sold, or traded by antiquers, you will find it here! Stamps, coins, firearms, postcards, books, autographs, sheet music, furniture, and genealogy are all regular features in this informative periodical. (Some dealers subscribe just to read the "wanted" advertisements, which completely fill the first six pages.) Send $1 for a sample copy to: *Collectors News,* 606 Eighth Avenue, Grundy Center, IA 50638.

For doll lovers and art glass connoisseurs, the venerable publication *Hobbies Magazine* is a must. Each thick issue contains thousands of advertisements for everything from vintage phonograph records to autographs and seashells. It's hard to imagine a more exhaustive coverage of the hobby of collecting. Write to: *Hobbies,* 1006 South Michigan Avenue, Chicago, IL 60605.

Last, but not least, is *Art & Auction,* published ten times a year by the Auction Guild. It contains all of the inside news (and titillating gossip) of the important auction houses, both here and abroad, and is a must for anyone who plans to consign goods to the world market. It offers lots of photos and prices—everything from vintage cars and airplanes to art, autographs, coins, stamps, and diamonds. A sample magazine, for $3.50, may be obtained by writing to: *Art & Auction,* 250 West 57th Street, New York, NY 10019.

If you want to deal in out-of-print or antiquarian books, the trade publication of the specialist book field is *AB Bookman's Weekly.* Over 9,000 book dealers, librarians, collectors, editors, book scouts, and publishers look to *Bookman's Weekly* for both

"For Sale" and "Wanted" titles. Many mail-order book dealers, or pickers called "scouts," derive a major portion of their income from the contacts within the trade that this weekly provides. (It's not cheap, but one sale could pay for the year's fifty-two issues at about $35.) Write to: *AB Bookman's Weekly,* P. O. Box AB, Clifton, NJ 07015. (Sample copies are $3 each.)

The stamp and coin trades have similar publications, which you can preview at local stamp and coin shops before subscribing. The bible of the gun trade is *Shotgun News,* or maybe you would like to subscribe to the (3,000 circulation) magazine *North American Decoys.* We could give an endless list of specialist publications; there is even one for collectors of World War I airplanes. The important thing is to convey to you that there is an active market out there for anything old and rare. You must expose any important finds to more than a local audience. To find the right trade publication or collector's tabloid for your specialized ad, consult either the *Ayer Directory* or *Ulrich's Periodical Directory* at the local library, or order sample copies of all the tabloids on the preceding pages (ask for an advertising rate card).

We once purchased a set of Rookwood dinnerware from a dealer in a country town. She knew what she had, but couldn't find any buyers at more than the $50 we gave her. After a year in our shop priced at $500, the set still had not been exposed to a real Rookwood collector. A $9.50 nationwide ad in the *Antique Trader* brought in letters and phone calls from a dozen serious bidders and the dinnerware was quickly sold to an Arizona dealer for over $750. (He broke the set up and sold each piece separately at shows throughout the country, eventually *doubling* his investment.) A gold mine doesn't have to be a hole in the ground. The broader your knowledge is of the entire field of collecting, the more apt you are to strike it rich. (You might even survive as an antique dealer if you read enough.)

Price Guides.   A retail merchant knows just what any product he purchases is going to sell for before he buys it! How does an antique dealer gain the same knowledge without a current sales catalog, or years of buying and selling experience? How can a novice buy for half of retail if he or she doesn't know the true retail price at which the "bread and butter" items move? "Show" prices are misleading at best, and many times shop prices are a third higher than the dealer will actually settle for. Antique "price guides" may fill this experience gap.

The most common mistake novice dealers make is to overpay for their initial stock. Another frequent error is a tendency toward underpricing some of the finer things that may have come out of one's personal collection—perhaps purchased several years back.

We all can learn from our mistakes, but for only a few dollars you may obtain a good basic library of value guides which will be of great assistance in eliminating potentially costly errors.

Suppose you have only been open for a day or two and in walks a pleasant woman with a worn-out hatbox full of dusty things from her deceased aunt's estate. She is trying to raise enough money to buy her daughter a piano, and is selling off the "less valuable" things first. What would you pay for the contents of this box?

- A five-by-seven-inch painting on a china plate signed Wagner and marked KPM
- An old wooden box camera with an unmarked brass lens and a stained developing tank built into the rear of the box
- A dusty copy of *Camera Works* magazine
- A rolled-up paper birth certificate dated 1825, hand lettered, and decorated in watercolors with a few bright tulips and green grapes
- A small black coffeepot with dull glaze over all and impressed Wedgwood on the bottom
- A shaving mug market R. S. Prussia, with a mirror base

DEALER: "Well, let's see. You have just six items here, Ma'am. . . . Ah . . . hmmm . . . would $60 be in the ball park?"
SHE: "No, Jane's Junque, down the street, has already offered me $250!"
DEALER: "Well, Jane is probably after that old coffeepot; Wedgwood is quite collectible! Let me know what you have for sale next time around, and thanks again for showing me this stuff."

About lunchtime you lock up and wander over to Jane's to see if she really thinks she can turn a profit on that expensive ($250) box of junk. She's on the phone to Sotheby's New York. They have just given her a minimum presale auction estimate on the whole lot of $8,900 subject to a closer inspection! (Jane hasn't been at this business much longer than you. How did she know what a bunch of sleepers she had there?) "Just a wild hunch," Jane says with a wink. As you turn, red faced, to leave, you notice a row of about three dozen colorful paper-backed books stacked on the shelf beside her desk. Most of the titles begin with the words "price guide."

Ten years ago there were only two popular antique price guides on the market. They were the pioneer efforts of a couple of farsighted dealer/collectors who were content with just breaking even on the first few editions. Today, there are hundreds of price guides available to collectors of everything from barbed wire to bottle openers. Those first two authors are both alive and well. Their price guides are now well past the twelfth printing with completely updated prices and new listings each year—sales to date, over one million copies each. A list of popular reference books and price guides appears in Selected Reading Material, on pages 223–41.

The dangers of relying upon only one or two price guide references to establish the market value of any antique are self-evident. *Where* was the item offered for sale—at a show, auction, or shop? In *what section of the country* did it actually sell? *What condition* was it in? *Was it of the period,* or an early reproduction? The most important use of price guides is to make sure that you don't "give" anything away (or grossly overpay for items you are not familiar with). Once you have identified an object and have a rough idea of its value, you are forewarned and forearmed to deal with advanced collectors or "specialist" dealers of that item. In the case of Jane's Junque, she knew, after consulting a guide or two, that she had something worth calling to the attention of an important auction house.

We own about a dozen "general" price guides, in addition to at least twenty-five specialized ones that deal in specific areas such as rare books, firearms, pocket watches, stamps, coins, glassware, Early American and Victorian furniture, silver, pottery, prints, toys, dolls, vintage cameras, and photographs.

Fire fighting toys sold at Parke Bernet PB-84 auction. Courtesy Maine
Antique Digest

These are areas of great diversity, and many priced and illustrated examples are very helpful. For instance, you don't have to look very far in a Scott's *Standard Postage Stamp Catalog* to discover that older unused U.S. stamps in the higher denominations are rarities. A quick look at a photographica—vintage photographs and cameras—guide will likewise inform you that outdoor and occupational images are scarce and that cowboys, Indians, miners, and shady ladies bring top prices.

Since there are hundreds of price guides currently on the market, one must exercise a great degree of caution in selecting practical guides that are not hastily printed compilations of ambiguous prices (a large percentage currently are).

Ask specialist dealers to recommend a favorite reference book or price guide. Examine book advertisements closely for a statement by the publisher as to the actual number of pages and illustrations. Many "official" price guides contain less than a hundred pages of outdated prices and a few blurry illustrations. Look for at least three favorable book reviews of a given title by antique and collector publications. Pick up several back issues of popular price guides. Never rely solely on the latest edition.

Many veteran dealers are quick to ridicule *all* price guides (and their readers). Just smile and buy the sleepers right out of their showcases! Remember that broad knowledge is the shovel of success in today's garden of antiques. You can't own too many good reference books or subscribe to too many collector publications.

The following is a recommended "price guide" library for the *novice dealer* in antiques and collectibles:

1. *Kovels' Complete Antiques Price List.* An annual price guide with 500 illustrations and current prices asked for 45,000 items. (Try to obtain a few back issues of this one.) Crown Publishers, New York, NY 10016.
2. *Antiques and Their Current Prices* by Edwin G. Warman. This 25-year-old publication (now in its 15th printing) is another widely quoted checklist for dealers and collectors. E. G. Warman Publishing Co., Uniontown, PA 15401.
3. *The Current Antique Furniture Style and Price Guide* by George Grotz. Over 1,000 prices and photographs of dealer wares

and auction offerings. Doubleday and Co., Garden City, NY 11530.

4. *Pictorial Price Guide to American Antiques* by Dorothy Hammond. The 5,000 items priced are all illustrated by photographs and keyed to the states where offered. E. P. Dutton Publishing Co., 2 Park Avenue, New York, NY 10016.

5. *The Antique Trader Quarterly Price Guide to Antiques.* This inexpensive magazine-size guide comes out four times a year and is available at many antique shops or directly from the Babka Publishing Company, Dubuque, IA 52001. (Also, try to obtain several back issues of this one.)

6. *The Used Book Price Guide* by Mandeville. This expensive three-volume set (about $84) is indispensable to anyone who has an opportunity to buy old books on a regular basis. The set contains 1,224 pages with 114,000 entries of retail prices asked by book dealers all over the nation. It is available only from the publishers at 525 Kenmore Street, Kenmore, WA 98028.

It is a good idea to keep a couple of general price guides in your automobile glove compartment. Many great bargains have been passed up by overcautious dealers only a few miles from home.

A word of advice to new dealers: don't pay more than a third of the guidebook price for any expensive items that you are not familiar with reselling, and be sure to find at least three references to purported value before applying this formula. We learned the hard way . . . buying a group of signed Russian samovars at "one-half of price guide" and finding them unsalable at any price locally.

Courtesy Tom Warren

Chapter 3
TWO OUT OF THREE FAIL

How to Project a Profit or Loss

Did you know that only *one out of every ten* new business ventures is what the Small Business Administration terms "very successful"? Another *two out of this ten* are termed "moderately successful," and the remaining 70 percent either go broke or struggle along for years, their owners barely making minimum hourly wages!

Two Out of Three Fail.   In the critical first twenty-four months of operation, two out of three, or 66 percent, of all new businesses either fail or are dissolved. Most of these failures can be traced to mismanagement; about a third of them stem from undercapitalization—you can't sell much from an empty wagon! Remember that the two most indispensable ingredients for success are adequate working capital and a firm set of plans to achieve your goal. High hopes and wishful thinking are not tangible business assets.

Partnerships Can Cause Problems.   The first thought that pops into almost anyone's mind after deciding to go into business is a suitable "partner." Don't feel guilty; it's a natural inclination to want to share the joys and responsibilities of starting a new business venture with a friend. But according to statistics, you may soon become bitter enemies! There are only two forms of workable partnerships—a silent partner who puts up half the money, for half the profit, and agrees to leave day-to-day business decisions up to you; and corporate partners (stockholders), who also leave day-to-day management up to you but who meet once a year to form corporate policy and decide whether you have performed well enough to stay on as the salaried manager (or be fired and revert to the status of other common shareholders). If you plan to use either of these forms of partnership, you will need a lawyer to draw up a "Partnership Agreement" or "Corporate Bylaws." Do not proceed past the planning stage in any tentative partnership without a written "partnership agreement." You can start with the standard ones that appear in basic business law books. Essentially, these agreements spell out exactly who has what authority, limits on individual expenditures, meeting and voting procedures, and buy-out stipulations for the inevitable dissolution of the partnership by death or disagreement (whichever comes first). Do you really need a partner?

Antique Co-ops. These are just about as successful as partnerships. A co-op is a share-the-work, share-the-rent concept that, in the long run, just doesn't work. If you are smart enough to talk several dealers into sharing a building, then you ought to be smart enough to be the landlord and subrent the spaces to them. Why bother with the hassle of group decision making?

Now that we have eliminated partners, let's get on with the planning of your speculative venture and try to eliminate as much of the speculation as possible. It is not difficult to actually project your profit (or loss) ahead of time if you have all the facts at hand. Most neophyte business owners don't discover the real facts until it is too late.

Let's analyze each expense item on the following "Hypothetical Investment Chart," and then you may construct a similar planning sheet.

Paint and Carpentry. These costs can be reduced by volunteer labor, but keep in mind that in many areas all wall coverings and wall-mounted fixtures must be of fireproof materials. This can double or triple your outlay.

Electrical Wiring and Lighting. Electrical work can run from zero to a thousand dollars, depending upon the condition in which the last tenant left it.

If Your Store Is in a New Shopping Center. You may be required by the terms of the lease to provide your own floor covering, heating, cooling, and lighting systems. The obvious solution is to try to find a previously occupied retail space that suits your needs without any major alterations. The subsequent savings in leasehold improvements can be invested in more inventory and could result in thousands of extra profit dollars over the life span of the lease.

Store Signs. They need only say "Antiques" in Old West or English-style lettering. Play down the name of your shop in the sign layout. The word "Antiques" has evolved into a self-explanatory visual symbol. The cost of a good hand-lettered signboard can run from $75 to $150. In some business districts, you may be required to use the same size and style sign as the neighboring shops. This could raise your costs substantially. The landlord doesn't pay for those huge, back-lighted plastic signs. You do. They run from $600 to $1,600 each for very modest storefront installations.

The Rent or Lease Deposit. Your landlord could ask for as much as two months' rent, plus a "security" deposit in some shopping centers. Private landlords rarely require more than the last month's rent, in advance, as a security deposit.

Legal Fees. Fees vary according to the services performed. You will want a lawyer to at least review any lease before you sign it. The money you pay him may save you several thousand at a later date.

Shopping Center Leases Can Be Very Binding. You may be required to join a *merchants' association,* abide by its rules, and pay dues. You may also be required to keep long shopping-center hours, like 9:00 A.M. to 9:00 P.M. six days a week, and noon to 5:00 P.M. on Sundays. This can wear one down quickly. You can't afford many employees in the antique business, and you will need time away from the store to follow up leads and attend auctions.

Bookkeeping. A bookkeeper or accountant will generally charge you from $100 to $180 to set up an initial bookkeeping system. The monthly charge, after that, will vary according to your sales volume and the number of employees you have. A *monthly profit*

HYPOTHETICAL INVESTMENT REQUIRED TO
START A RETAIL ANTIQUE BUSINESS

Starting Expense	Indoor Market Stall	Rural Roadside Building	Suburban Business District	Older Downtown Location	Established Shopping Center
Paint & Carpentry	$ 50	$ 300	$ 350	$ 500	$ 1,800
Electrical & Lights	20	150	150	200	1,000
Sign Installation	50	100	450	250	850
Shelving & Showcases	150	250	350	350	850
Office Equipment	150	150	350	350	925
Utility Deposit	—	25	60	60	150
Sales Tax Deposit	50	75	160	160	500
Business License	15	20	25	25	50
Rent/Lease Deposit	250	200	600	600	1,750
Legal & Accounting	115	125	180	180	200
Advertising, Printing	25	75	275	275	350
Supplies, Sacks, Etc.	$ 25	30	50	50	75
Subtotal	$ 900	$ 1,500	$ 3,000	$ 3,000	$ 8,500
plus Inventory Cost	6,000	9,000	14,000	15,000	22,000
Total Starting Expenses	**$6,900**	**$10,500**	**$17,000**	**$18,000**	**$30,500**

MONTHLY EXPENSE AND PROFIT PROJECTIONS

	Indoor Market Stall	Rural Roadside Building	Suburban Business District	Older Downtown Location	Established Shopping Center
Rent/Lease Payment	$ 250	$ 200	$ 350	$ 275	$ 800
Maintenance, Bldg.	10	15	20	17	175
Utilities	—	45	85	85	100
Telephone, Inc. Ad.	25	35	50	35	75
Subscriptions, news	10	10	10	10	15
Admissions & Fees	15	—	10	10	20
Advertising	10	25	45	25	100
Supplies & Postage	12	12	20	20	50
Refinishing & Labor	30	50	80	80	300
Taxes & Licenses	10	10	15	15	25
Insurance, fire & P/L	20	20	32	20	70
Bank Charges	3	3	8	8	15
Interest, bank loans	—	—	20	20	25
Vehicle, gas & maint.	75	75	100	100	125
Travel, food, motel	50	15	50	25	100
Deprec. truck & fixt.	60	60	80	80	120
Accounting	20	25	50	50	85
Employee Wages	—	—	250	250	800
Total Monthly Expense	$ 600	$ 600	$ 1,275	$ 1,125	$ 3,000
Total Yearly Expense	7,200	7,200	15,300	13,500	36,000
NET COST OF INVENTORY	6,000	9,000	14,000	15,000	22,000
Retail Value Inventory	12,000	18,000	28,000	30,000	44,000
ANNUAL TURNOVER	2½X	2 X	2 X	2 X	3 X
Projected Annual Sales:	$30,000	$36,000	$56,000	$60,000	$132,000
COST OF GOODS SOLD	-15,000	-18,000	-28,000	-30,000	-66,000
Gross Profit	$15,000	$18,000	$28,000	$30,000	$ 66,000
Less Annual Expenses	- 7,200	- 7,200	-15,300	-13,500	-36,000
NET PROFIT TO OWNER	**$ 7,800**	**$10,800**	**$12,700**	**$16,500**	**$ 30,000**

Important Note: *Gross sales are largely predicated on the size of a shop's inventory. A larger investment in inventory at any of the above locations should produce a marked increase in sales and profits.*

and loss statement will run you at least $75 in addition to your tax reports. You can save this amount by learning to post your own expense ledger and making most of your own entries from cash receipts and checkbook records. Some dealers don't keep any books at all; they just throw all their bills and check stubs into an apple box and give the whole mess to a tax service at the end of the year. This type of "bookkeeping" can end up being very expensive. Your shop could be well along its way to bankruptcy before the revelation of a midyear accounting!

Shelving and Counters. Use actual old-time store fixtures. You can still find older hardwood showcases (with glass tops that need replacing) for under $250. The antique furniture that you offer for sale will serve nicely as fixtures for the display of bric-a-brac and primitives while also inspiring more impulsive purchases.

Avoid fixed wall shelving. You will be moving odd-sized furniture in and out of your shop every month. Your entire display area should remain flexible enough to accommodate any salable piece of furniture that you buy. More about store display later.

Advertising and Printing. Expenditures should include no more than an initial series of weekend classified ads and a couple of thousand printed business cards. Save most of your advertising dollars for the telephone book's Yellow Pages and a direct mailing to doctors, lawyers, businesses, decorators, and known collectors in your area. A fixed return on advertising dollars spent in the antique business is rare. You're not a plumber or a shoe store; people don't need you. They want to discover your shop! Spend that extra thousand dollars on inventory and a few more signs along the highway. If your shop is hidden among other small retail establishments in a suburban shopping district, have a sign painter boldly letter the side of your van or station wagon with the simple message "ANTIQUES—buy, sell, trade." Park your portable advertising near the sidewalk or street and wait for the inevitable action.

Shopping Center Fixtures. The fixtures needed—locks, gates, and so on—are estimated at three times those of a conventional location because of stringent fire codes and the number of lockable showcases needed for the display of small valuables that always seem to tempt a certain percentage of the general public.

Office Equipment. In an antique shop the office equipment generally consists of a large desk, a swivel chair, wastebasket, filing cabinet, bookcase, adding machine, and a cash drawer or register. A large burglarproof safe will more than pay its way in reduced insurance premiums and peace of mind if you plan to carry rare coins, vintage firearms, fine watches, sterling flatware, jewelry, and other small but valuable *objets d'art*.

Utility Deposit. This is sometimes waived if you are a local homeowner and already a paying customer; otherwise, it may be the equivalent of one month's billing.

Sales Tax Deposit. Usually required at the time that you apply for a resale number from the State Tax Board, the deposit is based on the size of your inventory, store rent, and projected gross sales. The lower your estimated business expenses and sales goals, the smaller your sales tax deposit will probably be.

City Business License Fee. This fee shouldn't run you much over $25 (in most areas) *unless* you state that you plan on hiring several employees. If you are working out of your home and want to obtain a resale number or business license, you may want to tell the clerk that you intend to do primarily a mail-order and antique-show business. Otherwise, local zoning laws might prevent your home-based enterprise from gaining a license in a residential neighborhood. Displaying a sign in the city suburbs is usually forbidden; county regulations are more flexible.

Store Supplies. All you'll need are a stack of cheap white wrapping tissue, a week's accumulation of newspapers, and some clean, brown paper sacks. People don't expect imprinted bags or fancy gift wrapping in a run-of-the-mill antique shop. The lack of these "extras" has not cost us a sale yet. A shopping center location could perhaps necessitate a gift wrap department that would set you back at least $150; look in the Yellow Pages under "Paper Dealers."

Refinishing Supplies. These supplies account for one of our largest monthly expenditures. Figure on at least $100 to get starfed with a couple of gallons of stripper, lacquer thinner, paint thinner, turpentine, and linseed oil, plus a variety of stains, spray finishes, sandpaper, and steel wool. This low estimate assumes that you already have a basic selection of shop tools; otherwise, as much as $1,000 might be needed.

Insurance. In a modest location, a basic insurance policy shouldn't run you much more than $300 a year. This *does not* include coverage for theft, which could be uneconomical in relation to the replacement value of a small shop's inventory. *Shopping center locations require full coverage, including protection for the landlord.* A blanket policy might run as much as $95 per month before an added premium for theft.

Transportation. A small van, truck, or station wagon is almost a necessity to the successful operation of a general-line antique shop. If you can't afford the initial outlay of several thousand dollars or lack a credit line, look into leasing a truck on a twenty-four-month contract. The "buys" you haul home from auctions will more than make the monthly lease payments of about $200.

Courtesy Tom Warren

Be sure to include at least an additional $150 a month in your projected operating costs to cover gas, oil, insurance, and maintenance for a pickup and delivery vehicle. Also, the actual cost of your vehicle is deductible as depreciation. There are several methods of computing depreciation; your bookkeeper or an IRS employee will help you at tax time.

Almost every expense that we have mentioned so far (except deposits and licenses) can be reduced through barter! We traded either antiques or labor (involving our own specialized skills) for many of these opening expenses. One of our contractors needed some old wooden wagon wheels; we exchanged them at the going retail ($75 each) for electrical work. Our accountant needed his dining room chairs reglued ($25 each). The $150 sign on the side of our van was the result of an advantageous trade for old advertising items that our sign painter collects; our net cost, $15. Run a small ad in your local paper offering to trade antiques for any product or service that you need. It works!

Now, let's hypothesize, or project, your survival (or failure) in the antique business, based on what we have just discussed. Turn back to the Hypothetical Investment Chart (page 26) and fill in your own monthly expense items, based on the size and style operation which you plan to conduct. A quick phone call to a local realtor will provide you with the going commercial property rental rate (per square foot) in your area. Unless you are selling jewelry, stamps, or coins exclusively, you will need from 600 to 1,200 square feet of floor space to conduct a reasonably profitable retail operation (unless you will use your own home). If you plan to bring in container-sized shipments from abroad, you will need a large unloading and get-ready area in addition to at least 1,600 square feet of selling space.

After you have projected a year's fixed operating costs, you can go on to your gross sales. Again, the old saying to the effect that "you can't sell from an empty wagon" couldn't be truer anywhere than in the antique business! You must have an adequate inventory on hand the first day you open your doors. If you went to the grand opening of a gift and greeting card shop and discovered that it carried just a hundred items, would you return at a later date to see if it had a larger selection? By the same token, one should not expect repeat customers from an understocked antique shop. Take a moment to examine the *retail inventory* required for each type of antique shop operation shown on the Hypothetical Investment Chart (page 26). Note that in the most optimistic projections the *annual sales* are only three times the retail value of inventory. Many less aggressive dealers report yearly sales of only one or one and a half times retail inventory totals. After deducting other opening expenses from your nest egg, multiply the remaining funds by two. This figure is your shop's *retail inventory* (plus items from home and consignments from friends). Multiply this inventory figure again by two and you will have a pretty good idea of a year's gross sales, based on fact, not fantasy. Now subtract one-half of this sales total as your *cost of goods sold,* and you have a hypothetical *gross profit* from which you must deduct the *annual expenses.*

The above being accomplished, we have a picture of what you might realistically expect to make from your own full-time, aggressively run antique business in a productive location. One plucky lady we met in rural Pennsylvania had talked her husband into moving her shop twice before she finally hit pay dirt. A state highway frontage home with shop attached was the final choice. It must have been a good one because we headed west with a vanload bought right out of her garage, in the middle of a pouring rainstorm!

If you plan on borrowing from a bank, *do it while you have a regular job*—just in case your application is rejected. You must tell the bank why you are applying for the loan, and banks can be uneasy about granting loans for a new business. Don't expect to receive any consideration at all from the bank unless you have prepared a written profit and expense projection (see Hypothetical Investment Chart).

Most major bank credit cards are good for a cash advance as well as consumer purchases. Use your credit card for a few household items that you would normally buy for cash and pay off the balance promptly. After you have established your credit, apply to have your credit card limit raised to a couple of thousand dollars. If your credit application is accepted, you will have access to several thousand dollars through your credit cards, and future loan applications are unnecessary.

Apply for a loan from the bank while you still have a good job!

If you are buying a home, you are probably already aware that in some areas you can borrow funds on a second or third mortgage loan. This is a good source of funds to tap for expansion—*after you have learned the business* (at least three years). Another source for ready cash is an employees' credit union.

Shoestring entrepreneurs, retirees, or ambitious housewives with limited working capital can get started in the antique business by using other people's antiques (in lieu of borrowing several thousand dollars). We wouldn't recommend this route to anyone who has to support a family, but it can provide a marginal income from a minimum investment. All that is needed in the form of capital is about two months' rent money and $100 for local advertising.

Nothing will draw prospective consignors or sellers into your store faster than the offer of a *free appraisal.* If you don't feel qualified to appraise an item offered for consignment, ask the prospect if you can give him or her a receipt and keep the object for a couple of days until an expert can examine it. (A reputable local appraiser will give you "verbal" estimates on several items for a few dollars.) Sotheby Parke Bernet has sponsored about a hundred "Heirloom Appraisal Events," which have brought in several million dollars' worth of impressive consignment merchandise for its auctions and many antique show promoters use the offer of free appraisals to increase attendance at paid admission events.

GRAND OPENING MARCH 15
THE ANTIQUE CONSIGNMENT
Turn your bric-a-brac, party clothes, antiques, collectibles, and fine used furniture into CASH! Phone 294-6371 or come in today for a FREE APPRAISAL

About three weeks prior to the grand opening you can start running weekend classified ads in your local newspaper. The wording should read the same as your window banner, except for the heading, which should be in double-sized, bold type, and read: **ANTIQUES WANTED!**

Flyers should also be run off and prominently posted at all public gathering places (for example, cocktail lounges, liquor stores, restaurants, beauty salons, barbershops, grocery stores, and gas stations). Door-to-door delivery of this announcement could produce a sizable number of quality consignments too.

Also look through the phone book for likely women's organizations that might be tempted to use your services to raise funds. You might add a handwritten postscript to these flyers, stating that two-thirds of the proceeds from any donated items will be forwarded to the club along with an itemized monthly statement.

Several simple typewritten consignment forms should be prepared ahead of time. Provide plenty of room to itemize and
number each piece. Give each consignor a special code number
(for your files and for the price tags). For example, consignor
#14's merchandise would be marked 14-1, 14-2, 14-3, and so
forth. Provide a space on the consignment form for the consign-
or's minimum acceptable price, as well as the actual amount that
the item sold for (the difference between the two is your commission). Also, note "date in" and "date sold" or returned to
consignor. Most successful consignment shops do not display
any item for more than ninety days. This keeps a constant
stream of new merchandise coming in and allows them to build
a regular clientele of buyers, as well as sellers.

Consignment merchandise is usually marked up by 50 percent
of the consignor's net asking price, thus yielding a one-third
gross profit margin; for example, on a $150 "retailer" the con-
signor receives $100 (two-thirds) and you get $50 (one-third).
Any markup over this figure may alienate regular consignors.
You can, however, start buying "off the street," for your own account, almost as soon as the doors open. Many people will accept your low cash offer rather than wait for an item to sell on
consignment. Do not commingle funds! Avoid the temptation to
use a consignor's money to purchase more stock for "a quick
profit." Put the consignor's cash (or checks) in separately labeled envelopes for pickup at a moment's notice.

Since you probably will not be able to insure the consignor's
merchandise against loss or damage, you had best include a
statement of nonliability on your forms—something to the effect
that "Carol's Consignment Corner will take every reasonable
precaution but cannot accept the responsibility for loss or damage to merchandise due to fire, theft, water damage, and so
forth." "Please check your homeowner's insurance policy for
coverage on items owned by you, but removed from your home
for display or sale elsewhere."

Below this statement, provide a line for both you and the consignor to sign, and date the form. A copy must be given to each
party, and one should be filed under the consignor's code number (to record sales from tag "code" numbers as they occur and
also to compare against merchandise descriptions in order to
prevent tag switching).

CONSIGNMENT FORM

STOCK NO.	DATE REC'D	DESCRIPTION	DATE SOLD/ RETN'D	RETAIL PRICE	CON- SIGNOR NET	SHOP NET

We agree to display the above described merchandise for sale in our shop in return for a fee of ( )% of the actual selling price. Shop is, / is not, authorized to reduce retail price by ( )% after 30 days exposure. Please note that all merchandise will be removed from the sales floor if unsold after 90 days. We do not have room for storage and must charge a fee of $( ) per week on items left over 100 days. Our liability on the above consignment shall be limited to $_____total   (due to loss, or damage, by any cause.)

_____   _____
CONSIGNOR   SHOP OWNER

_____   _____
ADDRESS   PHONE

Try to buy at a figure of one-half of "quick retail" when you are investing your own hard cash. Shoot for a better markup on large lots and lesser quality items. You should at least triple on these because they help to offset the abnormally low profit margin on consigned goods.

Chapter 4
PAPERWORK CAN BE FUN

Inventory and Cash Control Forms

As stated earlier, the two most common causes of business failure are undercapitalization and mismanagement. Most of us are somewhat undercapitalized, but there isn't any excuse for mismanaging an antique business. All that's really involved is self-discipline!

Set Up an Inventory System.   Doing your own basic bookkeeping can alert you to most problems before they become serious enough to bury you. Your earliest recordkeeping should start right now, with a *perpetual inventory system*. Every item that you have purchased for eventual resale should be recorded (preferably in its order of acquisition). The actual date of purchase, your stock number, description, source, net cost, and retail asking price should be entered in a large notebook. As each item is sold, cross it out with a transparent colored marker; this gives you a running record of the cost of your inventory as well as a "perpetual" total of all unsold items remaining in stock. We insert a carbon in our notebook to have an "Insurance Copy" of this inventory (which we keep in a fireproof box at home).

The advantages of a perpetual inventory system are many. First of all, it makes it easy for an employee to at least act knowledgeable in your absence. Since the stock number on the price tag is keyed to a complete description opposite the same number in the inventory log, it's a simple matter to answer most customers' questions (for example, how old is it, country of origin, pattern name, and so forth).

A retail price appearing in the inventory opposite the stock number gives your clerk some degree of protection against customer tag switching (a rare occurrence). Also, if a price tag is lost or blurred, you can readily replace it by recalling the approximate purchase date or looking up the tag number of another item purchased on the same day. (The "lost" tag number should be on this page too.)

Entering the name and address of the source of an item is a worthwhile effort. It eventually gives you dozens of vendor prospects to call if you run low on merchandise. (It also protects you against being convicted of running a fencing operation for stolen goods.)

This inventory record can also be an aid in determining what you should pay for replacement stock, how fast specific items move, when the retail price should be raised or lowered, and, finally, which store-sitters are ready for the auction block.

Figuring your *gross profit* margin for the year is facilitated by this particular system because your *net cost* is routinely recorded and can be totaled quickly on an adding machine tape directly from the logbook (this beats leafing through hundreds of check stubs, or trying to find cash purchase receipts at the end of the year).

Each year's "sold" merchandise should be lined out of the inventory log with a different color of transparent marker so that your "cost of sales" can be determined for any specific year (for example, 1980—yellow; 1981—light orange; 1982—sky blue, and so forth).

Cash Flow.   Next you should set up a system for controlling and reporting your firm's *daily cash flow.* A cash register is really nothing more than a fancy adding machine with a drawer underneath. You don't need to spend $900 on the latest electronic register to keep track of the cash generated in an average antique shop. You do need to make a written invoice of each transaction that includes the stock number, description, price, sales tax, down payment, terms, and balance due. You should also note whether payment was made by cash, check, or bank credit card. (Never refund cash on an item purchased by credit card; use a refund form provided by the bank.) A local stationery or office-supply firm will be able to provide you with inexpensive sales books that have spaces provided for most of the preceding information. These sales invoice books are available in one- or two-carbon styles. You will need a third copy on layaway sales, so it might pay to keep a separate sales book exclusively for

INVENTORY FORM
(Purchases for Resale)

BUY DATE	STOCK NO.	DESCRIPTION	PURCHASED FROM	COST	SELL PRICE	PAID BY
1/15	001	VASE, sil. pl. ca. 1910	J. Brown	15⁰⁰	29⁰⁰	cash
"	002	CHAIR, oak, cane, 1890	(picker) on file.	27⁰⁰	55⁰⁰	"
"	003	WATCH, coin sil, Elgin (needs $35.00 repair)	C. Reed 116 3rd	32	125⁵⁰	"
"	004	LAMP, brass, oil. Rayo	" "	60	120⁰	"
"	005	QUILT, hand sewn, 1900	" "	45	100	"
1/16	006	MIRROR, art deco, 1920	Auction Sale,	24	50	ck. #33
"	007	BRIDE'S BOX, orig. 1840	Eagles Hall.	100	195	"
"	008	DRESS, victorian lace		12⁵⁰	25	"
"	009	SIGN, tin root beer, 1940's	"	15	45	"
1/17	010	WINDOWS, leaded glass	Antique Whole-	50	95	ck.
"	011	(from English pub.) 20x30	Salers Inc.,	50	95	#34
"	012	CLOCK, mantle, 1880⁵	Downtown	100	225	"
1/18	013	CANE, ivory carved head	Flea	25	75	cash
"	014	TINTYPE, photo, indian	Market Hwy 12	2	25	"
"	015	PIN, art nouveau, sterl.	at bridge	15	30	"
"	016	TABLE, cherry, 1860	road.	200	395	"
"	017	POSTCARD ALBUM (break up & sell seperately at 1⁰⁰ to 5⁰⁰ each)	"	30	✓	"
"	018	PAINTING, oil portrait (Denmark 1778, need restoration)	Photo Studio 10th & B	35	250	ck #35
"	019	CAMERA, studio, 1895	street	75	180	"
1/19	020	TOOLS, woodworking (refinish & sell individually)	Drive-in Swap meet	45	200	cash "
"	021	TEA CADDY, 1790's mahog.	"	50	195	"

layaway transactions. The third copy of each layaway invoice goes into an alphabetical card file under the customer's name, and each payment on account is similarly written up and filed. The customer is always given a copy of any purchase invoice or payment on account.

At the end of each business day, you should total the day's sales invoices and your own petty cash expenditures on a cash control form such as the one on page 42. (You can type up a dozen of these simple forms in twenty minutes.) Your bookkeeper will appreciate this extra effort.

A daily record of sales can come in handy when you decide that you are tired of staying open seven days a week. One can review a few months' transactions and identify the "slow" days—the best time to take off. After a couple of years in the trade, you will be able to spot certain periods when you could close up for a week or two without a significant loss in revenue (usually in July, August, or January). These are the best weeks for planning a buying trip or a family vacation. At all other times we urge you to keep very regular hours. Post the days and hours you are open on the front door and keep to them religiously! You can't build a regular clientele by keeping irregular hours.

Another good reason for balancing the cash daily on a form is to enable you to spot employee "till tapping." Or more often, when an absentminded customer swears that she gave you a twenty instead of a five, you can quickly add the day's "cash sales" to the "starting cash," subtract the "paid outs," and know exactly how much money should be in the till!

Treat bank card sales as cash transactions, and count the bank vouchers as cash in the till. Be careful to put a written slip in the drawer for any cash paid out, including "draw" slips for personal cash removed. No petty cash expenditure is too trivial to record! If you neglect to itemize such incidentals as paper towels, Windex, soap, coffee filters, turnpike tolls, light bulbs, and postage stamps, you may be cheating yourself out of several hundred dollars a year in legitimate business tax deductions.

Some of your sales invoices will have a combination of "cash" and "charge" sales on them. If an item is sold for $25 with a $5 deposit and $20 due in sixty days, record the down payment in the "Cash Sales" column and the layaway balance due under "Charge Sales." Merchandise returns, refunds, and unredeemed layaways should be deducted from each day's cash or charge sales, as they occur. If you are kind enough to return a canceled layaway deposit, you would enter the refund as a "minus" cash sale and the unpaid balance as a "minus" charge sale. (This eliminates any sales tax due on the previously reported transaction.)

Profit and Loss. "Current" records (like those we have just described) are kept on a *day-to-day* basis at the time that each transaction or expenditure takes place. "Cumulative" monthly and yearly records are also necessary for both your own and Uncle Sam's enlightenment. Every dime that you spend for business purposes should be recorded somewhere and eventually find its way into a cumulative record-keeping system! Bookkeepers and accountants are paid by the hour, so keep your petty cash slips and check stubs in an orderly fashion. Mark your copy of any bills paid as to the method and date of payment (for example, paid 3/20/81, ck #142; or, paid "cash" from drawer 3/20/81). If you want to try your hand at preparing a monthly *profit and loss statement,* you can make your own summary on a simple typewritten form (page 43).

A close examination of the Profit and Loss Worksheet gives us a fairly accurate view of the month to month sales, overhead, and profit potential of a typical mom-and-pop antique shop—capitalized at $20,000. Note, first of all, that about $15,000 is the amount invested in inventory (at cost). This figure would produce a $30,000 retail value store stock, which should turn over twice a year and result in sales of approximately $60,000 (an average of $5,000 per month). In many areas the antique business is highly seasonal—this shop is no exception. Note the slow sales in April and August with a marked increase for October. By the time November rolls around these people will probably obtain a ninety-day bank loan to build up their inventory for the Christmas season. If they do not, and continue to draw full living expenses from their day-to-day revenue, sales could plummet drastically as a result of the dwindling inventory. Again, gross sales are linked directly to the dollar value of the inventory and the number of square feet devoted to its display—especially in a business where replacement stock is not as close as the nearest telephone or regional warehouse!

DAILY CASH CONTROL FORM

MONTH _____ YR. _____

	Starting Cash In Drawer	Payments Received on Account	Cash & Bank Card Sales	Personal Draws & Cash Pd. Out	Today's Bank Deposit	Ending Cash & Drafts	Cash Over/ Under	Cash & Bank Card Sales	Charge/ Layaway Sales	Total Daily Sales	
1											1
2											2
3											3
4											4
5											5
6											6
7											7
8											8
9											9
10											10
11											11
12											12
13											13
14											14
15											15
16											16
17											17
18											18
19											19
20											20
21											21
22											22
23											23
24											24
25											25
26											26
27											27
28											28
29	100.+	20. +	180. ‒	50. ‒	150. =	100.	‒0‒	180. +	70. =	250.	29
30											30
31											31

WORKSHEET FOR COMPUTING
MONTHLY PROFIT OR LOSS

	JAN	FEB	MAR	APR	MAY	JUN	JUL	AUG	SEP	OCT	NOV	DEC
Rent/Lease Payment		300		300		300		300		300		
Maintenance, Bldg.		10		16		10		20		20		
Utilities		65		45		40		40		65		
Telephone, Inc. Ad.		45		35		45		45		35		
Subscriptions, news		8		10		10		6		16		
Admissions & Fees		10		2		6		4		6		
Advertising		40		25		-0-		15		50		
Supplies & Postage		50		60		75		50		95		
Accounting		25		25		25		25		25		
Taxes & Licenses		5		10		5		5		10		
Insurance, fire & P/L		26		25		25		25		25		
Bank Charges		6		6		5		5		8		
Interest, bank loans		30		30		14		-0-		50		
Vehicle, gas & maint.		80		75		90		75		80		
Travel, food, motel		95		-0-		50		50		25		
Deprec. truck & fixr.		50		50		50		50		50		
Employee Wages		60		-0-		-0-		-0-		130		
Refinishing Labor		75		26		-0-		35		10		
TOTAL MONTHLY EXPENSE	$ 980.		740.		750.		750.		1,000.			
Beginning Inventory (at actual cost)		15,000		14,000		12,000		12,000		11,500		
Resale Purchases	+	1,000	+	1,000	+	2,000	+	1,000	+	3,000		
Total Goods Available	=	16,000	=	15,000	=	14,000	=	13,000	=	14,500		
Ending Inventory (at cost)	−	13,500	−	14,250	−	12,500	−	12,000	−	11,750		
COST OF GOODS SOLD	= 2,500.		= 750.		= 1,500.		= 1,000.		= 2,750.			
MONTHLY NET SALES ▶		5,000		1,500		3,000		2,000		5,500		
Cost of Goods Sold	−	2,500	−	750	−	1,500	−	1,000	−	2,750		
Gross Profit	= 2,500.		= 750.		= 1,500.		= 1,000.		= 2,750.			
Monthly Expenses	−	980.	−	740.	−	750.	−	750.	−	1,000.		
NET PROFIT TO OWNER	$ 1,520.		$ 10.		$ 750.		$ 250.		$ 1,750.			Monthly Totals

Note: *All above figures are taken directly from check stubs, petty cash slips, perpetual inventory log sheets, and monthly sales receipt book totals.*

Now let's take another look at the *gross profit margin*. It should average 100 percent of an item's cost (a discount of 50 percent from retail). This is the minimum average you must strive for! Survival would be difficult on any smaller margin. Yes, we are aware of the fact that prominent dealers often pay certain prices at public auction, adding only a modest markup of 15 or 20 percent before selling to a wealthy client or institution. In most of these cases, the dealer is acting as a buying agent—no risk of time and personal capital is involved. It is true that one might mark up a fine, ready-to-sell piece of higher-priced furniture only a third while, on the other hand, doubling on medium-priced goods. When the bank borrows from your savings account at 6 percent, and lends the funds to overextended consumers at 18 percent, they are making a full 300 percent profit. Jewelry stores and clothing boutiques commonly triple their costs of acquisition. Butchers, bakers, candlestick makers, gift and hobby shops, candy stores, garden centers, and hundreds of categories of small retailers double their money on over half the items they sell. They have to in order to remain in business. Why should antique dealers even consider working on any smaller margin of gross profit? We can't begin to find, clean, fix, and restore enough merchandise to keep up with our retail competition.

Finally, observe the bottom line, the "moment of truth." Mom and Pop don't make enough to live on if their sales drop much below $4,000 a month (when fixed overhead looms at $700 to $950 every thirty days). Four or five months in a row with gross sales of under $3,000 would put this hypothetical business deeply in the hole, or out of operation entirely if there was no financial cushion. That's what the charts and forms are all about. *Keeping close track of your own sales and expenses can alert you to trouble before it controls your destiny.* If you can predict, by a comparison of former months, the slow periods, the times when cash flow may not meet overhead—then you are prepared to take direct action to increase sales and revenue. Perhaps these are the months you should devote to doing out-of-town antique shows, or possibly consigning a large portion of old store stock to an auction house. Maybe spending every Sunday sitting under an umbrella at a large flea market will turn the tide—there are many ways to increase sales by $1,000 a month in this business.

In the early days, my wife and I would hold a garage sale at the home of a different friend or relative every weekend. Many of these sales produced over $800 of needed cash in a two-day period (holiday weekends were flops).

Other avenues available to antique dealers who wish to increase retail sales are hauling, mail-order merchandising, picture framing, and furniture refinishing. A less drastic approach might be to broaden one's inventory to include giftware and reproduction items. (We have found collectible costume jewelry to be a profitable addition to our own stock in trade.) If you have a busy sidewalk outside your store, there is no end to possibilities for increasing income. We recently met an enterprising antique dealer who has turned his entire front window over to the display of electronic metal detectors and is doing quite well with them. A vintage furniture dealer I am acquainted with finally hit pay dirt by adding wine and cheese to his inventory. The move entailed a weekly restocking trip of forty miles into town, but the food has doubled his furniture volume. One enterprising young woman in our city moved her entire stock of very feminine antiques into her boyfriend's barber shop. Sales tripled in less than a month.

Innovate—be creative! Has anyone in town thrown a "Tupperware" party using antiques instead of the traditional plastic? Do you know some person with idle acreage that could be utilized for a weekend flea market during the tourist season?

There aren't really any secrets in the retail trade today. If any area of merchandise looks like an interesting possibility for addition to your line, you can reach the sources through trade publications or manufacturers' directories available at most public libraries. Simply send off a few dozen neatly typed letters of inquiry and wait for your mailbox to fill with catalogs, samples, and sales pitches from wholesale distributors. The giftware marts listed in Chapter 23 are an excellent place to start your quest.

Courtesy R. G. Canning Enterprises

Chapter 5
THE GREAT AMERICAN GARAGE SALE

Basic Backyard Capitalism

Okay. You've undergone psychoanalysis, paid off all your installment debts (or declared personal bankruptcy), attended weekly antique auctions for the past six months, bought all the books we've listed, and subscribed to at least half a dozen antique publications for a year or more. If you still have reservations about opening a full-time business, maybe a part-time entry into antique dealing would be wise.

Let's examine the most basic form of backyard capitalism—the garage sale. In the teeming suburbs of sunny southern California it is not uncommon for a weekend yard sale operation to gross $1,000 or more. (My wife does, twice a year.) Several books have been written on the subject of conducting garage sales. These burgeoning suburban businesses have become so fashionable that Neiman-Marcus recently offered a prepackaged garage sale kit, complete with instructions, signs, price tags, and marking pens.

Your first sale might be a simple housecleaning effort. Most of us who have lived in one place for more than a couple of years have accumulated a good deal of what we now consider to be "junk." If you haven't used something in the last year or two, sell it and invest the proceeds in antiques. Ask the kids if they have any toys they want to get rid of. Call up your mother-in-law and offer to clean out her attic and basement for "nothing." The more you get into it, the more endless the possibilities seem. Your gross sales will be in direct proportion to the amount of goods you have to offer, so hustle up a huge inventory! The next step is to call up the local newspaper and place a classified ad in Friday, Saturday, and Sunday's garage sale column.

Professional garage sale merchants (they do exist) tell us that they don't skimp on their advertising budgets. If you have a good-sized, well-rounded inventory and want a fair shot at a large profit, you must expect to spend from $35 to $60 for weekend advertising. First, try to think of an attention-getting headline (which could be in two-line height, bold-type capital letters), for example:

MOTHER-IN-LAW
CLEANING ATTIC—
20-YR ACCUMULATION
MUST GO!

If you're selling strictly antique items, you must likewise sensationalize a bit to get people to drive twenty-five miles to view the contents of your garage (when they could be going to a flea market instead). Antique buffs love "unloading sales." If they think that fresh merchandise has just come in from two thousand miles away, they will beat your door down to be the first to see it! Here is a headline that we used recently to good advantage (we sold out):

GREETINGS FROM PENNSYLVANIA

Ron Barlow returning Fri. morn. with load from Lancaster County. Lots of stoneware, kitchen stuff, tools, toys, thimbles, and sewing items. Rocking chairs, small chest, and 3 doz. Amish hand-loomed throw rugs. Come on out and look us over Fri., Sat., & Sun., 9–5.

Other than an attention-getting headline, the most important element in your advertising copy is an itemized listing of almost everything that you have for sale. This will attract the widest attendance, and people may buy other items once they arrive. A typical listing that might provoke action is "tools, toys, clothes, sports equipment, baby things, bric-a-brac, old radio, TV, lots of books, old furniture, costume jewelry, and some antique items." This copy must not be too slick, too commercial, or an attempt to be overly clever or funny. Write like a homebody, not a Madison Avenue type! Sometimes it is best to omit the use of a phone number because of the potential loss of impulse buyers who might "screen" your event. A three-day sale is a good idea, if possible. It gives you time to benefit from additional "word-of-mouth" advertising and also a final day in which to cut your prices in half and move it all out.

Where do garage sale dealers get their merchandise? From swap meets, auctions, other garage sales, rich relatives, and the trash bins behind small factories and retail businesses.

The night before the sale should find you and your helpers cleaning and pricing all the goodies and deciding which valuables should be next to the checkout table or in a locked display case. The evening before is also a good time to paint a few large directional signs that should be placed (that same evening) at busy intersections up to half a mile from the sale. Don't put off pricing or sign placement until the morning of the sale. Veteran garage sale goers will be pounding on your door at 6:00 A.M.!

Most cities have a law about how many garage sales you can conduct from your home in a year. The women in our neighborhood get around this by alternating locations each month. They simply code their individual merchandise with their initials and settle up after the sale. This "partnership" also cuts advertising expenses to a negligible amount and spreads out the workload among three or four participants.

We don't want to spoil your weekend by making you paranoid, but you must expect that a few thieves and tag switchers may try their hand at your event. Drill your helpers about the prices on the most valuable pieces, and put all the small stuff in a safe place. Cashboxes and purses lying around are a no-no. Keep your change on your person.

GARAGE SALE CHECKLIST

- Wash, polish, vacuum, or press everything. Remove rust if possible and rub with light oil. Wax dull painted surfaces.
- Price according to what you would expect to pay at a garage sale, not an antique shop.
- Use different colored markers or initials to code tags in multiple family sales.
- Set everything up and group it in an area away from items that are not for sale.

- Remove items to be put on sale from the house ahead of time. Your home is *off limits* to shoppers.
- Put a $10 limit on check cashing. (You don't have to accept any.)
- Smile and greet each customer. They're going to make you rich!
- Be prepared to accept less than your initial price—you can't go broke making a profit!
- Send the kids to a swap meet with all the stuff that didn't sell. (They will have no qualms about selling too cheaply.)

Chapter 6

FLEA MARKET FORMULAS

The Secrets of Successful Operators

Flea markets, or swap meets, as they are called on the West Coast, are the next step upward on the ladder of antique dealing. At about 5:00 A.M. on any given Sunday morning, some 150,000 seasoned swap meet dealers roll out of bed, dress in several layers of peelable clothing, grab a thermos of coffee, climb into vehicles ranging from Volkswagen Beetles with roof racks to semitruck and trailer outfits, and head for one of the nation's hundreds of flea markets or swap meets. These weekend "people's markets" are nothing new, but their numbers and popularity are mushrooming at an unbelievable rate!

Newsletters and magazines devoted to swap meet advertising are being circulated by the thousands. *Swap Meet U.S.A.*, a nine-by-twelve-inch sixty-two-page magazine/directory (from Cranbrook House, P. O. Box 272, Saginaw, MI 48606), lists 1,047 weekly events that take place on a regular basis. Included in each listing are directions for finding the market, the cost of a seller's space, the opening and closing time, the number of dealers and customers attending, and the manager's telephone number. Another good guide is *Fleamarket U.S.A.*, a national directory (six by nine inches, 100 pages) published four times a year by Charles and Dorothy Clark, Route 1, #470, Cantonment, FL 32533. A check for $4 will get you a sample copy from either of the publishers above. (We use both guides.) The huge Nashville Flea Market, operating out of both the Nashville and Memphis (Tennessee) State Fairgrounds, publishes its own *Flea Market Newspaper* (available at $2.25 a year from P. O. Box 155D, Fairview, TN 37062).

Some swap meets are unadvertised, informal affairs that might typically take place among a grove of trees in a farmer's field. Others are gigantic enterprises with their own advertising

Aerial view—Rose Bowl Flea Market—2,000 vendors, 50,000 custom-
ers. Courtesy R. G. Canning Enterprises

and public relations people. Some, like the Canton, Texas, "Trade Days," are community-sponsored affairs; but most are privately owned and are operated strictly for a profit.

R. G. Canning Enterprises, Inc. (P. O. Box 400, Maywood, CA 90270) owns and manages the nation's largest flea market at the famous Rose Bowl in Pasadena, California. (Canning also runs the Ventura Flea Market and the semiannual Santa Barbara Antique Show.) The Rose Bowl event began in 1968, and attracted an opening crowd of about 5,000 eager shoppers and 300 vendors. Today over 50,000 buyers vie for the antiques, collectibles, and handicrafts of up to 2,000 space holders on the second Sunday of every month, "rain or shine." The premium selling spaces (immediately around the perimeter of the stadium) are sometimes sold out a year in advance! Where else can a flea market dealer have the opportunity to mingle with Hollywood's celebrities and perhaps sell a couple of thousand dollars' worth of antiques in a single six-hour spree? The unreserved spaces on the outskirts of the parking lot are sold on a first-come, first-served basis. The lineup of vendors' vehicles at the gate sometimes begins the day before the market opens.

Another 2,000 dealers converge three times a year upon the little town of Brimfield, Massachusetts. Gordon Reid's Auction Acres started it all twenty years ago. Today three huge markets share the action with a myriad of tag sales and baked-goods tables set up all over the village. This extraordinary event takes place in May, July, and September. It is considered the place to sell, or shop for, Americana. Space holders return to the same spots every season and some shoppers stay all three days. For show dates, write the Gordon Reid Co., 138 Kispert Court, Swansea, MA 02777.

No advice to fledgling flea market vendors would be complete without the mention of Renninger's famous "extravaganzas." These huge indoor/outdoor markets draw thousands of buyers from New York, New Jersey, Philadelphia, Pittsburgh, and Washington; dealers attend from all over the nation. Renninger's No. 1 is located in Lancaster County, PA, on Rt. 272 near Adamstown, one mile north of the Pennsylvania Turnpike, Exit 21. Number 2 is located in Kutztown, PA, on Nobel Street, one mile south of the center of town. A brochure is available from Renninger's, Box 107, Adamstown, PA 19501.

Only antique and collectible dealers are welcome. Reproductions and swap meet junk are not allowed. Both locations are open the year round. (#1), Adamstown, on Sundays from 8:00 A.M. to 5:00 P.M. (#2), Kutztown, on Saturdays, same hours. Both markets charge a regular set-up fee of $10. Reserved space at their thrice yearly "extravaganzas" is $30 for two days. Over 800 sellers show up at these events.

A little-known, but obvious fact is that several high-geared western dealers have permanent salaried buyers (and commissioned pickers) who do nothing else but attend these weekend markets and ship their finds back to California or Texas on a regular basis. Both Renninger's and Brimfield are dynamic marketplaces for sellers of Americana.

The average-sized swap meet does not require advance reservations or weeks of preparation on the part of the seller. If you pull up to the gate by 7:00 A.M., chances are that you will secure a pretty good selling spot for $5 or $10 at a worthwhile event.

Flea market sellers are generally admitted an hour or two before the general public. At the large eastern "extravaganzas," they are allowed to set up the night before and camp out on the spot.

Between daylight and 8:00 A.M., there will be a flurry of activity as "smart" dealers buy from "dumb" dealers (and vice versa). By opening time, a third of your stuff may be on a "regular's" table and a third of his stuff may be stashed in your van. This dealer-to-dealer trade is one of the great phenomenons of the antique business. (The same intercourse takes place at antique shows before the general public is admitted.) Can you imagine a hardware dealer buying from a hardware dealer or a baker buying from a baker? Market-wise collectors just can't pass up underpriced antiques if they know of a better "home" for them.

We are acquainted with a professional picker who pays for his selling space in advance of every weekend meet. Early Saturday or Sunday morning he drives an empty van into the middle of the selling area and proceeds to fill it with "sleepers" from the stalls of novice dealers, before the general public is permitted to enter the field. By 10:00 A.M. he is ready to set up his own booth with his newly acquired "inventory." It takes years of experience to pull off a performance like this, but professional buyers often use the same technique to gain first chance at the goodies displayed among any large gathering of sellers.

Spending two or three days a week as a regular flea market vendor can produce a livelihood for you if you learn what sells and where to obtain a dependable supply. Take a good look at what the "regulars" in your area are stocking in their booths. At our local swap meet, there is a "Toy Man," a "Basket Lady," a couple who stock nothing but antique reproductions in brass and copper, a baked-goods table, a fishing-tackle dealer, a used-tool specialist, a gem-and-mineral man, a few general-line antique dealers, the normal array of jewelry and T-shirt sellers, and, of course, the ever-present produce stalls, pitchmen, and auto-parts vendors.

At swap meets that pull from the larger metropolitan areas, you will find "big-time operators," who reserve up to four full spaces every Saturday and Sunday and proceed to unpack the contents of twenty-foot vans. You wouldn't see them there every weekend if they weren't making money! (Those truck and trailer rigs cost a small fortune.)

We know of more than one couple who make a weekly buying trip to big city antique wholesalers for a load of European hall trees, wash stands, refractory tables, framed mirrors, chair sets, lamp tables, clocks, and quilt racks. Most of this furniture is small and lightweight; all that is required to haul it is a second-hand Step Van (like the ones that milkmen and United Parcel drivers use). If these couples are able to move a dozen, $100 items on a typical two-day weekend, they can gross $5,000 a month. Most of the furniture is sold in the same condition as (carefully) bought. A little rubbing oil or "restore-a-finish" applied with fine steel wool is all the upgrading that usually takes place. Since the source of supply is constant and the units of sale are large, these itinerant used-furniture dealers can work on slightly less than a "double" markup. They offer free delivery and also carry a VISA bank card imprinter to encourage impulse buying by charge card customers. I would reckon these folks have a total cash investment of about $8,000 including the used Step Van. Deduct their small overhead, and a monthly net profit of $2,000 would not seem unrealistic in the spring and summer months. If things get tight, or the weather is unusually bad, they can "turn" their inventory at auction or by having a couple of garage sales a week in different locations throughout the state.

Another operator I am acquainted with supports a wife and three kids entirely from his swap meet income. This young man obtains his inventory primarily from garage sales and local auctions. To keep his garage/warehouse full of merchandise, it is necessary for him to attend at least two or three auctions every week. He makes his best buys at regular used-furniture events that are not widely advertised or heavily attended. Books, radios, tape decks, picture frames, trunks, primitives, and paper items are frequently mixed in with the furniture offerings at these low-key evening auctions. This young man's gross sales are a steady $35,000 per year. His cost of all items sold is about $12,000. Overhead consists of gas for a Datsun pickup and $40 a month in swap meet space rental fees. He prefers to reserve space at the same event for several months in advance. This rigorous schedule has enabled him to develop a wide following of regular customers who unfailingly stop by his truck to see if he has anything "put away" for them to purchase. The secret of his success is simply constant hard work and a selling schedule of two swap meets every week!

Reproduction merchandise such as glassware, lamps, toys, brassware, porcelain, and other decorative accessories is readily available from hundreds of sources at the gift and merchandise marts in all major market areas. Catalog houses such as A. A. Imports, at 4244 Olive Street, St. Louis, MO 63108, also offer a broad line of antique reproductions to the trade. Don't approach these wholesale sources without first securing a state tax number and a printed letterhead or business card. Some firms sell "wholesale" to anyone who remits a check with an order, while others will wholesale only to established retailers dealing from open shops. See Chapter 23 for sources near you.

Picking the right flea market to sell from is as important as choosing the correct location for an antique shop! Since traffic is the name of the game, make sure that there are at least one hundred sellers and a few thousand prospective buyers at any market you plan to try. It may pay you to drive as far as two hundred miles to get this kind of exposure. Many dealers try to hit a different swap meet every weekend, feeling that their merchandise looks "fresh" to new customers. Others prefer to price their stuff cheap enough to sell out at each event and start anew with goods that are indeed fresh.

The psychology of successful selling at a swap meet is subject to varying opinions. I have always felt that it is important to mark one's merchandise clearly with the price, wait for a prospect to offer a little less, then close the sale by meeting him halfway in between. But there is more than one way to skin a cat! We frequently travel to a large indoor flea market with a dealer friend who has an advanced degree in psychology and many years of swap meet experience. While I am busy setting up an attractive display of plainly priced merchandise, he is dumping his stuff out on a large red cloth on the ground in an unpriced and unsorted potpourri of fine things ... mixed in with pure junk! Within an hour this con artist is usually half sold out and ready to cut his prices to the bone on the rest. (He thinks it's bad luck to take anything but cash home from a swap meet.) I rarely sell more than a third of my carefully displayed antiques and collectibles, so you must draw your own conclusions.

Generally speaking, good merchandising methods at flea markets are the same as those of successful retail shopkeepers. Break the ice! Greet the customers with a smile and a friendly "Hello. How are you today?" (Some kind souls will buy from you just because of your sparkling personality.) Watch your valuables and carry your cash (don't leave purses or change boxes lying around). Arrive early and dress for the weather. Bring your own food and drink. There are only a few prime selling hours, and you must make the most of them before packing up for the next event. A summertime job with a traveling carnival might be a good way to prepare for a flea market career!

Chapter 7
THE SHOW MUST GO ON

How to Make a Living on the Road

Hardly a week passes without a major antique show being promoted in at least one of the major market regions of the United States. These collector-oriented events take place anywhere a large crowd and their automobiles can be accommodated. Indoor shows are the most popular, but some pretty sophisticated gatherings take place in open fields on the East Coast.

Shopping malls are becoming very popular settings for general interest exhibitions because of their immunity from bad weather conditions and also for the new customer contacts they often provide. These largely public-attended affairs are likely to be weekend events in which part-time dealers can participate. A typical mall show may charge $175 for a three-day run from a twelve-by-eighteen-foot selling space. Larger booths are $250 and up—West Coast prices are higher.

A strong trend toward more specialized events has recently developed. Doll shows, toy shows, postcard exhibits, vintage automobile meets, and gun and relic shows are a few among those one can now attend.

Many shows are juried, or vetted, and only leading dealers are invited. At this end of the spectrum are the prestige charity shows of the East Coast. The annual Eastside House Settlement Winter Benefit Show in New York City draws a first-night crowd paying $180 per couple for the privilege of attending the gala preview. Preshow sales of $10,000 to $15,000 items are not uncommon.

The economics of exclusively dealing at shows are not complicated. The overhead mainly consists of travel expenses and booth rental fees. If a well-heeled dealer, with a good clean $20,000 inventory, did three shows a month, the profits might justify the efforts of maintaining a "portable" antique shop.

Display by Joy Piscopo, President, F. O. Bailey Co., Portland, Maine

There will be individual variations in travel and living expenses, but let's suppose that one limits his or her efforts to shows that are within a day's drive of home; living full-time on the road is a lifestyle that only a few hardy souls are equipped to handle anyway! Hypothetical expenses might be:

Booth rental (36 shows)	$7,000
Food and motels (100 nights)	5,000
Gas and maintenance (10,000 miles)	2,000
Annual expenses	$14,000

Some dealers could get by on a third less overhead, while others might spend more, but you can readily see that full-time "showgoers" have about the same overhead that "stationary" shop owners do. In order to break even, a yearly gross sales figure of $28,000 would have to be achieved. If we divide thirty-six shows into $28,000, we come up with a minimum break-even target of $778 in gross sales per three-day show, or about $260 a day. Anything above this would be 50 percent clear profit. A couple, averaging sales of $2,000 per show (from a $20,000 inventory), might net $500 in clear profit from a three-day event after all travel expenses. In the back of every dealer's mind is the hope of unloading a "windfall purchase" at top retail and perhaps "making the year" at one event.

Most promoters of antique shows advertise them many months in advance. They reach dealer prospects by screening attractive booths at events sponsored by competitors and through widely read ads in popular antique and collector periodicals. Some antique shows are always well attended while others are routinely flops. Talk to several traveling dealers, find out which sponsors are consistent winners and which promoters are "first timers" or lukewarm advertisers. It's better to pay an extra $150 for space at a large, well-attended gathering than stare at empty aisles from a budget rental table in a church bazaar!

Antique shows can be exhausting, exciting, and rewarding. Dealer-to-dealer sales are quite common, and many sleepers are sold two or three times at the same event (sometimes doubling in price at each change in ownership). The advantages of exposing your merchandise at shows rather than just in your shop are obvious. Fifty or a hundred quality dealers under one roof attract a very sophisticated "buying" clientele. After all, they have paid cash just to get in and see the wares—they are mentally prepared to buy. Many dealers use shows to gain regional visibility. The 10,000 collectors who pass by your table at a well-attended show may well equal the exposure provided by ten years of normal shopkeeping. A three-day appearance at an important event will bring forth dozens of new customers who may buy regularly from you throughout the year. Expect long waiting lists but better results from top-grade shows; expect to be disappointed at mediocre events.

Projecting your anticipated gross sales from a show is not altogether impossible. Veteran dealers tell us that they can reasonably hope to sell from 10 to 20 percent of their inventory at a well-attended event. Some hardworking furniture haulers have been known to sell out their entire stock—particularly if it has been well chosen, finely finished, and attractively priced. The more you can haul, the more you should sell. Carry a wide selection at first and narrow down or specialize as you find what moves best in what areas.

Traveling antique dealers often spot regional price differences and can capitalize on their ability to haul particular items from areas of abundant availability to areas of scarcity and higher prices. Some show dealers advertise their "wants" in small-town newspapers, well in advance of their arrival date. This on-the-road buying technique allows them to replenish stock and make new "picker" contacts at every major layover.

A couple we know spends the winter in California and Arizona and the summer months in New England. They do weekend shows in all the states along the way and a few state fairs in the Midwest. This enterprising pair leaves California with a Dodge maxi-van full of English curio cabinets (circa 1920), several boxes of brand-new art objects from the Orient, a stack of hand-woven Mexican-Indian rugs, primitive paintings, charcoal irons, spurs, scales, and "jail keys" (also from Mexico). In Arizona and New Mexico, they stop at a couple of large swap meets to purchase better Indian-made silver and turquoise jewelry at very competitive prices, and then move on to Kansas and Iowa, where they begin to sell their "western" wares to both dealers and collectors.

By the time this couple reaches New England the van is empty, and they begin to fill the truck for the return trip with smaller antiques that are still common in the Northeast. They try to buy things that will fit into old humpback trunks (the trunks themselves are going for from $100 to $175 in Los Angeles). Victorian prints, picture frames, postcard albums, tintypes, old advertising, early radios, weather vanes, carnival dolls, sewing items, handmade linens, salt cellars, and stereo viewers are but a few of the items which might make up a load for the return trip to California. This pair aren't getting rich, but they are having the time of their lives and have made good friends in every state between California and Connecticut.

Experience as an on-the-road dealer can be invaluable when it comes to quickly learning which antiques to purchase for resale and when to pass up "bargain" items that must be continually packed and repacked. It is this "eclectic" bent that makes show dealers the best customers of many tastefully stocked small shops and pickers.

A seasoned trouper will happily pay close to the asking prices of most rural and suburban shops for items that have proven themselves as show sellers. If you have a steady supply source for such staples as silver spoons, vintage jewelry, fine pocket watches, art pottery, small primitives, early dolls, toys, and textiles, it will pay you to contact show people personally. Offering a 15 percent discount from your retail prices will encourage volume purchases and repeat business.

In summarizing "Show Business," we can only relay the advice of several successful operators:

1. Check show dates against the calendar. Avoid participation in any production that would have to share the limelight with other crowd-pulling events, such as county fairs, local and national sports events, high school and college graduation ceremonies, holiday weekends, and so forth. Some promoters overlook local distractions, but you can't afford to!
2. Choose your show carefully. Does the sponsor have a good track record? Is the event an annual affair or is this the first time it has been produced in the area? How much advertising space has been actually purchased in local and trade periodicals?

3. Bring a few outstanding "props" to draw showgoers into your booth. The unusual always attracts attention!
4. Smile and greet every customer. Don't spend floor time with your nose buried in a book or eating from a plate on your table.
5. Don't fill up your booth or the aisles with an assortment of relatives, or friends, and their belongings. They take up valuable space and will discourage serious shoppers from entering your area.
6. Invite collectors to register their areas of interest; a card file of wanted items can produce big dividends on return trips.
7. Bring three times as much merchandise as you hope to sell. You can't close a sale on something left at home.
8. Try to schedule two or three shows in a row when on road trips. It saves a lot of preparation time and eliminates lost motion in removing and storing a large inventory between events.
9. Do not display extremely valuable items at flea markets or other "open admission" events. More than one dealer has been followed to his motel room and relieved of both cash and inventory.

If you are carrying high-priced merchandise in a van or station wagon, camouflage it with junk piled on top. Always park your vehicle directly in front of your ground-floor motel room door. Even large trucks have been towed away in the dead of night by clever thieves.

So much for paranoia! I have been swap meeting and showgoing for twenty-five years and have never seen an act of violence (but several eastern dealers have, and wanted me to add their comments).

Chapter 8 KEEP ON TRUCKING

Cross-Country Hauling Opportunities

If you are young, husky, and adventurous, and own a fairly good-sized truck, you might want to try your hand at cross-country antique hauling. "Haulers," as they are known in the trade, are capitalist truck drivers who buy semiantique furniture (or anything else they can make a buck on) from dealers, pickers, and auctions in the northeastern United States, and haul it to auctioneers in the Southeast, Southwest, or wherever the current action is. Few haulers stick with this kind of work for very long. Some of them become dealers or auctioneers, while others get into contract hauling where a fixed profit margin is more or less assured.

Making a Steady Income at Hauling Antiques. You'll have to work at hauling full-time, perhaps making seven or eight coast-to-coast trips per year and refinishing furniture all winter long. Some West Coast dealers run local newspaper ads in advance of buying trips. In these ads, they offer to haul local household goods for private persons to eastern destinations at reasonable fees (less than a moving company would charge). Frequently, western dealers who fly east to buy at auctions employ produce-truck drivers to carry their purchases back home in vegetable vans. Others rent large U-Haul rigs or pay moving-and-storage van companies to transport higher-ticket furnishings.

Some haulers do not confine their efforts to furniture or antiques exclusively. A few of them have found it more profitable to call directly on manufacturers of reproduction furniture, pottery, picture frames, textiles, and so forth, and buy a wholesale semiload of goods for resale to dealers in other states. A friend of mine picks up two loads a year of cast-iron ranch bells, stoneware crocks, and butter churns at a Texas factory and sells them as far north as Oregon (at twice his acquisition cost of $12,000 per truck and trailer load). In between these "working" trips, he dabbles in antiques. Another acquaintance is in the advertising antiques game. "Advertiques," as they are called, are a rising star in the collectibles field. This fellow does not need to drive anything larger than a station wagon; in fact, he flies to most of the specialized auctions, which are his major sources of supply. One week may find him at a tobacco factory closeout in Iowa. The next week, he will be on a plane to San Francisco attending a brewery auction. In between these trips, you might spot him at any major flea market or antique show in the country making new dealer contacts for the wholesale marketing of his vintage advertising labels, cans, trays, signs, and salesman's samples.

A beginning dealer would not be able to capitalize on the opportunities that these two gentlemen do. We would suggest at least a couple of years of shop or swap meet dealing before hitting the road with a big rig and $15,000 in your money belt. In the meantime, if you do have an opportunity to buy several thousand lots of anything collectible, or even usable (at a giveaway price like 10 cents on the retail dollar), don't be timid about advertising it for sale nationally or calling on likely retail outlets in person. Having been a gift and stationery shop owner, as well as an art and picture frame buyer, I can attest to the many free-lance truck driver and station wagon jobbers who sell "closeouts" to retail merchants every day of the week. All that it takes to get a store owner's interest (and order) is a good clean item offered in wholesale lots at a price substantially below what he would have to pay a regular supplier. Anytime you can offer a good $10 retailer to a merchant for under $4.50, he is likely to give you an order. If you can price it at $2.50, he may take the whole load and wholesale it to his friends!

The Economics of Hauling Are Simple. It takes about five days to drive a small rig across the United States (if you eat three square meals a day and stop at night to sleep). One way expenses for a medium-sized truck with a sixteen-foot covered bed might run something like this:

Food and motels	$200
Gas or diesel	500
Taxes and tolls	50
Tires and maintenance	200
(A one-way U-Haul truck runs more.)	Total $950

If you return home with an empty rig your expenses are going to be about $1,900 for the round trip. If you can find something to buy in the East (or West) that can be resold back home for a profit, you may be able to amortize the return trip by selling to dealers along the way. (One Arkansas antique dealer we know picks up a load of leather jackets at the Mexican border for resale in his home state.) The profit potential of this type of venture depends on six key factors:

- How cheaply you are able to buy
- How quickly you can fill your rig
- How many pieces of furniture you can haul
- How many small items you can profitably buy to fill up the drawers in the furniture
- How dearly you are able to sell
- The ability to haul a payload in both directions

If you hope to double your money on a load, before expenses, then you must buy in the East for less than half of southern or western "auction prices." When we say "auction prices," we mean less than retail shop prices. Some haulers who are not in a hurry have found that they can sell directly to big-city dealers and save an auctioneer's commission. Some even try to bypass dealers and sell directly to the public at swap meets or from the home of a relative, via a newspaper advertisement.

The advantage of dealing with an established auction house is that you can have your money the morning after the sale and be on your way with no further selling expenses. We would advise a preliminary visit to likely out-of-state auction outlets before you buy your first load for resale. (They advertise in the *Antique Trader Weekly* for Haulers.) Take notes of the actual prices realized. Talk to dealers in the crowd (they're in the back row). Ask if this was a good or a bad night for consignors. Inquire about the auctioneer's reputation. Is he a "slow pay" or otherwise hard to deal with? You might even call the local Better Business Bureau to see if it has any complaints on file. Never consign a load without a signed written contract that itemizes each piece you are selling and the commission terms and cash settlement date. Most of the auction houses that advertise regularly in antique publications are reputable firms, but a written agreement can eliminate any potential misunderstandings.

Listen to an Auctioneer. A good antique auctioneer can tell you in a minute what sells best in his area. Most of them will practically guarantee certain prices on specific items. Again, it is important to take copious notes in order to buy "right" in your own area, for resale in another. I have a three-year written record of the prices that my favorite auction house has realized. For instance, almost any common chair will bring $15 to $45; beds go for nothing. Highly illustrated books and bound volumes of certain antique newspapers bring $15 to $35. Hoosier kitchen cabinets are almost always good for $500. Humpback trunks go cheap at auction, but are very high in shops. Rocking chairs are $60-to-$150 sellers, and lamp tables are about the same. Old advertising tins, signs, posters, and imprinted products bring almost retail at auction; country store stuff really takes off. Coffee mills and butter churns are other local winners, and cut glass of the Victorian period is also very good here (art glass is not). Farm primitives sell well in shops but usually fall flat at auction! Firearms command premium retail prices at this auction, while edged weapons rarely yield more than $25. Table lamps of the twenties are top performers (often bringing $150 to $350 with glass shades), but local collectors just don't get fired up over oil lamps. This list could go on and on, but its validity is limited to the fashions and prices of one auction house in a remote corner of the United States!

The Auction Game. Buying at one auction for the purpose of selling at another auction is a very tough game, but there are still people playing it. The trick is to *buy* at poorly attended rural or neighborhood sales—and *sell* at well-promoted collector-oriented auctions. Sometimes oversupply can work in one's favor. Medium-quality bowfront china cupboards that sell for $300 in

You never know what you may find at a country auction. Courtesy Don Kader Advertising

New England are going for $850 at West Coast events. Netsukes and Nippon, which abound in southern California, sell at a profitable premium in Iowa.

You will find regular antique or household auctions taking place in almost any small town on a Friday or Saturday night or Sunday afternoon. These are "buying" auctions. Some of the larger flea markets, like "Shipshewana" (Tuesday and Wednesday in northern Indiana, Rt. 5, about five miles from the Michigan border), feature half a dozen auctions conducted at one time during the spring and summer season. Country auction notices are generally posted at courthouses, liquor stores, farmer's markets, and other public gathering places. The local weekend editions of most newspapers also feature upcoming sales. Better yet, go straight to the horse's mouth and call up a few auctioneers to see what they have on the agenda. You might even be invited to a private "preview."

A lucky hauler may be able to fill a sixteen- or twenty-foot truck bed with vintage furniture acquired at one good auction. More often than not, it will take two or three auctions and several purchases from local pickers to complete a buying trip.

In the Northeast, local dealers, or pickers with a basement or barn full of furniture, may be found by attending flea markets, using the telephone, or, most commonly, by scouting the winding secondary roads that parallel most major freeways. In the spring, summer, and early fall (before Thanksgiving), you will likely spot many a homemade sign along the roadway.

Experience has taught us that only about 10 to 20 percent of any one dealer's stock will be priced low enough for profitable resale, but you can still fill a truck in a few days of concentrated buying in the lower Great Lakes region during the summertime. Currently, haulers are also finding good quality furniture, glassware, and farm primitives in Kansas, Missouri, Illinois, Indiana, Iowa, Pennsylvania, and upstate New York. Do your shopping at least twenty-five or fifty miles away from major cities. Sell your wares in highly populated downtown or resort areas. You will get premium prices in upper-income communities.

My friend, with fifty years in the trade, sums it all up when he says, "Antiques are like orphans; they just need to be placed in the proper homes." Your job is to find them a prosperous home.

1880s ad for mail-order manual.

Chapter 9 MAIL-ORDER MERCHANDISING

Selling Antiques from Your Own Home

Buying through the mail has been a popular pastime in the United States ever since the pioneer firms of Sears Roebuck and Montgomery Ward & Co. printed their first catalogs at the turn of the century. Even in this day of abundant regional shopping centers and countless local retail establishments, mail-order selling continues unabated. As late as 1979, the *Saturday Evening Post* boldly proclaimed that 70 percent of its 3 million readership still firmly believed in buying by mail. (In the same letter, they invited antique dealers to buy classified advertising at the rate of $2.30 per word.)

Over the years many major antique dealers have issued their own mail-order catalogs. Some of these printed pieces have become valuable reference tools in themselves. Oriental rugs, paperweights, firearms, and fine furniture are frequently purchased, sight unseen, from these prestigious firms. A glance through the pages of *Antique Monthly* newspaper will find several such catalog offerings.

A successful mail-order dealer is the envy of all who would aspire to make an honest profit from as little work as possible. More "get rich quick" books have been written on the mail-order business than on horse racing and the stock market combined! Catalog printers thrive on the business generated by would-be mail-order magnates, and the nation's magazines and pulp tabloids continue to accept ads from all comers. Weight reduction, bust development, balding remedies, and "limited edition" collectible manufacturers are successful advertising-space buyers, and have been for the past twenty years. At the turn of the century it was cheap pocket watches, custom corsets, piano lessons, quack cures, and knitting machines. One wonders what mail-order wizardry will captivate the fancy of the next generation.

Today there are still many legitimate mail-order opportunities in the antique and collectible field. I am personally acquainted with three gentlemen who garner their entire livelihood from various forms of mail-order endeavor. The most prosperous of these entrepreneurs sells electronic components to ham radio operators. The most sophisticated is a fellow who sells his own color slides of the world's great art to university art departments and slide libraries. Jon, the most widely traveled of the three, sells military antiques by mail and flies a private plane all over the country, replenishing his stock from dealers, pickers, and the estates of collectors.

What do these successful mail-order operators have in common? Specialization and a catalog! They offer, in depth, a selection of items that would be impossible to find in a retail shop, anywhere. Their businesses took years of careful cultivation to produce sustaining incomes.

Only five out of every one hundred mail-order advertisements that you see will ever be repeated (95 percent fail). An even more startling statistic is the well-researched fact that only 1 percent of all "single product" offerings are profitable! The pros are happy if they can harvest a hundred new names for their catalog lists and break even on an ad.

Copy Success.   An old mail-order maxim that bears repeating is "Copy Success." The procedure is simple. Look through a year or two's issues of a popular antique publication and clip out the advertisements that have been repeated time after time, month after month. These people aren't throwing money down a well! They are onto something that at least pays for the ad and produces some degree of profit. It is a logical assumption that if "Miss Alice's Antique Silver Matching Service" has been advertising for two or three years in the *Antique Trader,* she is doing something right. (The fact that the advertisements may end abruptly after an extended period may mean that Alice has recruited enough steady customers to keep her busy.) You can't be "all things to all men," but you can be a very important member of the mail-order fraternity if you are the only antique zither dealer in the country. So specialize and put out a catalog

if you are serious about making a living from your mailbox!

Some collectibles have been sold for years through the mails. Remember the ads that used to appear inside the covers of comic books? I bought more than my share of "Worldwide Stamp Packets" for $1. Coins are also regularly sold by mail. Old postcards are a mail-order staple, and political memorabilia, Depression glass, beer cans, and American art pottery are also marketed by mail. What do these products have in common? They are already well documented and easily identifiable. The prospect can know from your brief description exactly what he or she is buying.

What Won't Sell. Things that generally don't sell well by mail are widely available goods like china, silverplate, and pressed glass (or one-of-a-kind items like original art). If your first ad doesn't pull, ask yourself if you would buy the same type of merchandise, sight unseen, from the brief description you have offered? Selling a Coca-Cola item or a popular brand of barbed wire by mail should be easy if the price is right. How many variations of a twelve-inch 1938 Coke thermometer or an eighteen-inch length of Johnson's galvanized flat twist exist? A statement of condition and the right to return are all that the prospective purchaser of these items needs to know before sending you a check.

Low-Cost Advertising. A distinct advantage of selling antiques or collectibles by mail is the comparative low cost of reaching prospects. A typical weekly tabloid with a circulation of about a hundred thousand collectors charges 19 cents per word, or $8.50 a column inch for classified advertising. Even the fancy monthlies have classified rates of under $10 per inch. If you've got something really hot, you can buy a full page for from $250 to $800 in many antique publications. If you think the entire nation might be your market, you can reach a million nostalgic readers through a full page in *Yankee* magazine for only $4,000, or 8 million *Better Homes & Gardens* subscribers for $43,550.

Mail-Order Laws Are Minimal. The few laws are mostly concerned with preventing outright fraud. There is no federal license required, and most state and local governing bodies are just concerned with your collecting and reporting the local sales tax on items sold within the state. All you need, to collect this sales tax, is a resale number from your local State Tax Board.

Most municipalities do not require a business license for mail-order selling from a home. Some cities do, however, frown on any business ventures being conducted from a residential dwelling. Find out before you ask them for a license. You may want to work from a post office box or a commercial mail drop.

If you conduct your business by the golden rule (and keep carbon copies of all correspondence), you probably will never run afoul of your local postmaster or any other authorities.

Don't Offer General-Line Merchandise. Occasional offerings of general-line merchandise from your shop's shelf stock will not be profitable. What incentive would people have to respond, unless they live in Alaska? Price alone may sell some run-of-the-mill things, but it generally does not pay to advertise $1 to $10 items for sale through the mails unless you have several dozen identical pieces to sell. Can you imagine the expense involved in returning twenty-five identical checks sent in for the same $3 Avon bottle? You can see why it is equally important to specify "S.A.S.E." (send self-addressed stamped envelope) in all of your advertisements!

Do not offer damaged antiques or collectibles via the mails. Invariably, even when the damage is described, these items will be returned for a refund. It is important to note even the slightest defects when advertising. Try to describe the item in as much overall detail as possible to avoid misunderstandings and motivate the prospect to send his or her check—rather than a letter of inquiry.

While we are on the subject of motivation, why do people buy antiques by mail? Perhaps the description rings a nostalgic bell, and they impulsively drop a small check in the mail. Maybe the item is not available locally and is needed for research, repairs, or to complete a collection. Often, antiques are purchased as gifts for friends or relatives. Some people seem to enjoy the gamble of buying by mail. Anyway, collectors are called "collectors" because they *collect.* They want to buy! All you have to do, in many cases, is find the right merchandise; it will sell itself. The selection of antiques that you offer is ultimately the deciding factor in the number of dollars that will find their way into your mailbox. (Again, don't expect to sell the commonplace by mail.)

Invoicing. It is a good idea to write up all mail-order sales on a triplicate invoice form (available from any office supply store). One copy is mailed to the customer the same day you ship his package. Another copy is inserted inside the package before wrapping. This is done in case the outer wrapper is damaged or lost (it also facilitates the goods getting to the proper person if initially unwrapped by an employee or relative). The original invoice is kept by you and filed alphabetically under the last name of the customer. Your own firm's name and address—as well as the complete mailing address and name of the intended recipient—should appear on all copies of the invoice.

Never mail or release all of the copies of the invoice or any subsequent correspondence with a customer. You would find it impossible to reconstruct the transaction should a dispute arise, or a claim for lost merchandise be filed, at a later date.

If you feel it necessary to hold a customer's order until his check clears the bank, you should note by return mail, on a copy of the invoice, that the merchandise will be shipped in three weeks. Under no circumstance should you ship any item prior to receiving payment. Bad checks in general mail-order merchandising can run to about 5 percent of all sales. Collectors, however, are honest 99 percent of the time, and less than one in a hundred of the checks you receive is likely to bounce (wait three weeks for clearance before sending expensive items).

Packing and Shipping.   Double box and double address all merchandise. If an antique has been packed properly for the U.S. mail, it should not be damaged by a toss across the room onto a concrete floor. Glass or ceramic items should be individually wrapped and padded, and inserted at least three inches apart in a box filled with shredded newspaper or plastic popcorn. This box is addressed and placed within another box that is at least three inches larger in all dimensions, and likewise padded on all sides, including top and bottom. If you take this extra care in mail-order packing, you will probably never have a claim for damage. Don't ship a heavy object in the same box with lighter-weight things. The weight of a sadiron can crush a porcelain teapot even though they are both well padded and six inches apart. Better to mail them separately or on opposite sides of a partitioned wine box. It's also a good idea to note the number of boxes you are shipping on the customer's copy of the invoice; separate packages may arrive several days (or weeks) apart.

Large items are best shipped by United Parcel or Motor Freight. Check with your post office for size and weight restrictions before packing. *Insure everything you ship or mail.* Pay a little extra for a "return receipt" on valuable packages.

Even if you do not list a telephone number in your advertisements, you can expect to get a few phone calls. Be extra cheerful and courteous to those who telephone. Today's caller may be next month's customer. Many callers will request that you give their telephone order preference over any other customers' checks that you might receive. Our experience has been that two out of three of these callers don't ever send a check (they have second thoughts and don't follow through). The best way to handle telephone customers is to thank them for calling and tell them your policy has always been to give preferential attention to orders accompanied by postal money orders or certified checks—if theirs arrives within three days, the deal is on!

Mailing Lists.   Be sure to save the names and addresses of all mail-order customers and file them under the headings of the items they collect. This file is a categorical cross reference of every customer inquiry you have ever received and is in addition to your alphabetical shipping invoice file. A "live" mailing list is an asset that can be mined repeatedly and sometimes sold or rented to others. The R. L. Polk Co. is a nationwide seller of mailing lists. For only a few cents per name it can supply you with thousands of gummed name and address labels covering every occupational group from dentist to dog catcher. (I recently availed myself of the excellent list of ten thousand libraries that buy "how-to" books.)

Mailing and Placing Ads. Some dealers send a printed list of all merchandise on hand twice a year to their entire mailing list. These semiannual mass mailings often produce a large volume of business. Since the advent of instant printing, it has become very simple to put out a Xerox or offset list. One need not scrimp on descriptions or line drawings when the cost is only pennies per sheet. You can go into a lot more detail here than in your regular classified advertising. You also have the advantage of being able to mail lists of particular collector interest to a specific group from your files. The return from a specialized mailing to only a dozen active collectors can be worthwhile.

Try placing identical advertisements in three or four collector publications on the same date. Key your return address in each ad to a box or department number, for example, Dept. A.T. (for *Antique Trader*) or Box C.N. (for *Collectors News*); you will soon know which publication's readership responds best to any particular offering. If you have a large quantity of any one item on hand, and it hasn't moved from an ad, try inserting a photo or a simple pen-and-ink sketch (along with a lower price) in your next advertisement. Stand behind all of your mail-order solicitations with an advertising statement that "Satisfaction is guaranteed or a full refund will be made on merchandise returned within ten days."

In the Event of a Lost or Damaged Shipment. The burden of filing forms and collecting from the post office has traditionally fallen upon the buyer. The buyer has in his or her possession the broken items, which have to be presented to the post office with the claim, and it would be a waste of valuable time and money to remail damaged goods back across the country to the seller. However, if the buyer wishes to return broken merchandise to the dealer (along with the original carton and packing), the dealer should file the claim. In either event the post office will confiscate the merchandise and provide the proper insurance forms. In the case of a United Parcel or private trucking company claim, it is also very important to retain the original shipping container and all of the packing material. We would recommend that you insert these instructions inside every shipping carton and also advise every customer that it is his or her responsibility to file any claim for loss or damage, in transit, directly with the carrier who makes the final delivery. Also indicate that you will provide assistance, if needed, in making the claim.

Above all, treat the customer as if he were a local over-the-counter buyer. Promptly acknowledge the order. Assure a return privilege. Ship merchandise within twenty-four hours of the order unless the customer advises otherwise. Treat all sales in confidence and be cheerful on the phone.

Evaluating Results.   Remember that it takes just as long to create a self-sustaining mail-order business as it does to establish an antique shop (about three years). Don't give up after running a couple of $10 ads.

Again, ask yourself if you would respond to your own ad? Is the merchandise in demand? Is the price attractive? Are the items illustrated or well described? Have you tried more than one publication? Was your headline an attention getter?

Since advertising for a direct customer response from mail-order ads can be scientifically measured (for example, no response = poor ad), several rules have evolved for successful mail-order copy writing. Although not all of them apply to selling antiques, we would do well to take note of the principles involved and apply them wherever we can. After all, as was mentioned earlier, one maxim of mail-order merchandising is "Copy Success"; why not go a step further and copy successful advertising?

The first rule is get the reader's attention (before he turns the page and misses your ad).

CLASSIC EXAMPLES OF SUCCESSFUL DIRECT MAIL HEADLINES

- **Do You Make Mistakes in English?** (ad ran for 40 years)
- **They Laughed When I Sat Down at the Piano!** (remember?)
- **To Men Who Want to Quit Work Someday** (who doesn't?)

- **When Your Horse Goes Lame** (an embrocation)
- **Still Less than $10** (is anything?)
- **FREE—This 1,339 Page Book!** (a Sears catalog)
- **Our Remarkable Offer for 1912 ... To You!** (use a date)
- **How It Feels to Earn $1,000 a Week** (good!)
- **What's Wrong in This Picture?** (a question)
- **Have You Heard About ...** (the "NEWS" approach)
- **Now, for the First Time ...** (a combination of "now" and "news")
- **An Easy Way to Make Money from Your Own Home** (is it legal?)
- **A Thrilling Surprise Each Month!** (is it moral?)
- **You May Think I Am Crazy!** (my wife does)
- **Test It 10 Days Free in Your Own Home** (enclose money)
- **How to Lose Weight and Still Eat as Much as You Want** (pie in the sky)
- **A New Shampoo That Leaves Your Hair Lovelier** (beer)
- **How to Wake Up the Financial Genius Inside You** (real estate)
- **Millionaires Are Not 100 Times Smarter than You!** (real estate)
- **The Lazy Man's Way to Riches** (positive thinking)

Obviously, you won't have room for this kind of headline writing in a $5 classified ad, but consider creative adaptations of these classic examples for any serious advertising effort. Remember that all good headlines contain one or more of these messages: news, information, bargains, health, wealth, love, or something else free!

After you have gotten the reader's attention with a successful headline, you should use as many words as necessary to convince him of the worth of your product and his need to respond to the advertisement at once.

Most professional mail-order advertising contains a coupon to cut out and remind the reader that he has made a decision and must get around to mailing his check. If you don't have room for a coupon, consider using a dashed border design and the words "Clip and Save This Ad."

Also, if you are going to do anything more than sporadic advertising, it is important to develop some kind of a "look," or image, to your ads—even if it's just putting your name in bold capital letters at the top of every offering. This image establishes you as a regular, respectable dealer (in the minds of some readers).

If the idea of conducting a mail-order business intrigues you, there are dozens of newsletters, magazines, and "how-to" books available on this fascinating subject. (Most of them are sold only by mail.) We have listed a few (without endorsement or guarantee) just to pique your curiosity. Your librarian can probably supply you with current mailing addresses of those still in business.

Advertising Digest
Business Leads Digest
The Direct Mail Manual
Entrepreneur Magazine
How I Made $1,000,000 in Mail Order by E. Joseph
   Cossman (ant farm and spud gun inventor)
Introduction to Mail Order
Mail Order Digest (good)
Mail Order Informer
Mail Trade
Mailer's World
Small Business & Mail Order News
Success in Self-Publishing
Venture Magazine (excellent)
Towers Club USA (self-publishing news and advice)

Chapter 10 LOCATION, LOCATION, LOCATION

A Make-or-Break Decision

Look for High Traffic and Low Overhead. The lowest possible overhead, combined with a high traffic count, can enable your shop to survive while others fail. Don't spend an excessive amount of money fixing up a building you don't own. Every extra dime you have should be invested in inventory!

Some dealers feel that beginners should locate among existing antique shops and take advantage of the clientele already coming into the neighborhood looking for antiques, but there are also disadvantages to such locations. One thing you might consider is the lack of "off-the-street" buying opportunities because of the competition from other dealers nearby. Another minus would be your dependency upon a "collector" clientele almost exclusively; you could miss out on the booming gift market in antiques. In many cities, small specialty shops seem to thrive near large civic, office, hotel, or hospital complexes, where the lunch-hour traffic alone can provide dozens of impulse buyers.

Antique shops are not normally found in major shopping malls or other high-rent retail centers. These locations are manned by merchants who have to turn over their inventories four or five times a year! The typical annual sales goal in such a center is $125 per square foot of floor space. A one-thousand-square-foot gift store is expected to do at least $125,000 per year. Why can't an antique dealer turn over his inventory more than one and a half or two times a year? Simply because "ready to sell" replacement stock is not immediately available.

Most antique acquisitions are in need of cleaning, fixing, research, or restoration. You just don't unpack them from a supplier's shipping carton and put them on the shelves. Normally you are your own buying agent. Rarely does anyone else sit through auctions, run down telephone leads, attend flea markets, or travel for you in search of good merchandise. It is the *simplicity of procurement* that enables a gift retailer to turn over his stock four or five times a year and, subsequently, pay the higher rents demanded of metropolitan shopping center tenants. (We might note again that most major shopping center landlords require a new tenant to put in his own floor, ceiling, heating and cooling, and lighting systems. It is not uncommon to spend $30,000 on space preparation in a new center.)

We live in the age of the automobile, and most businesses feel they have to provide ready parking space for these conveyances. A high auto traffic count is important only if the cars are traveling slow enough to take notice of your wares. When potential customers pass your building, they should be able to see you and turn around easily within a block or two. Foot traffic is a real plus! Shoppers can be enticed into a store by creative window and sidewalk displays. (Your shop *does* have a display window, doesn't it?)

Who Are Your Potential Business Neighbors? Good neighbors are "people pullers," like beauty shops, fabric stores, florists, post offices, bookstores, banks, hardware stores, coffee shops, escrow offices, drug stores, ice cream shops, cinemas, furniture stores, and wall covering or paint outlets. Don't settle for the first vacant building in your neighborhood; see a realtor and tell him or her of your need for a "people-pulling" location. Chances are that he knows of a vacancy soon to occur. If you live in an unzoned rural location, you will need to rent some sign space on the main highway (in several locations up to five miles away). Tourists love to "discover" antique shops!

Antique Supermarkets and Shopping Marts. A relatively new concept in the United States, these markets allow large groups of dealers to get together under one roof to offer their wares. Permanent or weekly shop spaces are leased to individual operators, usually within large barns or warehouse-type buildings often consisting of several floors. The attraction and advertising power of so many dealers is much more than any single shop could hope to offer. The environment is similar to a farmer's market or flea market, except that the event is indoors and the shopping spaces can be secured with the merchandise left safely overnight or until the next weekend. We recommend these antique marts to the beginning dealer because a small amount of working capital will go a long way. Walls are ready for display. Heating, cooling, and electrical systems are already in. Advertising is cooperative, and other dealers may even help you to price your antiques realistically. Because of the amount of traffic generated, a specialist can hope to survive here. Larger antique marts frequently feature used book and paper dealers, doll and toy vendors, candy or coffee shops, furniture dealers, glassware and china shops, stamp and coin dealers, arts and crafts people, and a myriad of collectors dealing in everything from beer cans to Disneyanna.

In this type of environment a beginner could conceivably start selling with a small personal collection and as little as $2,500 in "buying" cash. A stall owner working out of a five-hundred-square-foot space, with an inventory of $5,000 (at cost), might eventually achieve monthly gross sales of $3,000 in a well-promoted market. Deduct the rent, insurance, supplies, and cost of merchandise, and you could come up with a net profit of $650 a month from this type of low-budget operation. It's better to spend a few months on the waiting list for a booth in an established market than to be one of a few understocked "early birds" in a brand-new antique cooperative. New shopping centers, from the humblest to the grandest, take about twenty-four months to fill up with tenants and actually generate sustaining traffic.

Before you sign a lease or rental agreement, talk to as many tenants as possible. There will always be a few disgruntled dealers in any large group, but you should also be hearing from some happy merchants and see real money actually changing hands. Spend a market day near your prospective selling space and check it out carefully. Are there enough electrical outlets available? Do they work? How is the overhead lighting? Is the dealer in the neighboring booth tolerable? Is there sufficient heating or cooling in your corner? Will the center of the room suit you best, or would you prefer a booth against the wall for the added display possibilities? If you are considering the rental of an unattended booth in one of the newer consignment malls, you had better look into the management's policy on theft. One couple we know pulled out of the nation's largest mall after losing a two-hundred-pound desk and a chest of drawers to clever shoplifters.

If the mart is a multiple-story affair, do your best to obtain a ground floor location. Two-thirds of the ground floor shoppers spend all of their money or energy on the first level and never make it upstairs. Think it over—don't rent in a day and repent for a year!

Choose the Largest Booth You Can Afford. Remember that a square foot of display space can produce sales of $125 per year in the very best retail stores. Your shop will do well to gross $50 a year per square foot of rented space unless you are a jeweler.

If you aren't turned on by the idea of sharing space with other dealers, the possibilities are endless. Imagine all the abandoned corner gas stations that dot the countryside. Drive by the vacant meat markets and empty neighborhood grocery stores. There are plenty of low-cost rentals for would-be antique and second-hand dealers, so be choosy.

Home-based Shops. The lowest possible shop rental (zero) would be your own garage, basement, or barn. All it takes are a few roadside signs to direct tourists and big city dealers to your location. A common practice among "resident dealers" is to put an additional small sign on the gate or front door saying "Blow your car horn for service." This allows one to go about regular household or farm chores without having to sit in an open shop. It also serves as a method of screening out all but the most serious buyers. (A casual "looker" is not going to blow his or her horn and wait fifteen minutes for you to open the barn door!)

We have done some of our best picking from the home-operated shops of the northeastern United States. It is not uncommon for a California or New England "city dealer" to spend $1,000 in an hour of buying from a country picker. If you are an auction buff and are willing to operate on a quick one-third markup, this type of low-overhead, dealer-oriented wholesale operation may be your ticket to financial independence. When you have accumulated a barnful, run a small ad in several collector publications advising out-of-town dealers of what you stock and your willingness to "wholesale to the trade."

A shot of our shop's wall display. Courtesy Tom Warren

Before we leave the subject of home-based antique shops, we might add that they are not limited to rural locations or wholesale only. A local doctor's wife takes three "vacations" a year in Europe, and ships home about $15,000 worth of bric-a-brac, clocks, and furniture after each trip, via a twenty-foot ocean "container." Twenty-three days later, the container clears Customs and is hauled to her back door by a local truckline. After inspection by Customs is completed, this enterprising lady gets on the phone and calls every dealer in town for "first pick" of the lot. When the dealers are finished, she runs small classified newspaper ads and sells most of the remaining antiques to the general public at slightly above wholesale. Can you think of a nicer way to travel (and net an extra $10,000 or $20,000 a year)?

Should You Rent by the Month or Lease by the Year? Terminating a month-to-month rental is just a matter of giving the landlord a few weeks' notice (or vice versa). If you've found the "ultimate" location, you should try for a long-term lease with an option to renew at the end of a three- or five-year period. The lease agreement may contain a number of standard clauses: cost of living index increases in rent, shared property taxes, maintenance fees, and merchants' association dues are among them. A *lease deposit*, amounting to the first and last month's rental plus a security deposit of a couple of hundred dollars, is not uncommon. Avoid *percentage leases* where the landlord gets a guaranteed minimum plus a percentage of your gross sales. Your overall rent should not exceed 8 percent of your gross sales. Again we note that the only way you can attempt to project your gross sales before you actually open for business is to multiply your actual beginning inventory cost by two, and multiply the total by two again. This formula assumes that you will turn over your entire inventory twice a year. If you are investing $15,000 in well-chosen antiques for resale at a $30,000 retail figure, you might gross as much as $60,000 per year, after your business gets going. Eight percent of $60,000 is $4,200 per year rent, or a $350 per month rental budget, which is a reasonable lease expense for this level of sales volume.

The rent and utilities are "fixed" expenses. Many new dealers get themselves into trouble by adding to their fixed expenses other contractual obligations that are completely unnecessary to the operation of an antique shop. Write down your fixed expenses and keep a running total of projected monthly overhead costs. It's a sobering fact to realize that you must sell twice this amount every month just to break even.

Chapter 11 MYTHS FROM MADISON AVENUE

A Short Course in Effective Advertising

Some Budget Warnings. Almost before the ink on your business license is dry, you will be besieged by an army of slick-talking salesmen who make their livelihoods selling blue sky and hot air.

Take Joe Doe, who has found a small shop renting for $250 a month with another $50 covering utilities and $25 for a telephone. He has a basic monthly overhead of $325, plus a truck and other extras that might add up to $500 per month in fixed costs. Along comes Mr. Slick, who sells him a computerized accounting service for only $125 a month (on a one-year contract). Just as Mr. Slick is leaving, in pops Emma Quickbuck with a monthly advertising program that "puts your name in every motel room in the county": another $50-a-month contractual obligation.

The next morning, as Joe is nervously arranging his stock, Mr. Able of "Accidents Always Happen" Insurance Company calls with "a golden opportunity" to get in on a "Small Business-man's Group Insurance Plan that is too good to pass up" ($25 per month). *Joe's cost of doing business is now at $700 a month and growing rapidly.*

Instead of bringing in a few paper bags from home, Joe has called the Pressure Pulp and Printing Company. Their commissioned salesman soon has him convinced that "every customer should be a walking advertisement for your store." A ten-thousand bag "minimum" order costs *only $900* and can be paid for over a period of a year or more. Another $73 a month is added to Joe's mushrooming cost of doing business.

An eighth of a page advertisement in the Yellow Pages will add another $147 a month. *Joe's little shop has now incurred a fixed monthly expense obligation of $920.* Incidental miscellaneous expenses quickly raise the figure to over $1,000 a month just to keep the shop open for business!

This fictional account is not exaggerated—it happens every day to small business people all over the country!

Don't throw away hard-earned cash by advertising in "business directories," church bulletins, coupon mailings, high school basketball programs, and yearbooks. Of course, you can't be a perennial Scrooge, but offer a modest door prize instead of a cash contribution. Your grandest white elephant probably cost you no more than $5, and it's a legitimate tax writeoff, at retail, when donated to a worthy cause (get a signed receipt).

What to Spend and How to Spend It. Plan to spend a few hundred dollars on advertising during your grand opening and the first month of business; after that gear your advertising expenditures to not a penny more than 2 percent of net sales. Your cash can be more wisely used in making good buys and building an attractive inventory. The emphasis within the trade is on buying wisely and letting the collectors know what is carried. "Price" does not necessarily sell antiques like it does shoes or groceries. Many a novice dealer can attest to "no takers" on a widely advertised 25 percent reduction sale. The same advertising funds would be more prudently spent in telling the public exactly what you have and what you are open to buy. Our closest relative, the gift industry, spends an average of 2 percent of its gross sales on advertising. This means that a typical small gift retailer grossing, say, $5,000 per month might allocate a maximum of $100 for keeping his or her name in the media.

As mentioned earlier, the antique trade is blessed with more than a dozen publications aimed at collectors only, some with circulations approaching 100,000 each. There isn't a cheaper way to get your message out than through these publications. Study the ads and prices of repeat space buyers. What works for them may well be good for you.

Advertising in your hometown daily need not be a complete waste—most shops spend their 2 percent budget on a seasonal basis. Don't do "panic" advertising when people aren't in the buying mood anyway! July, August, and September are vacation and back-to-school months, and January through April is a period devoted to income tax worries. These are periods in which to concentrate on buying and refinishing antiques. If you're out of cash, better to visit a banker or auctioneer than waste money on nonproductive advertising.

Ask any veteran retailer what his most successful or most widely used advertising method is—chances are that he will quickly reply: "direct mail." Your mailing list can be your most valuable business asset. The time to start building such a list is the day you open your doors. Keep a guest register with a column for the customers' specific collecting interests. Indicate on a small sign near the register that inclusion puts one on the "mailing list" (everybody likes interesting mail). Insist on a current mailing address when accepting credit cards and personal checks. It's a good business practice and it can add several dozen names to your mailing list each week.

When we sold our art supply store, after ten years of somewhat successful operation, we had accumulated over three thousand names and addresses of active art supply and picture frame buyers in our area. Postage costs of $450, spent mailing to this group, easily produced over $5,000 in additional monthly gross sales (if the right products were featured).

Large antique "wholesalers" use weekly or monthly mailers to dealers almost exclusively. Some of these wholesale sources don't even appear in newspaper or Yellow Pages advertising. (It will pay you, as a retail dealer, to get on several antique wholesalers' mailing lists; they get hungry occasionally and offer some sensational wholesale buys.) One large firm with warehouses on both the East and West coasts has a once-a-year half-off sale to clear the floor before inventory tax day. Most wholesalers who receive regular "container shipments" inform their mailing lists of the day of arrival and unpacking. Auctioneers are also active direct-mail users. Use your mailing list to announce new shipments, services, and products, or just write a "newsy" antique-oriented letter to let customers know what you have been buying recently. (There is a lot of truth in the old adage that "out of sight is out of mind.") Try direct-mail advertising as soon as you have a few hundred names, or launch a campaign today by sending an illustrated price list to every doctor, dentist, lawyer, and interior decorator in the local phone book.

Repeat another mailing to the same list at least two more times before trying other prospects (type all of your mailing labels in *triplicate*).

The Yellow Pages. Another popular advertising medium among antique dealers is the Yellow Pages section of the local telephone directory. Perhaps one reason is that it doesn't require any monthly creative effort (or the licking of a thousand or so stamps). Seriously though, there isn't a more economical way of letting the buying (and selling) public know where you are, what you buy, what you sell, and when you are open.

Many sophisticated dealers use the Yellow Pages as a buying vehicle as well as a selling medium. If you want the first look at every picker's load that comes through your area, say so—in the Yellow Pages. It takes real guts to advertise as a buyer, rather than as a seller, because one might feel obligated to buy from every individual who presents his wares. Not so! Professional buyers run huge ads implying that they pay the highest prices, while in reality they screen out 99 percent of the prospects over the phone and buy from only the poor souls who are willing to sell for half of wholesale.

I know the driver of a CB radio equipped auctioneer's truck who has never paid more than $1,600 for a houseful of modern furniture, and that usually includes whatever he can find in the garage or attic! His firm's (price-wise) telephone answerer screens out all but the most desperate callers and keeps in contact with three full-time driver/buyers. A divorce, bankruptcy, illness, or other personal financial disaster can motivate reasonable people to sell for ridiculous prices! I am not implying that you should adopt these purchasing methods, but we repeatedly emphasize that it can pay great dividends to advertise both in the Yellow Pages and in the local newspaper's classified section as a cash buyer.

Let's examine the most common forms of antique shop advertising in their approximate order of productivity:

- Direct mail to known collectors, upper-income households, interior decorators, and fellow antique dealers
- Yellow Pages telephone directory advertising to buy and sell

- Advertisements in antique- and collector-oriented publications (to reach out-of-town prospects)
- Local classified newspaper advertising on a seasonal basis
- An inexpensive flyer showing the location of every antique shop within a ten-mile radius. Each dealer on this map should agree to display it prominently and provide free copies to all customers
- Specialty advertising items—imprinted matchbook covers, postcards, bookmarks, and calendars—that will keep your name in front of the customer daily

Keep a running total of every dollar you spend on advertising. Under no circumstances should it exceed 2 percent of your gross sales. Remember, your best advertisement is a satisfied customer!

Wise merchants "key" all advertising by using a coupon or department number to measure the response of each ad. Using this technique, you may quickly ascertain that only a small portion of your advertising budget actually pays for itself.

Never make an advertising decision while a space salesman is present. Sleep on all your written "copy." A clearheaded, early morning editing job may save the day.

Chapter 12 *BUYING "RIGHT"*

What to Buy, What to Pay, Where to Buy It

Good sources for volume buying are auctions and wholesale container importers. Secondary sources for beginning dealers are flea markets, garage sales, giftware and reproduction distributors, professional pickers, and private individuals.

An item "well bought" is as good as sold the minute you unload it from your van, but before you go on a wanton buying spree count to ten and read these basic rules for beginning buyers:

1. It is not necessary to plan an initial cross-country "buying trip." Many novice dealers wrongly feel that the grass is greener in another state. Your best buys will almost always be made within a day's drive of your own hometown!
2. Don't buy any of your beginning inventory from local dealers. They are not going to sell you any fresh goods that can absorb a 100 percent markup.
3. Don't buy in haste. Better to pay rent on an unopened store building, for a month or two, than to open with the wrong stock purchased at the wrong price.
4. Don't buy more than 10 percent of your opening stock from any single source. This rule is "insurance" against wrong buying and, if observed, will expose you to at least ten sources of supply.
5. Buy the very best quality you can afford.

If you've got ready cash, and someone who knows local market values to assist you, try running an "antiques and bric-a-brac wanted" advertisement in your local newspaper. Don't expect immediate results from a "buying" ad. It takes at least a weekend or two of newspaper exposure to produce meaningful results. An advertising budget of $75 will produce many, many buying opportunities (a $15, one-time-only ad may not produce a single call).

All many people need is an "invitation" to sell their family heirlooms (not everyone appreciates antiques). Be cheerful and courteous to all callers and refer them to other dealers (or auctioneers) if you are not interested in their wares.

Your best purchases will be made from the very young, the very modern, the unread, the untraveled, and, sadly enough, from people with an alcohol problem. The shrewdest sellers are the proverbial little old ladies in tennis shoes! Buy with your eyes, not your ears. Disregard any stories that come with offerings! Heirs often assume that old family pieces are priceless treasures. Handwritten notes and oft-repeated tales are not documentation.

A good rule of thumb for beginners is to offer about one-third of what you feel an item might sell for in your shop. If, before buying, you pause to ponder whether or not you can possibly triple on your investment, you will automatically pass up all but the real sleepers! After allowing for mistakes, you will be fortunate to average the normal 100 percent (double) markup on most of your early purchases.

More Important than Where You Buy Is What You Buy. There are thousands of antiques that have no monetary value! Age has little to do with desirability. (Most of the rocks in your backyard are eons old.) Indian arrowheads and Roman coins are typical examples of ancient artifacts that are still in abundance and rarely worth acquiring. Of more recent vintage, and also little esteemed in the trade, are old newspapers, Bibles, encyclopedias, and religious pictures. You won't have any trouble finding a host of hundred-year-old silverplated flatware, unmarked pieces of porcelain dinnerware, pretty pattern glass, and Victorian garden tools; these are shelf sitters that can grace a shop for a lifetime! You must open shop with a salable selection of sought-after items, not just a potpourri of old things purchased cheaply.

What, then, does one buy to insure having a desirable, salable inventory? Chances are that if it's easy to buy it will be difficult to sell! Begin by finding out what people in your immediate area are collecting and how they decorate their homes. Spend a few weekends visiting shops within a hundred-mile radius of your own. Nothing will loosen the tongue of a fellow dealer quicker than a sincere compliment and a few dollars spent in his establishment. Ask the dual question of "what's moving best and what are the slowest items in your stock?" You will be surprised at the number of helpful hints you'll receive and the genuine interest that many antique dealers will express in your enterprise.

Look at the classified advertising sections of several antique periodicals. If specific collectibles are offered, or advertised for consistently, then you can be reasonably assured of their popularity with the antique-buying public. But remember that the novel, the unusual, the unique, and the flawless will outsell the commonplace by ten to one.

This is by no means a complete list, but below are some of the staple items most frequently asked for in antique shops. Your inventory will be very well balanced if you can offer clean and attractive items from half of the categories listed.

Advertising	Glassware	Postcards
Banks	Kitchen tools	Pottery
Bells	Inkwells	Prints
Books	Ironware	Quilts
Bottles	Ivory	Sewing tools
Brassware	Jade	Shaving items
Bronzes	Jewelry	Souvenir spoons
Candleholders	Lighting devices	Sterling silver
Clocks	Locks and keys	Stoneware
Coins	Military items	Tinware
Copperware	Needlework	Toys
Dolls	Paintings	Textiles
Farm items	Photos	Watches
Furniture	Porcelain	Weapons

A successful dealer friend of mine, with over forty years in the trade, asks himself five questions before he buys anything: Is it old? Is it small? Is it beautiful? Is it functional? Does it have defects that would be expensive or time consuming to repair?

Avoid the temptation of buying chipped, broken, or otherwise damaged merchandise. These "bargains" will sit in your shop

Restored oak barber shop shaving mug rack, circa 1880–1900. Courtesy Tom Warren

for years and cast the rest of your inventory in an unwanted light.

We could write a separate book about the cost of restoring art work and antiques, but there is really no good reason for a new dealer to tie up working capital in anything other than the best shop-ready merchandise he can afford. While Mr. Fixit is busy finding spare parts, or getting repair bids, a dealer down the street (who is all thumbs) is out doubling her money two or three times over on good, clean antiques.

An accomplished woodworker or refinisher can, however, make a great deal of money buying "problem" furniture if shop-work is his bag. The trick to turning a buck in this pursuit is to concentrate on the higher ticket items. It takes no longer to re-finish a $400 table than it does a $49 kitchen chair, and a re-stored candle stand will bring ten times the price of a wardrobe trunk.

Figure your labor at $50 a day *before you buy!* If you can't dou-ble your cost and your labor on an item, pass it up; other buying opportunities with better resale potential will invariably occur!

Chapter 13 GOING, GOING, GONE

How to Buy Successfully at Auctions

As discussed in Chapter 2, frequent auction attendance (and participation) is one of the most important prerequisites to entering the general-line antique business today. Auction houses are taking a larger and larger share of both the retail and wholesale markets and more and more dealers are supplementing their "cash flow" by selling at auction when retail customers become scarce. Many dealers actually buy and sell at the same auction. You should buy what you know moves quickly in your area, and sell the "store sitters" that have been on your shelves for a year or more. One month we sold over $1,500 worth of books, paper items, and glassware at an auction, where we simultaneously purchased a truckload of furniture. For us, it is much easier to buy bric-a-brac and paper over the counter; however, we save miles and miles of driving by purchasing most of our antique furniture at local auctions.

Basically, there are two types of auction sales: *uncataloged auctions,* where items are put on the block at random or by request, and *catalog sales,* where each lot is numbered and described on a printed sheet or brochure and sold in its proper sequence. Country auctions and farm sales are the most fun, but great buys can be made at any auction. A customer of ours recently related how he had bought a trunkful of antique cut glass for $15 at an industrial equipment sale in Anchorage, Alaska.

Some auction houses require a substantial cash deposit for a bidder number. Don't let this scare you off; pay your cash and get a receipt. Get in on the bidding early if you are interested in a piece. This way, you are assured of obtaining the auctioneer's attention. Late bidders who wait for the last "going, going, gone" frequently have their bids overlooked (or ignored). Don't forget rule #1. Be prepared to buy! Bring a van, truck, or trailer to every auction. It gives you tremendous mental reinforcement to know that you can haul home a $2,000 grand piano that is going for nothing, while others hedge their bids for lack of positive transportation.

On the West Coast, evening auctions of about four hours' duration are very popular. The number of lots offered rarely exceeds three hundred items. In the Midwest, all-day affairs are commonplace, with auctioneers working in shifts until midnight if necessary. Some auctions are three- or four-day events with spectators coming and going at all hours. This type of interest (or buying power?) has as yet to manifest itself on the West Coast, where sun and surf are more popular diversions.

The "house sale" or "estate" auction season in the eastern United States starts in early summer and ends with the beginning of the July heat wave. Recently, there were as many as one hundred house sales going on every weekend in a five-county area of southeastern Pennsylvania during the month of June. Regular auctions are held indoors all year long, but most of the outdoor activity takes place between April and October. The same thing is true of eastern flea markets—many close down or dwindle drastically just before Thanksgiving. (Call ahead!)

A rather sensational example of the buys that are possible at uncataloged sales was recently reported by *Antique Monthly* newspaper. A young schoolteacher (turned antique dealer) attended a Brown Brothers Auction in Buckingham, Pennsylvania, to bid on a Civil War cannon. Upon losing the cannon to another bidder, the young man wandered out to a shed where some broken-down furniture and picture frames were awaiting their turn on the block. In one of the dirt-encrusted frames, he noticed a small oil painting in very rough condition, having been split in three places over a span of many years. Not wanting to drive home empty handed, the young dealer bought the picture and several other empty frames for $4. Back at his shop he noticed the name Benjamin Lay in old lettering on the reverse side of the panel. No Benjamin Lay appeared in art reference books, but an assistant curator of prints at the Winterthur Museum knew of a rare engraving of a Mr. Lay (an eccentric eighteenth-century dwarf who dressed in fine clothes while living with his wife in a cave near Abington). One discovery led to another, and it was determined by museum experts that this was the original

Auctioneers at work under the tent in Amherst, Massachusetts. Courtesy Maine Antique Digest

work of the eighteenth-century English painter William Williams, who immigrated to Philadelphia from England to ply his trade. After a $400 restoration, the painting was reportedly going to be offered for sale at a conservative $65,000 figure.

Briefly, let's review the rules for auction buying once again:

1. Bring a truck, van, or station wagon. You must compete psychologically with other bidders who are equipped to buy.
2. Arrive at the preview showing at least an hour or two before sale time. Also attend the previous day's showing if one is offered; many items get "hidden" the day of the sale.
3. Bring the tools of your trade: a magnifying glass, flashlight, notepad, penknife, and, in the beginning, a glove compartment full of price guides.
4. After close examination, write down the prices you are willing to pay opposite the catalog numbers or, if there is no

Auction goers examine Oriental carpets. Courtesy **Maine Antique Digest**

catalog sheet, alphabetically on a notepad. Do not exceed these predetermined "wholesale" buying prices.

5. Get a seat in the front row or stand behind the back row. Either place gives you the freedom to jump up and examine late entries with ease. I prefer the back row because I can observe all of the action and sometimes can tell when another bidder is about to drop out. (In this case I may exceed my predetermined bid by 10 percent on a very desirable item.) On uncataloged sales the front row is best because you can see exactly what you are bidding on.

6. Don't believe anything you hear about the merchandise! Serious buyers sometimes spread disparaging rumors about good antiques *they are after*. Examine the merchandise carefully and *draw your own conclusions*.

7. You are there to buy—get your card in the air when the bargains appear. Don't be afraid to buy more than your vehicle will carry. Most auctioneers will store your purchases overnight or arrange for a local hauler to deliver the goods at a reasonable rate.

English container shipment on display at Unicorn Antique Wholesalers, San Diego, California.

Chapter 14
WHOLESALE IMPORTERS

A Handy Resource for Beginners

Many antique shops use the word "wholesale" on their signs and letterheads, but few buy "well" enough to offer a dealer discount of 30 or 40 percent from true retail. Those who do are usually located in huge warehouses that are open to "the trade only" (and a business card and resale number are required to get past the front desk). These wholesale outlets import from one to fifteen, forty-foot container loads of "antiques" from England and the Continent every month. Most of this furniture dates from the early 1900s, with occasional "period pieces" thrown in when they are available. The largest of these importers moves up to five thousand items a month by aggressive selling to auctioneers, interior designers, restaurant decorators, antique dealers, and the general public. In outlets where the public is also admitted, the dealer prices are generally coded in the stock number so that shop owners or decorators can bring their clients through the showrooms and quote them retail prices at will.

Most container dealers advertise their wares in the Yellow Pages under "Antiques, wholesale" and also in classified newspaper ads under "Antiques, to the trade only." Frequent wholesale advertisements appear in dealer-oriented antique periodicals, such as the *Antique Dealer*, the *Antique Trader Weekly*, *Collectors News*, *Antique Monthly*, and *Maine Antique Digest*. It pays to shop wholesale operations just as you would any retail store. A particular container importer may have the best price on wooden dining tables, while another might be running a special sale on sets of chairs. The Annual Wholesale Sources issue of the *Antique Dealer* magazine lists hundreds of firms that solicit dealer trade. (Send $4 to 1115 Clifton Avenue, Clifton, NJ 07015.)

New York City is probably America's largest wholesale antique center. One could easily spend a week exploring the four-block area that is bounded by 13th Street, 5th Avenue, 10th Street, and Broadway. Over thirty important sources plus several famous auction houses will make your trip an educational experience.

If you find yourself spending over a couple of thousand dollars a month buying from wholesale sources, it might pay for you to look into importing your own forty-foot container load.

Chapter 15 *BUYING ABROAD*

Container Costs and Logistics

Hundreds of American antique dealers and decorators have of late "discovered" the auctions, shops, flea markets, and wholesale houses of Europe. It all began in the early 1960s when a few tourists and military employees of the American government began to ship home more than just luggage. By the 1970s, several New York importers had all but cleaned out the "bargain basement" countries (especially France, where prices are the highest today). Growing tourist interest in antiques quickly spawned a proliferation of the existing shops, flea markets, and sidewalk vendors throughout Europe. It wasn't long before reproduction firms began to mass produce many items.

In 1968, John Byrns wrote a timely little pocket guide entitled *Europe's Hidden Flea Markets and Budget Antique Shops.* This book has since gone through several printings and is still available from the original publisher (Robert Long, 634 Bellmore Avenue, East Meadow, NY 11554). Another widely used handbook is the annual *Guide to Antique Shops in Britain,* which lists hundreds of trade sources and how to find them. It is distributed by Apollo Books at 391 South Road, Poughkeepsie, NY 12601.

Today, one can still make good buys at the provincial markets or from shops on the outskirts of the larger cities, but by and large, most American dealers abroad buy at auction or directly from antique warehouses open to the trade only. Commercial quantities of antiques are currently available from shippers in Austria, Belgium, Britain, Denmark, Portugal, France, Hong Kong, Holland, Ireland, and Scotland. In the early days of container shipping, you could safely buy "blind" and make a profit. Today, one must develop a relationship with suppliers by selecting much of the merchandise in person, or by working with a "resident" agent whose ability comes highly recommended from others in the trade. (The price of a plane ticket is a fraction of the overall expense, anyway, so why not pick your own load?)

The advertisements of major European shippers, packers, auction houses, and wholesalers appear weekly in the two English trade publications mentioned earlier in this book. They are: *Antiques & Art Weekly* (in care of) Independent Magazines Limited, Bridge House, 181 Queen Victoria Street, London EC4V 4DD, England; and *Antiques Trade Gazette,* Metropress Ltd., Langley House, 116 Long Acre, London WC2E 9PA, England. (Sample copies of either publication are available from the above publishers for a couple of dollars each.)

Importing from Great Britain. Great Britain is a country where 11,000 antique dealers and a hundred packing and shipping firms all can be found in a 50,700-square-mile area no larger than our states of Alabama or North Carolina. The easiest method of container buying is to establish contact with a reputable antique packer and shipper (also sometimes listed in English telephone directories under "Furniture Removers") and have a representative meet you at the airport. One such firm, Michael Davis Shipping Ltd., 111 Mortlake Road, Kew, Richmond, Surrey TW9 4AU, England, advertises a basic fee that includes:

- Pickup of all your purchases from London area dealers
- Warehouse storage while assembling load
- Arranging for antique authentication of purchases
- Wrapping and packing of the antiques into the final ocean shipping container (includes packing small pieces in the drawers of larger furniture, and so forth)
- Preparing export documents
- Trucking the container to the pier
- Ocean freight charges to the port of entry in the United States

For an additional fee, they will arrange pier-to-door delivery almost anywhere in the United States, or you can work through your own private *Customs house broker* at a port of entry. Customs house brokers are listed in the Yellow Pages.

If you are not in a hurry and have time to roam the English countryside attending auction sales and visiting rural shops, we suggest that you rent a van ("lorry") of your own for smaller purchases and arrange for the pickup of larger furniture by a packer/shipper. Most English auctioneers are very familiar with the needs of container load customers and will be happy to assist you by obtaining temporary storage for larger items (check before the auction). We will discuss several methods of shipping small parcels at the end of Chapter 16. Here we will concern ourselves with the logistics of a "container" shipment.

Basically, there are two sizes of containers: the smaller 20-foot length with a capacity of 1,100 cubic feet, and the 40-foot-long size that holds 2,400 cubic feet of shipping goods. Both of these "boxes" are 8½ feet high and 8 feet wide, and are specifically designed to bolt onto a flatbed truck trailer for transporting from the dock to your door. The containers are generally owned by the steamship companies and spend their entire lives going back and forth across the world's oceans. Since the fee for ocean shipping is based more on bulk than weight, it is important for you to utilize every nook and cranny in the container (and also the unused spaces inside the drawers and recesses of all the furniture within the container).

A 40-foot container will comfortably hold the following shipping goods in addition to hundreds of smaller filler items: This group of 170 pieces, plus smalls, would quite amply stock a 1,600-square-foot shop space or provide enough furniture and bric-a-brac for a two-session auction sale (600 lots).

10 marble-top washstands	2 upright pianos
10 wood hallstands	2 rolltop desks
10 wood wardrobes	10 mixed-style china cabinets
15 drawleaf dining tables	10 wood secretaries or desks
60 wood dining chairs	5 beds
20 mixed-style occasional tables	6 grandfather clocks
10 wood sideboards or dressers	plus hundreds of smaller filler items

The economics of container shipping are not complex—you pay for what you get! If you want a special packer/shipper to travel all over Europe and pick up your purchases, you are obviously going to have to pay him plenty. If you purchase all of your goods from one wholesale supplier, you should receive a substantial discount on packing, documentation fees, and delivery to the dock for export.

The acquisition cost of a medium-quality 40-foot container full of turn-of-the-century furniture and bric-a-brac can run from $10,000 to $29,000—and again, we are talking about enough goods to completely fill up a retail shop of 1,600 square feet (a 40 × 40-foot display area).

The shipping costs depend on the port of entry. Freight to U.S. West Coast ports is, at this writing, about $3,000 for a 40-footer, and $1,900 for the 20-foot-length container. East Coast destinations are about 10 percent less, and Midwestern ports, through the Great Lakes, are more.

Customs duty on documented hundred-year-old antiques and original art is zero, but most "shipping goods" will fall under the classification of wooden furniture at the current rate of approximately 8 percent of valuation. If you have $10,000 to spend for a container load of semiantiques, you can figure on an additional $500 for Customs fees, $200 for insurance, $250 for basic Customs house brokerage services, and from $1,900 to $3,000 for shipping, plus an additional $1,600 to $2,600 for pickup and packing in England (if you buy at auction).

A rule of thumb is to add 50 percent to the purchase price of medium-quality "collectible" furniture to estimate its total cost delivered to your door (for example, a $10 chair costs you $15 landed). This expense becomes considerably less of an overall percentage of the purchase price as quality goes up because you are dealing with a fixed cost per cubic foot. If you ship a $100,000 load of legitimate hundred-year-old antiques, you could be paying packing, shipping, and brokerage fees of only 5 percent of your cost, while an $8,000 "bargain" container load of 1920s furniture and porcelain could end up costing in excess of $16,000 when delivered to your door! Delivery by ocean freight takes from twenty-five to forty-five days, depending on how soon your packer gets the goods to the dock. A $100 deductible insurance policy for damage or loss runs about 2 percent of total value; a "loss only" policy would cost less than 1 percent.

If you wish to fly to England to purchase antiques, we suggest that you make your first trip in the off season to insure against room shortages and traffic problems—don't go in the summer. Leave your greenbacks at home—you almost always get a better rate of currency exchange overseas for traveler's checks than for U.S. funds. Remember that cash talks just as loudly to British shopkeepers as it does at home. They will go to great lengths to avoid their repressive tax system.

Let's review the steps for buying abroad:

- Obtain copies of overseas trade publications, antique buyers guide books, and dealer directories.
- Correspond with several specialist packer/shippers abroad who specialize in antiques. Ask for U.S. references.
- Talk to a private Customs house broker near your hometown.
- Talk to your banker about opening a checking account in London.
- Make reservations and inquire about transportation rentals abroad (travel agency).
- Contact U.S. Customs for the latest information before you leave.
- Get a passport and shots.
- Take along someone who has already been through all this, pay for his or her trip, and consider it a bargain.

a objects,
Auction,

are. 11.00.
RE & SON
, Lichfield
oton. Tel:
and effects.

UDGE &
h Street, East
Tel: 24101).
ts. 12.00.

BIDDLE & ...
Row, Birmingham 15. ...
4380). Collective antiques. 11.00.
BRACKETT, STOKES & CO.
(27 & 29 High Street, Tunbridge
Wells, Kent. Tel: 33733).
Furniture and effects. 10.00.
CHAPMAN, MOORE & MUG-
FORD (Newbury House, Gilling-
ham, Dorset. Tel: 2244). Furniture
and effects. 6.00.
CHRISTIE'S (8 King Street,
St. James's, London SW1. Tel:
839 9060). Fine pictures by Old
Masters. 10.30.
FRAZER'S (28-30 Church
Street, Inverness. Tel: 32395).
Furniture and effects. (Part 2).
11.00.
HAMMOND & CO. (The
Auction Rooms, Cambridge
Place, Cambridge. Tel: 56067).
Furniture and effects. 10.30. (NC).
HOBBS & CHAMBERS (Castle
Street, Cirencester, Glos. Tel:
2562). Household furniture and
effects. 10.30.
THOMAS LOVE & SONS LTD.
(St. John's Place, Perth. Tel:
24111). Household furniture and
effects. 11.00. (NC).

Me. ...
des Cheau-Lco ...
Versailles).
A: Old master paintings and
drawings, musical instruments,
antique furniture, French and
other European faience and porcelain—April 1.
B: Modern pictures and drawings,
etc.—April 8.
Me. BLACHE (5 rue Rameau,
Versailles). Original prints by
Picasso—April 1.

ceramics, and 19th cen...
masters—April 10-11.
paintings—April 10-11.

NETHERLANDS

AMSTERDAM;
MAK VAN WAAY (Rokin 102;
Amsterdam C). Paintings—April
2.

SO
Str
49
an

M
(

GERMANY

BERLIN
THEODOR PRUCHA (Ranke-
strasse 3). Jewellery—May 9 and
June 27.
*LEO SPIK (1 Berlin 15, Küfur-
stendamm 66). Paintings, furni-
ture, antiques, silver, porcelain—
April 4-5.
*GERDA BASSENGE (1 Berlin,
33-Grunewald-Erdenerstrasse 5a).
Spring Auction—May 22-26.

COLOGNE
*KUNSTHAUS LEMPERTZ
(5 Köln, Neumarkt 3).
A: Auction No. 532. Modern art
—May 3-4.
B: Old master paintings—June
6-8.
*KUNSTHAUS AM MUSEUM
(Köln, Drusugasse 1-15).
Furniture, works of art, jewellery,
prints—June 13-15.

DUSSELDORF
CHRISTIE'S (Alt Pempelfort 11a,
4 Dusseldorf). Expressionist, 19th
and 20th century paintings,
Medieval and Renaissance works
of art—May 23-24.

FRANKFURT
KARL HEINZ ARNOLD
(6 Frankfurt am Main, Bleich-
strasse 42). Antiques, paintings,
furniture, porcelain, carpets—
March 31.

HAMBURG
*DR. ERNST HAUSWEDELL
(2 Hamburg 13, Pöseldorfer
Weg 1).
A: Art and Non-European works
—May 11.
B: Rare books and autographs—
May 22-23.
C: Paintings, drawings and prints
—June 5.
D: Modern art—June 6-7.

HEIDELBERG
*DR. HELMUT TENNER
(69 Heidelberg, Bahnhofstrasse
63). Books and decorative prints
—May 9-12.
ARNO WINTERBERG
(69 Heidelberg 1, Zähringer-
strasse 3). 15th-20th century
paintings, watercolours, drawings
and prints—May 5.
GERD ROSTAN (69 Heidelberg
1, Schlzgasse 10). Furniture,
carpets, paintings, antiques—April
13-14.

KREFELD
H. SCHOHS—Paintings, furniture, antiques, etc.—June 4-5.

LINDAU
...9001indau, ...

SWEDEN

STOCKHOLM
BUKOWSKI (111, 47 Stockholm,
Arsenalsgatan 2). Furniture, silver,
porcelain, old and modern paintings, carpets—April 4-7.

SWITZERLAND

BERNE
GALERIE DOBIASCHOFS'
(CH-3008 Bern, Laupenstrasse
Paintings and antiquities—
11-12.
KORNFELD & KLIPST
(3000 Bern, Laupenstrasse
Old prints and modern
June 20-23.

GENEVA
CHRISTIE'S (8 Place
Taconnerie, 1204 Genève)
Continental silver and p
Russian works of art, go
and fine French furnit
9-10.

LUCERNE
GALERIE FISCHER
strasse 19, Luzern). C
national Auction—Ju
July 4-7.

ZURIC
SOTHEBY'S (8C
Bleicherweg 18).
A: Strasbourg ar
century faience—A
B: Jewellery—Ma
GALERIE KC
Zurich, Ramistra
furniture, silver
June 9.
PETER INEICI
watches—May

U

LOS
SOTHEBY
(7600 Bev
Angeles, C
portant 19
April 8-9

SOTHEE
(980 Ma
10021).
A: Goc
decorat
B: M
Ameri
C: Pr
D: Ir
ings
E: R
F: K
G: C
H:
I:
inc

STRIA

VIENNA
EUM (1010 Wien,
assell). Art Auctions—
13, May 22-25 and

BELGIUM

BRUSSELS
RIE MODERNE (rue des
Carnes 41 (Sablon) 1000
les). Paintings, furniture
works of art—April 16-17,
14-15 and June 18-19.

DENMARK

COPENHAGEN
RNE BRUUN RASMUSSEN
redgade 33, 1260 Kobenhavn
).
: Danish paintings and antiques
—April 3-13.
B: Old master paintings and
antiques—May 9-10.
C: Danish paintings and antiques
—May 11-17.

FRANCE

ANGERS
Me Lô DUMONT (12 rue des
Arènes, Angers). Antique furniture, objets d'art and collective
antiques—Apri 8.

CHARTRES
Me. Jean LELIEVRE (8 rue
Famin, 28000 Chartres).
A: Pictures, furniture, books,
carpets, collection of butterflies—
April 1.
B: Edged weapons and firearms—
April 8.

CLERMONT-
FERRAND
Mes. BAIF, DAVID & VIDAL
(19 rue des Sa ins, Cermont-
Ferrand). Objets d'art, antique
furniture, general antiques—April
4-7.

EVREUX
...ON (Hotel du Grand
... Evreux).

SATURDAY
APRIL 14

CLOWES, NASH & THURGAR
(6 Tombland, Norwich, Norfolk.
Tel: 27261). Furniture and effects.
10.00 (NC).
DEBENHAM COE (79-85 Old
Brompton Road, London SW7.
Tel: 589 2422). English water-
colours. 2.30.
DOWELL'S (65 George Street,
Edinburgh. Tel: 225 2266).
Household furniture and effects.
(Murieston Road). 11.00.
J. & R. EDMISTON (The Mart,
164-166A Bath Street, Glasgow
C2. Tel: 332 4664). Furniture and
effects. 11.00. (NC).
HARRODS AUCTION
GALLERIES (Arundel Terrace,
Barnes, London SW13. Tel: 748
2739). Collective antiques. (Part
1). 10.00.
HOUSE & SON (Lansdowne
House, Christchurch Road,
Bournemouth, Hants. Tel: 26232).
Household furniture and effects.
(Part 2). 10.00.
LALONDE (71 Oakfield Road,
Bristol 8. Tel: 34052). Household
furniture and effects. 11.00.
THIMBLEBY'S (1 Reading
Road, Pangbourne, Berks RG8
7LR. Tel: 2151). Fine arts, china,
glass, pictures, books.
WATSONS (26 North Street,
Bishop's Stortford, Herts. Tel:
7261). Selected antiques. 10.30.
... CO. (Croydon
... London

Chapter 16 CUSTOMS REGULATIONS

Instructions for Proper Clearance

Customs procedure in the case of a full container shipment is as follows. The container arrives at the U.S. seaport and is placed on the dock. You or your private Customs house broker are notified of its arrival by the shipping company. You, or your broker, then file a set of *"Customs entry forms"* with the Customs officer at the port. This involves presenting the type of invoice required, showing the cost, description, date of manufacture, and country of origin. (This is also information that you should get on the invoice when you make the original overseas purchase.) On the Customs form you will also be asked to indicate the *proper tariff classification* (of any items under one hundred years old). Upon completion of the paperwork, you are required to pay the *estimated duty* and post a *surety bond,* which includes a provision for the payment of increased duty that the collector may find due later (a rare occurrence).

The Advantages of Utilizing the Services of a Licensed Customs Broker. A broker is not only familiar with the many hundreds of tariff headings, but is also able to classify the non-antique goods in a way acceptable to Customs at the lowest possible rate of duty. Other services offered by these privately owned Customs brokerage firms are payment of freight, Customs duty, dock dues, and arranging for the delivery of the container to the shopkeeper's door. You will find Customs house brokers listed in the Yellow Pages, ready to quote prices and ancillary services. Current basic fees for processing the paperwork on a container load are about $200 to $250 on the West Coast. All other shipping, freight, storage, insurance, and duty fees are extra.

Almost always, the U.S. Customs officer will allow a properly documented commercial container to be taken (under seal) out of the immediate port of entry to the shopkeeper's premises or to a bonded warehouse for later unpacking and Customs inspection. In the case of an inland destination, the container would be forwarded by a trucking firm, traveling *"in bond"* under Customs seal, to an inland port of entry for final Customs clearance. This procedure postpones final Customs formalities and payment of duty until the goods arrive at their inland destination.

If you have a small shop and handle only objects of virtu, you can send many of your overseas purchases home by prepaid Parcel Post and carry the most valuable items in your baggage. (Do not rely on retail shopkeepers to pack and mail any purchase.) The U.S. Postal Service sends all incoming foreign mail parcels to Customs for examination. Make sure that you include antique documentation in the parcel. Packages free of Customs duty then go back to the Postal Service for home delivery. If any duty is required, the Customs officer will attach a form showing the amount to be paid. Your postman will collect this duty and a postage handling fee when he delivers your package.

For heavier packages of valuables than postal regulations allow, air freight is a convenient method of shipment. Usually the air freight forwarder in the foreign country will handle all the necessary "paper" arrangements, including clearance through Customs in the United States by a Customs house broker. The air freight fee that you pay abroad does not include anything other than your parcel's airplane ride to the nearest port of arrival in the United States. You will be charged all of the inland travel and Customs fees when the package is delivered. It's much cheaper to pick up air freight at the airport.

Most international household removers and specialist packer/shippers of antiques will accept less than container load shipments at a flat rate per cubic foot. Michael Davis Ltd. recently advertised a door-to-door 54-cubic-foot package deal from London to any destination in the United States for less than $800. (This included collection and packing in London and Customs clearance, door to door in forty-five days.) You can pack an easy $8,000 worth of antiques into a 54-cubic-foot space. An example might be a corner cabinet, a serving table, lamp table, curio shelf, chair, footstool, silver flatware set, vases, figurines, porcelain service, and assorted small glassware. As we mentioned earlier, if you purchase a substantial amount of goods from one wholesale trade supplier, you can expect a reasonable amount of help in packing, documentation, and shipping.

Before you travel, contact a packer/shipper for current price quotations. Also, write to the Bureau of Customs, Washington, DC 20226, for its latest Customs hints brochure, which includes the rates of duty on nonantique items or reproduction goods that you might wish to include in your shipment.

Chapter 17 BUYING PRIVATELY

Estate Lots, Walk-Ins, and the Law

The "average" antique dealer does only about a third of his or her buying from individuals. Newly established dealers find it especially difficult to begin buying privately—while those who have been in the trade for many years rely almost entirely on pickers and private contacts.

Again, we emphasize how important it is for you to begin at once to ADVERTISE as a *cash buyer* for antiques and collectibles. Many veteran dealers (and some aggressive auctioneers) advertise their wants daily in both metropolitan and suburban newspapers. Sometimes a weekend ad may bring in only a single seller, but rarely is the money misspent. We have been buying steadily from a little old lady who saw our ad in the local classifieds over a year ago. We have not pressured her about visiting her home because she seems comfortable bringing in a few items every week. Eventually we may be invited to purchase larger items.

A dealer friend of ours, who does most of his buying in small country towns, runs his wanted ad several months in advance of his trips. He always stays at the same motel in each town he visits, and invariably there will be several telephone messages or letters waiting for him from anxious local prospects.

The Yellow Pages section of the telephone book definitely does produce regular buying opportunities for those who use it wisely (frequently at a much lower monthly cost than newspaper advertising). Remember that the phone book works for you twenty-four hours a day, seven days a week! Since it takes from six months to a year for a new business to get a Yellow Pages listing, it is important to plan ahead. In some areas you can secure a display ad that gives a post box number as the business address. This gives you an opportunity to use an answering service to accept calls before you have a regular business location.

Early in the game you will learn to screen out potentially un-profitable calls from those that offer some promise. Does the caller really want to sell, or are you being used as a sounding board for current market value? Is the furniture nondescript peeling veneer, or handcrafted hardwood? Do the collectibles consist of early mayonnaise jars, or mint Coca-Cola trays? Is the seller knowledgeable and looking for "retail," or will the price depend upon your offer? Have other dealers already examined the goods? If all the clues are positive I will drop everything, close my shop, and rush to the prospect's home before another dealer or an antique-wise neighbor is called in. On more than one occasion we have been the only dealer in town "open to buy" or, in many cases, the only one in the phone book who could be reached at a particular hour. Give serious thought to listing both your home and shop telephone numbers in all of your "Wanted" advertising. Some telephone companies offer a system that automatically rings your home number if the shop phone goes unanswered after three rings.

Head your newspaper or phone book ad with a bold **WANT-ED** statement (see next page). Then proceed to list everything in which you are interested.

One method of buying that eliminates the possibility of giving a free appraisal is to make only one offer on an entire group of items. If the prospect asks for individual prices, you might indi-cate that you would be glad to provide an itemized appraisal for a fee and leave the buying to other dealers whom she might wish to call in.

A good starting point in any buying negotiations is to try to extract the seller's idea of what he feels his items are worth. This way you won't blow the whole deal by offering the wrong price before you eliminate the one or two objects that will invariably be overvalued in the seller's mind. Most often, though, the pros-pect will refuse to quote an asking price. This is where patience on your part will eventually pay off. Don't rush, be cheerful, be enthusiastic; but be sure to point out flaws in the goods that the seller may not have taken into account in his or her original preconceived price. The final dialogue might go something like this:

DEALER: I am really interested in the whole lot, Ma'am. What rough figure do you have in mind?

PROSPECT: I just don't know. You're a dealer, what's a fair price?

DEALER: Well, I am not sure about some of these things; they are desirable but they might sit for years before the right buyer comes along! What amount would you feel satisfied in getting for the china and silverware alone?

PROSPECT: I don't know. You will be fair with me. You know what they are worth, what is your offer?

At this point, you mentally pick out the *very best items,* which are sure sellers within a week, and offer one-half of their quick market value for the whole lot (fair is fair).

DEALER: I can pay you $250 for everything here or perhaps you would like to remove an item or two and take a little less.

The game can go on and on, but *the longer you play it, the lower the price will get.*

When buying away from the shop, it is important to follow a few basic maxims. When a price is agreed upon, pay for the goods (with cash, if possible), load them up, get a signed receipt, and leave. Many a purchase made the day before is canceled by the seller if no money changes hands or the goods are left to be "picked up later."

If you have paid a top price for the items, leave a card and request that you be called if anything else becomes available (perhaps a neighbor might have antiques to dispose of, too). On the other hand, if you have gotten a very good buy (way below wholesale), it is best to remain somewhat anonymous.

"Estates" is an overworked word that implies much more than it delivers in today's antique marketplace. Because of the recent widespread popularity of antiques and collectibles among young married people, and the public in general, not many estates arrive intact on the auction block, or for sale privately. By the time the maid, the gardener, and sundry friends and relatives of the deceased have had their fingers in the pie, little is left but the crust.

Here on the West Coast few, if any, legitimate antique households are offered within a year's time. This is also true in other areas of the country that were settled within the last sixty to eighty years, where the competition for antiques is fierce, and very few second-generation occupied homes exist. A lot of southwestern towns were not much more than mud forts prior to the turn of the century. The real migration of entire families in the middle and upper classes took place after World War II. (I am descended from a long line of fruit pickers, car washers, and bricklayers who came West during the Great Depression. Our family, and others like us, did not bring along houses full of fine furniture and fragile bric-a-brac.)

If you are willing to work very hard and direct 90 percent of your efforts at estate buying or liquidation, a few may come your way. Who places estates on the market? These are the people at whom you must direct your telephone and direct-mail campaign. Aim your message at bankers, trust officers, title companies, lawyers, and surviving relatives (see the obituaries). Other persons privy to the information you may need are real estate brokers, public administrators, sheriffs, and apartment and mobile home park managers. Aggressive auctioneers often call every law office in the telephone directory once a week to see if any estates are available for outright purchase or liquidation.

Regular weekend newspaper ads indicating that "Estates" are your specialty may eventually produce a client. Also look into placing an ad in local legal newspapers and other periodicals subscribed to by bankers, realtors, and lawyers.

Tag sales at the homes of the deceased often resemble small wars! The people who conduct them have learned the hard way about written contracts, food catering, crowd control, security methods, furniture logistics, and legal requirements. Dealer percentages charged for estate liquidation vary from area to area, but 25 percent would not seem excessive considering the responsibilities involved. It is no wonder that so few dealers specialize in this segment of the antique business.

Estate administrators are human beings who may be inclined to want to do as little work as possible, while at the same time attempting to get a fair price for the heirs. Your "image" must be one of broad knowledge and high-level dealing. The bidder who offers to handle the whole ball of wax, from diamonds to automatic dishwasher, is the one who usually gets the cake!

"Buying off of the street" is a term dealers use for the unsolicited purchases they make from people who come in *"off the street"* offering valuables for sale. It is a risky way to buy, at best; but many dealers depend upon off-the-street contacts for their entire stock! There is always the possibility that you may be dealing with a petty thief or even a professional who buys from

one shop, *pays with a bad check,* and drives on to the next county, *where he sells to another unsuspecting dealer for cash.*

If a dealer, private owner, or law officer spots stolen merchandise in your shop, it may be confiscated by the court with no remuneration to you. Once the merchandise is proved to be stolen, the full burden of proof is placed upon the shopkeeper to prove that he did not have prior knowledge that the goods were stolen and that he made a reasonable effort to ascertain that the seller was indeed the legal owner, or his agent, with full permission to sell. Section 496 of the California Penal Code is reproduced below; other states have almost identical statutes.

California Penal Code

§496. Receiving Stolen Property

1. Receiving knowledge; concealment; punishment.
Every person who buys or receives any property which has been stolen or which has been obtained in any manner constituting theft or extortion knowing the property to be so stolen or obtained, or who conceals, sells, withholds or aids in concealing, selling, or withholding any such property from the owner, knowing the property to be so stolen or obtained, is punishable by imprisonment in a state prison for not more than 10 years, or in a county jail for not more than one year; provided, that where the district attorney or the grand jury determines that such action would be in the interests of justice, the district attorney or the grand jury, as the case may be, may, if the value of the property does not exceed two hundred dollars ($200), specify in the accusatory pleading that the offense shall be a misdemeanor, punishable only by imprisonment in the county jail not exceeding one year.

2. Secondhand dealers; inquiry; presumption.
Every person whose principal business is dealing in or collecting used or secondhand merchandise or personal property, and every agent, employee or representative of such person, who buys or receives any property which has been stolen or obtained in any manner constituting theft or extortion, under such circumstances as should cause such person, agent, employee or representative to make reasonable inquiry to ascertain that the person from whom such property was bought or received had the legal right to sell or deliver it, without making such reasonable inquiry, shall be presumed to have bought or received such property knowing it to have been so stolen or obtained. This presumption may, however, be rebutted by proof.

3. Secondhand dealers; inquiry; burden of proof.
When in a prosecution under this section it shall appear from the evidence that the defendant's principal business was as set forth in the preceding paragraph, that the defendant bought, received, or otherwise obtained or concealed, withheld or aided in concealing or withholding from the owner, any property which had been stolen or obtained in any manner constituting theft or extortion, and that the defendant bought, received, obtained, concealed or withheld such property under such circumstances as should have caused him to make reasonable inquiry to ascertain that the person from whom he bought, received, or obtained such property had the legal right to sell or deliver it to him, then the burden shall be upon the

defendant to show that before so buying, receiving, or otherwise obtaining such property, he made such reasonable inquiry to ascertain that the person so selling or delivering the same to him had the legal right to so sell or deliver it.

It is important that you obtain a signed receipt for each purchase of secondhand merchandise. Many dealers go a step further and require unknown vendors to fill out a form similar to the one below.

Some cities supply used merchandise dealers with similar forms and require a copy to be forwarded to law enforcement officials before any purchases from private individuals are resold. A waiting period of several weeks is usually required.

Vendor Information Form

Seller's Name	Please Print		Date
Home Address			City
State	Social Security #	Age	Sex
Vehicle Make	Year	License No.	Driver's License #

Quantity	List complete and accurate description of property you are selling	Amount Received	

Under penalty of perjury, I certify that I am the legal owner of the above items and have received payment in full for my property.

_____
Signature

Never judge a picker by his cover.

Chapter 18

PICKING A PICKER

Independent Treasure Hunters

Department stores have *"buyers,"* and antique shops have *"pickers."* The difference is that pickers are usually self-employed and working on their own capital. Usually, they are people who love to buy antiques but don't want the responsibility of maintaining a shop. Pickers buy from the same sources that dealers do, but they are in the field more often and seem to "live" at auctions. Typically, a picker does not spend much time cleaning, repairing, or otherwise upgrading his finds. He or she is most often quite content to make 20 or 30 percent on a fast turnover (like one day)!

To keep your pickers happy, you must not haggle too much or turn down very many offerings. If a picker can count on you to take at least half of his load each time, you will probably be the first dealer he contacts after a "find." We tend to overspend on our first transaction with a picker who brings in interesting things. We know that if we send him on his way with at least $100, he will be back again soon. If your picker insists that you buy his "dogs and cats" along with the good stuff, you can pack the duds up in box lots and unload them through a local auction house of the "used furniture" variety. Making a profit on the duds is not important; moving them out of the shop and getting your cash back is!

Traveling salesmen make excellent pickers (maybe if you are a salesman, you would like to try your hand at it). When out of town, they have spare time available between appointments plus evenings free. We know an industrial chemical salesman who has made thousands of dollars over the past fifteen years picking in small towns in Illinois, Indiana, and Michigan. He is a "good ole boy" who plays the role to the hilt. Typically, his Sunday afternoons on hot summer days might be spent walking down a dusty street in the residential section of a small town where people still congregate on their front porches during warm weather. His opening pitch goes something like this: "Hi ya, folks, I'm buying old pitcher (sic) frames and bric-a-brac. You folks got any old china or glassware for sale? How about that shed there? I'm buyin' old woodworkin' tools, too!" Once our friend has made an initial purchase, he really warms up and asks the kind of questions that eventually lead to the purchase of more valuable items, such as sterling silverware, gold pocket watches, and vintage firearms. He has purchased entire bowfront china cabinets (full of fine porcelain) for less than $50.

Not too many years back, this same picker was selling some janitorial supplies to the resident priests in a defunct Indiana seminary, when he just happened to mention that he was looking for old picture frames. One thing led to another . . . and the picker ended up helping the retired Fathers clean out the basement in return for three stacks of ornate walnut picture frames and two bushel baskets full of tin candle molds (used in the heyday of the institution to provide all the candles for student dormitories).

Another picker (the one who gets mail and phone messages at his motels) bought an entire Catholic church in Missouri—complete with stained glass windows, oak balcony, and several marble statues—for less than $3,000 last year. Currently he is negotiating to buy a defunct carnival that he spotted rotting away in two sheds on a vacant lot across the street from a cafe where he had stopped for breakfast.

One thing that pickers share in common is their constant questioning of any and everyone that they meet, from the corner gas station attendant to a waitress in the local greasy spoon! Some pickers have international connections, but their methods are the same. They tend to avoid costly warehousing in preference to turning over the merchandise quickly at a one-third markup. We have recently begun dealing with a Mexican national who has dual citizenship. He flies to New York monthly with brand-new "pre-Columbian" artifacts, then back to Mexico with a truckload of used clothing following him. The next week may find this Latin entrepreneur in Japan arranging for a drop shipment of transistor radios directly to a purchaser in Los Angeles. While in Mexico City, he buys primitive charcoal irons, spurs, saddles, branding irons, jail keys, and balance scales for sale to dealers like myself in southern California.

Finding pickers on the road when you are on out-of-state buying trips takes a little detective work. Ask at local business establishments if "anybody in the area refinishes furniture or has a barnful of old stuff for sale." Other possible sources are war surplus stores, pawn shops, coin dealers, sign painting establishments, picture framers, used bookstores, printers, scrap dealers, house wreckers, and automobile junkyards. When you drive through a small town, any business is a prospect. Remember that obsolete store stock of just twenty years' vintage has value in today's collectibles market.

Get a swap meet directory and try to attend some of the larger events where several hundred picker/dealers are assembled. Every state has several such gathering places.

We have listed but a few of the hundreds of events where you might meet a good picker:

ARIZONA Phoenix, 3801 E. Washington, Greyhound Park, Sat. & Sun. mornings.

CALIFORNIA Aromas, 1000 Highway 101, Sat. & Sun. A.M.
Costa Mesa, Orange County Fairgrounds, 88 Fair Drive, Sat. & Sun. A.M.
Rose Bowl, Pasadena, 2nd Sun. every month A.M. (rain or shine).
San Jose, 12000 Berryessa Road, Hwy. 101 (13th St. offramp to frontage road), Sat. & Sun. A.M.
Saugus, 22234 Soledad Canyon Rd., at the Speedway, Sun. mornings only.

INDIANA Shipshewana, 5 miles from Mich. border on Rt. 5 at south end of town, Tues. & Wed. 6:00 A.M. until dusk, spring & early fall.

MASSACHUSETTS Brimfield, Golden Reid's on Rt. 20, 6 miles west of Old Sturbridge (750 dealers). Write for upcoming dates to Auction Acres, Brimfield, Mass. 01010. (Three other important flea markets in the area, over 1,500 dealers.)

OHIO Aurora, on Rt. 43, several miles south of Aurora, Sat. & Sun. A.M.
Hartville, a mile west of town on Rt. 619, Mon. & Thurs. mornings.

OKLAHOMA Okla. City, Mary's, Hwy. 62 east at Spencer city limits. Every weekend.
Tulsa, Fairgrounds, Sat. 8 A.M. till 6 P.M.

PENNSYLVANIA Adamstown & Denver. There are five great flea
markets on Rt. 222, north of the turnpike, Exit 21,
Sun. mornings.
TENNESSEE Nashville, State Fairgrounds, 4th weekend of every
month except Sept. & Dec.
TEXAS Canton, first Monday of every month and the weekend before that Monday; thousands of dealers.

Many pickers have found that by specializing in a specific area
of collector interest they can increase their income and decrease
the chances of making the bad buys that all of us do from time
to time. Just last week a young fellow from Mississippi came
through our town buying up quantities of sterling silver flatware
(spoons, knives, forks) from any dealers who would give him
good wholesale prices. He maintains that most of the active
trading in sterling silver pieces is done at the dealer level and
that few of us sell much of the stuff to the general public. I am
not sure about this point; but it was certainly educational talking
with a self-assured country boy who confided that he was "mak-
in' as much as most of yer doctors 'n lawyers and not workin'
half as hard either"!

This specialist picker and his partner tour the country most of
the year—stopping only at antique shops to inquire if they have
anything made of "sterlin' silver fer sale." If this pair of entrepreneurs makes fifteen or twenty calls per day, the law of averages enables them to get at least a couple of good buys. He
confided that many country shopkeepers don't even display
their sterling silver. He always asks, and is frequently rewarded
with a drawerful at bargain prices! As soon as his scrap amounts
to about 1,800 troy ounces net, he ships it to a friend in Los Angeles, or New York City, who in turn sells it to a large refinery
that pays up to 98 percent of the New York spot silver price for
industrial quantities. (See Chapter 31.)

While we are on the subject of both pickers and specialization,
let me tell you about another aggressive young man who makes
his living buying and selling vintage photographic images and
cameras (photographica). Tom has memorized the names of
about 150 turn-of-the-century photographers and studios that
are currently in vogue with the photo collecting cult. Most of
Tom's best buys have been paper photos rather than hard cased
images. It is much easier for him to spot a sleeper in the form

of a 1920s studio portrait or landscape than the more commonly known occupational collectibles. His finds are quickly resold to one of a dozen or so photographic galleries located in either Los Angeles, San Francisco, or New York.

Incidentally, one of the most celebrated photographic finds of this decade was the discovery of seven circa 1846, daguerreotype photographs of United States government buildings in Washington, D.C., including the White House. The discovery was made in 1972 at a San Francisco area swap meet by two photographica collectors who paid $29 for the lot. A friend of theirs traded them some vintage cameras for the "dags" and immediately mailed his booty to the Library of Congress for identification. The library subsequently purchased six of the views for $12,000 and a private collector bought the White House image for $14,000. (It's tales like this that keep us on the swap meet circuit.)

If you are interested in learning more about dealing in old photographs, we recommend the following titles for further study:

- *Collecting Photographs: A Guide to the New Art Boom* by L. Dennis. E. P. Dutton, New York, NY
- *An Identification and Value Guide to Vintage Cameras and Images* by J. Maloney. Books Americana, Florence, AL
- *The Photograph Collectors Guide* by L. Witkin and B. London. New York Graphic Society, Boston, MA
- *The Photographica Collectors Price Guide* by G. Gilbert. Hawthorn Books, New York, NY

You will also benefit by subscribing to the *Photographica Auction Catalogs* of Phillips, Sotheby's, and Christie's. All three of these New York firms conduct regular sales of rare photos, books, and cameras.

Chapter **19** *BACKYARD BARGAINS*

The Gold in Your Neighbor's Garage

House sales, barn sales, yard sales, and garage sales all are essentially the same thing. Hopefully, they are the efforts of private persons to sell accumulations of unwanted household articles, tools, toys, trash, and trivia that tend to pile up anywhere people live for five or ten years. Of late, these home-centered sales have literally become second sources of income for many enterprising persons. In southern California, on a sunny Sunday afternoon, one can find a garage sale sign in every block of suburbia. Most of the "antiques" offered by these sophisticated sale givers are not giveaways at all. It is not uncommon to spend a day in the field without ever finding anything for sale at less than the going retail price, but as in any other pursuit, the early bird usually gets the worm!

If you are willing to rise at 5:00 A.M., three days a week, and map out a battle plan from the morning newspaper's classified advertisements, you may hit pay dirt. Try several different neighborhoods before giving up for the day (usually the more affluent the homes, the better the pickings). It's best to be parked at 7:00 A.M. across the street from the morning's most likely prospect. If you are in luck, there won't be more than half a dozen others waiting there with you by the time the garage door is raised at 8:00 or 9:00 A.M. Then the real battle ensues!

Pick up everything that interests you quickly without asking the price (you can do that later). Better yet, take someone along to sit on your pile while you scurry around looking under tables and in boxes for other hidden treasures. You must likewise *guard* your purchases even after you have paid for them. One clerk may *resell* the stuff that another clerk has already sold you. Sometimes, you may be the only buyer present. This leaves time for inquiring about other things that are for sale but not on display. Veteran garage sale pickers don't quit in disgust at 10:00 A.M. They work at it all day long on the theory that fresh merchandise may be put out as the day progresses (or that an innocent "inquiry" might produce big dividends).

One of our customers recently purchased a cupful of "children's" costume rings for 30 cents each. Upon cleaning away the grime, she was quite impressed with the quality and style of the settings. Her jeweler appraised these Victorian era dinner rings at from $100 to $400 each. They had been the personal adornment of a very tiny, and wealthy, lady!

A cement finisher I am acquainted with takes every Friday off to spend the day attending garage sales. Recently, he bought an 1898 lever-action carbine at a neighborhood sale. It was hanging from a tree limb in its original leather scabbard with a $10 price tag affixed where no one else had seen it.

An auctioneer we deal with spends every Sunday afternoon on the garage sale circuit. His theory is to go late, after the sellers are tired and perhaps dreading the ordeal of putting everything away. If there are enough worthwhile antiques in sight, he makes an offer on the whole works based on one-half the quick market value of the antiques alone. This way, he doubles on the good stuff and makes a couple of hundred bucks on the rest in the form of "box lots" at his monthly auctions.

No matter how well kept a secret is, if more than one person knows about it, the word soon gets out. A case in point is the Thursday morning line-up of garage sale enthusiasts waiting for the 8:00 A.M. edition of the weekly Coronado Island newspaper outside its storefront office here. Coronado is no longer the mother lode of antiques she once was, but fond memories don't fade quickly. One devotee we interviewed has been coming faithfully to this weekly event for twenty years. The lineup starts at about 7:30 and usually grows to about fifty participants by the time the office doors open. Everyone has the exact change ready, 15 cents, which he or she flings down on the counter before grabbing a still warm copy. Outside, they jump into cars left with motors running, or onto bicycles, motorcycles, or skateboards, and the chase is on! Up and down alleys behind the stately Victorian mansions they race, each hoping to be the first to view the contents of a garage full of collectibles. By 9:00 the game is over—winners and losers alike trek to the local ice cream parlor for a double shot of dessert. In the early days, not a few things from the attics of this wealthy retirement community made their way to the Los Angeles auction showrooms of Sotheby Parke Bernet.

Nowadays, finding enough antiques to stock a shop would be difficult indeed if one had to depend entirely on garage sales. Pickers tell us that they often attend ten or twenty events before finding anything worthwhile, but alas, once you have discovered the gold in your neighbor's garage you may be hooked for a long, long time!

Chapter 20
THRIFTY SALVATION

Buying from Charitable Institutions

The thrift shops operated by charitable institutions used to be a fertile field for finding antiques to resell, but the current widespread distribution of price guides has changed things considerably. More often than not, any antiques that survive the previewing by truck drivers, warehouse helpers, sales personnel, and their assorted friends and relatives are either overpriced or undesirable. (One of our best pickers was a thrift-shop employee who bought daily for resale to antique dealers.)

If you live or work near a thrift shop, a weekly visit might eventually pay some dividends. Be friendly with the sales help. They may advise you in advance of any markdowns or backroom stock due to go on display. It might even pay to mail frequent "Wanted" lists (printed on stamped self-addressed postcards) to all the thrift shops in your area.

Quality secondhand stores in some cities are worth a weekly visit, junk stores are not. The prices displayed or quoted are to be taken with a grain of salt. If you offer half the asking price, in cash, be prepared to take the item home with you. Here again, no harm can come from leaving a self-addressed stamped postcard and your specialized "Wanted" list.

Church rummage sales are often overlooked as sources of supply because of the mediocrity of the merchandise on display. Insiders do quite well, however, buying antiques and collectibles before they ever reach the carefully arranged sales tables. The key factor is to know someone who is helping in the backroom or perhaps the administrator herself. Usually, an honest appraisal and an offer of half the market value will land the goods (these are not retail establishments). Put every church in town on your mailing list and send them frequent offers to buy or appraise.

Chapter 21
SWAPPER'S GUIDE

Nationwide Swap Meet Buying Opportunities

Last, but not least, on our list of common dealer sources for antiques are flea markets. As we mentioned earlier, there are over one thousand regular weekend swap meet locations in the United States today. Source: *Swap Meet U.S.A.,* a flea market directory available from Cranbrook House, P. O. Box 272, Saginaw, MI 48606 ($3 per copy). If you are on a cross-country buying trip, plan on an *early morning* stop at one of these outdoor markets. Saturday and Sunday are the most common market days, but midweek or evening openings are not uncommon in some areas. Consult a flea market directory or local Yellow Pages for information when traveling; you are probably within minutes of a swap meet (in any state except Montana).

Don't overlook farmer's markets and livestock auctions as possible sources for merchandise or contacts leading to local pickers. A good example of a typical farming community flea market, where antiques and collectibles are also available, is the famous *Green Dragon Farmers Market and Auction* on twenty green acres in Ephrata, Pennsylvania. Once you get used to the smell of fresh "cow" and the startling sight of black-garbed Amish countryfolk, you can get down to the business of buying. We recently attended this charming event (during a thunderstorm) and purchased one hundred brand-new Amish hand-loomed rag throw rugs for $5 each. Back in California, we sold them all to other dealers (in forty-eight hours), doubled our money, and took orders for next year (I hope the salesman is as easy to deal with in fair weather). If nothing else appeals to you, you can always buy a vanload of Amish cheeses and pastry for resale. Indoor and outdoor shopping is available every Friday from 10:00 A.M. to 10:00 P.M. Look for the Green Dragon sign just south of the lumberyard on Rt. 272, north of Ephrata, Pennsylvania.

For pure Americana, it's really hard to beat the flea markets of Pennsylvania. The Adamstown area is the home of several vintage flea markets, including Renninger's, Black Angus Mall, Shupp's Grove, Hummer's, and others, off Rt. 222, north of turnpike exit 21.

The flea markets of the Northeast are as different as night from day when compared to those of the western states. In California, at a typical drive-in theater event, you will be lucky to find more than one or two "quality antiques" priced low enough to resell. A West Coast dealer I know does 50 percent of his yearly purchasing at eastern flea markets. In his words, "I thought I had died and gone to heaven the first time I attended the Brimfield Massachusetts Market ... everything there was old!" He was, of course, referring to Gordon Reid's famous, thrice yearly, outdoor market at Auction Acres on U.S. Route 20, six miles west of old Sturbridge Village, Massachusetts.

Massachusetts boasts thirty seasonal markets; Connecticut, twenty-five; New Hampshire, twenty-five; New York, one hundred; Ohio, seventy-five; Pennsylvania, one hundred twenty-five; and New Jersey, fifty. California and Florida host hundreds of weekly events. Clark's quarterly *Fleamarket U.S.A.* keeps tabs on these and also hundreds of midwestern swap meets ($7 a year, Rt. 1, #470, Cantonment, FL 32533). Some events are best attended for buying, while others are attended strictly for selling purposes. Within a year's time, a *"buying market"* may become a *"selling market"* or vice versa. It all hinges on the population migration, levels of income, and the local supply of currently "popular" collectibles.

Word travels fast in the antique trade. Right now, furniture haulers are picking up some real bargains at the seasonal *Shipshewana Auction and Flea Market* on Rt. 5 in northern Indiana. Starting at 6:00 A.M. every Tuesday morning (summer until early fall), hundreds of Amish farmers and local pickers converge in an open field at the south end of this crossroads town. Half a dozen barking auctioneers walk up and down row after row of wagons and truck beds piled high with country furniture and farm primitives. The action doesn't end until Wednesday evening, when over three hundred sellers pack up for the long ride home. By the time you read this, Shipshewana may have become a "selling market."

Meanwhile, back in California, my own Sunday morning schedule often consists of rising at 6:00 A.M. and driving forty-five miles to attend a rural swap meet that has yielded big dividends in the form of "picker" contacts, tools, and farm primitives. It takes me about an hour and a half to cover this five-acre event, taking the time to speak with each stall holder. By 10:00 A.M., I am back in the city visiting a couple of drive-in theater markets, where occasionally we are able to find a sleeper or two. One day I bought a nineteenth-century brass and wood, Seth Thomas ship's clock for $60 from a picker who had purchased it earlier in the morning for $20. This was my first major clock purchase because I had always been too cheap to pay much for anything that didn't tick. A local clockmaker got it going, complete with bells that rang on the quarter hour. The first ship's clock collector who saw it in our shop peeled off seven $50 bills and laid them on the counter.

A couple I know does all of their picking at flea markets. They travel constantly, spending spring, summer, and part of the fall in the East and winter in the southern and western United States. Last year in Pennsylvania they purchased a signed Handel ceiling light fixture, with ruby glass intact, for $100, right out of a greasy wooden box behind a local picker's table. This lamp was washed off with a hose and resold a few miles down the road, at the Kutztown Flea Market, for more than $2,000.

We have also talked with dealers who have tried buying at a swap meet without results and quit in dismay. They didn't start early enough in the morning and also didn't "fish in enough ponds." It's like garage sale buying; you've really got to work at it to produce worthwhile results! Sooner or later the law of averages will work in your favor.

Beginning dealers are sometimes inclined to rush up and down row after row of flea market goods, looking for the obvious bargains. This "foot race" technique may produce results during the first half hour of an event, but after the opening flurry it takes a calm, cool picker to score with any degree of consistency. Take your time—look under the tables and inside the beds of pickup trucks. Talk to each stall holder. Ask about things that may not be on display. Nobody brings all his items to any one event. When you run into someone at a flea market who has lots of other goodies for sale at home (perhaps a barn or shed-ful), make a firm appointment to view the stuff that very after-noon. We have never failed to make a profitable buy when invited to follow a picker home.

The rewards are still out there for the patient, plodding per-son. Late one Sunday afternoon I asked a friend of mine why he was wasting his time going through every box of old books re-maining on display. . . . I figured that we might as well call it quits and head for home. Bob replied that he wasn't in any hur-ry. "I might find another $4,000 book," he said with a wry smile. The reason for his persistnce: A year before at this same swap meet, about a mile from my shop, Bob had bought a rebound first edition of *The Last of the Mohicans* by James Fenimore Coo-per (it now resides in a bank vault).

If you plan on doing any serious swap meet picking, take heed of the Boy Scout motto and "Be Prepared." You may find your-self miles from home, food, and friends, with only a few pre-cious hours to spend in your quest.

Check These Simple Rules for Productive Flea Market "Picking":

1. Set your alarm for 5:00 A.M., eat a hearty breakfast, and pre-pare a sack lunch for midday. Carry a canteen that you can fasten to your belt or shopping cart on summer days; water fountains are few and far between.
2. Wear a hat and sunglasses. Put on your most comfortable pair of shoes or hiking boots; never go barefoot. Wear layers of clothing that can be peeled off as the day progresses.
3. Carry a large burlap sack, backpack, or folding shopping cart for your purchases. Better yet, buy a selling space in the mid-dle of a large event and move your van in early in the morn-ing. You won't have to work nearly as hard to get a load!
4. If you have a buying "partner," have him or her start at one end of the meet while you start at the other. (Give your part-ner a duplicate key to your car or van so that he can get in out of the weather if he finishes first.)
5. Haggle! Very few swap meet sellers expect to receive the ask-ing price. Express an interest in the things that you want; if

you stand there long enough admiring an item, the price usually will come down!

6. Avoid displaying large amounts of cash! Use good common sense and you will probably never have a problem.

7. Remember that no matter where you are in the United States, on any given Saturday or Sunday morning there is a flea market or swap meet within driving distance of your motel room! If you start early enough in the morning, you can sometimes cover up to three good-sized buying events.

Time: 11:00 A.M. *The professional buyers have already covered this event. Courtesy R. G. Canning Enterprises*

Chapter 22

REPRODUCTIONS AND LIMITED EDITIONS

Proceed with Caution

King Solomon once said, "There is nothing new under the sun," and he wasn't far from the truth. Just about everything ever produced by mankind has been a modification of something else already in existence. Ninety percent of the new furniture and giftware on today's market is of classical design, in the sense that it relates to forms that were significant before modern times. Perhaps this is why sophisticated collectors place so much importance on "period pieces"—those produced in the era when a style was first popular. .

Art and antiques of great value (or in great popular demand) have been reproduced since the beginning of recorded history. In the days of Augustus, the demand for works of earlier periods prompted the production of thousands of copies as well as outright forgeries. Michelangelo, in his youth, created a classical statue of "Cupid Asleep" which he *antiqued* by burying for a few years and subsequently sold in Rome in 1496 as an authentic antique. In America in 1926, the fakers were still turning out anything the public took a fancy to. William A. Dyer wrote in the twenties that the American antique market literally teemed with fraudulent reproductions and that he personally knew of two gentlemen who had made fortunes in the worm hole game.

Today, many museums actually license, manufacture, or sell quality reproductions of universally popular classic art and important pieces from their own collections. Tooling up for the production of a replica can run into thousands of dollars. Most museum gift shops prefer to buy from specialist firms, such as the American Heritage Publishing Company, or directly from other institutions that may have an excess of reproductions manufactured from their own originals. It is interesting to note that museum gift buyers are often seen at the semiannual wholesale giftware shows, buying from the same sources as the neighborhood card shop. (Perhaps there is a shortage of better quality replicas available to the trade at prices the public can afford.)

Our nation has celebrated two centennials. Each occasion has prompted alert manufacturers to produce thousands of souvenir and reproduction items to satiate the collecting passion which also seems to be an integral part of our national heritage. Over the mellowing span of years many of these reproductions themselves have become heirlooms, commonly called centennial pieces.

Today, the question of whether or not you should handle modern reproductions in your shop is not so much one of ethics as of economics. If you have a ready supply of good salable antiques in a price range that your customers can afford, then obviously you don't need to stock reproduction merchandise. On the other hand, many antique shop owners in high traffic locations are facing an acute shortage of acceptable antiques and have subsequently turned to reproductions as a major source of revenue. The best way to display reproductions (according to a major trade supplier) is to segregate them from antiques and tastefully label them for what they are. The words "Antique Recreation" or "Heirloom Reproduction" frequently appear on such labels. Domestic manufacturers are not trying to fool anyone; they are just doing a good job of filling the gap between supply and demand in the middle-income area that thousands of antique and gift shops cater to.

A lot of unsophisticated consumers actually feel more comfortable buying a reproduction than they would trying to select a legitimate antique. They are a market group that must be reckoned with. A certain percentage of this market group is also eagerly collecting "limited edition" prints, plates, medals, figurines, and furniture. Persons who would never dream of playing the stock market or betting on horse races are spending a major portion of their incomes gambling on the future of limited edition collectibles! A recent edition of a popular antique periodical devoted fifty pages to the paid advertisements of limited edition promoters. We take the liberty of using the word "promoters" because many of these manufacturers have taken extraordinary liberties with the word "limited." In the sense that

Shaving mugs and mustache cups, circa 1967. Courtesy A. A. Importing Co., St. Louis, Missouri

the word has traditionally been used by artists and authors, these factory-produced limited editions are not limited at all! Can you imagine Hemingway sitting down in a warehouse for two weeks to sign 15,000 "limited" first editions? Or picture Rembrandt signing an etching "one of five thousand."

We recently called a major medals producer to inquire as to how many medallions of a widely advertised limited edition would actually be struck. After an embarrassing pause the manager replied, "Why, however many are actually ordered in the next sixty days. After that, the subscription period is officially closed." *Caveat Emptor!*

The hotbed of porcelain plate collecting is currently centered in the Midwest, where some 15,000 enthusiasts gathered recently for a Plate Collectors Fair. According to a 1980 market survey, almost 4 million Americans (mostly women, over age thirty-five) were actively buying, trading, and hanging this relatively new "art form."

Many porcelain "collector plates" are issued in preannounced quantities of five to fifteen thousand copies, while others are limited only to the quantity produced in a thirty-day firing period. These production runs do not, in my opinion, justify retail prices of $25 to $50 for transfer-printed pieces of machine-made greenware run through an automated kiln and probably produced at a cost of under $5. Who knows? The current limited edition craze might even reach the stages of advanced "Tulipmania." A few hundred years ago in Holland, thousands of otherwise sane people quit their jobs to get in on the tulip raising and trading fad that was sweeping the country. Speculation was rampant in the larger cities. By 1634 some varieties of colored tulips had become priceless; new bulbs changed hands for thousands of guilders each. Eventually, the bubble burst and there were no more buyers for tulips or the inflated paper stocks and bonds of the larger growers. The government banned trading and the whole Dutch economy went belly up! Banks failed, businesses collapsed, and unemployment was rampant.

In the minds of many astute investors, ready-made collectibles hold little, if any, potential for financial appreciation over the long term. If you go to the trouble to telephone some of the firms that advertise for collector plates under the "Wanted" headings in several antique publications, you may find that they

Courtesy A. A. Importing Company, St. Louis, Missouri

are not really buying at the advertised prices which appear in their ads. A typical response to a selling offer is, "We have enough of that issue on hand right now and are not buying." And yet you may see the same "Wanted" ad repeated month after month. What many of these advertisers are looking for is a distress situation, where the respondent will offer to sell for much less.

We can't blame any dealer for trying to buy right, but deceptive advertising does not elevate the collectible trade in the minds of consumers. We have also heard of instances where false buying ads were supposedly placed by manufacturers to prop up the retail prices on issues that were undersubscribed or overproduced. Almost any gift shop owner can buy "back issues" at the regular 50 percent trade discount from distributors, as long as there is any inventory left in the manufacturer's warehouse, in many cases for several years after introduction of the original "limited" issue. (There are, of course, some plates and figurines that are sold out, in short order, after being placed on the market.) The *real aftermarket* in the antique business is verified daily by auction room sales. You will find no such legitimate aftermarket for most limited edition items. We have seen $50 porcelain plates of the "limited" variety go for $2 at well-attended auctions. We have also seen limited edition silver ingot pieces go for meltdown prices at public auction. Most limited edition collectibles have little, if any, intrinsic value and, like other new goods bought at retail prices, they can seldom be resold at a figure approaching the original purchase price. Many gift shop proprietors are urging customers to buy two of everything, "one for their wall and one for investment." It is only a matter of time until the real aftermarket will be tested, en masse. We would urge antique dealers not to stock these "instant collectibles" in depth or to attest to their investor qualities!

Chapter 23 THE GIFTWARE GAME

Thousands of Wholesale Sources

While some antique dealers have struggled along for years punishing eyes, lungs, and bloodstream with sawdust and toxic chemicals, many of their counterparts in the giftware business have grown rich. Why fight the trend? Many in the antique trade are moving slowly but surely toward selling gifts and decorative accessories in addition to "vintage" merchandise—especially in tourist areas.

A trip to one of the "markets" near your city may prove to be a very profitable experience. These market buildings house from dozens to hundreds of tenants who wholesale greeting cards, gifts, home furnishings, and wall decor. A business card and resale number are usually required to gain entry into these showrooms. (Take along someone who has these "credentials" if you do not.) If you are too far away to visit a wholesale center, we suggest that you write to the mart's manager for a list of tenants and then write for individual wholesale catalogs from the various representatives.

You might also want to subscribe to a few of the giftware industry's trade publications. Among them are:

- *Decor* (pictures, prints, and frames). 408 Olive Street, St. Louis, MO 63102
- *Gift & Tableware Reporter.* P. O. Box 2152, Radnor, PA 19084
- *Gifts & Decorative Accessories.* Geyer McAllister Publications, 51 Madison Avenue, New York, NY 10010
- *Giftware Business.* 1515 Broadway, New York, NY 10036

You will find the displays at gift shows so appealing that you may be tempted to buy from every booth. A word of caution, however; those cardboard or plastic containers with their "cute" advertising messages will not add to the turn-of-the-century environment you should be trying to create. You want your shop to look like a room setting or a general store, not another "plastic" gift department. Smart boutique buyers limit themselves to items that look earthy or handmade. Textiles, woodenware, cast iron, stoneware, brass, copper, porcelain, and pewter accessories lend themselves to display among antiques. Stainless steel, aluminum, pressed wood, Plexiglas, and other synthetic materials do not.

Your first order need not be in tremendous depth. Normally, the minimum order from any single gift supplier is below $100.

In addition to the firms displaying reproductions at gift marts, there are several catalog houses that do a large portion of their business with antique shops. Among these are A. A. Importing Company, Inc., 4244–48 Olive Street, St. Louis, MO 63108; A-America Inc., P. O. Box 46372, Seattle, WA 98146; Colonial Lamp & Supply, Inc., P. O. Box 867, East Arrowhead Drive, McMinnville, TN 37110; Merritt's Antiques & Reproduction Clocks, R.D. 2, Douglassville, PA 19518; Ritter & Son Reproduction Hardware, Gualala, CA 95445; and Sign of the Crab Brass Works, 8101 Elder Creek Road, Sacramento, CA 95824.

A final word about buying from catalogs: Don't put full faith in anything you haven't seen for yourself.

Many English concerns specialize in producing or distributing antique reproductions. One Richmond, England, firm advertises in the London-based *Antiques & Art Weekly* that they are suppliers to the trade only, of all of the following reproduction items:

Antiques	Decorators' Pieces	Jewelry Boxes
Bells	Doorknockers	Lamps
Brassware	Doorstops	Lead Articles
Brass Weights	Engravings	Maps
Candelabra	Garden Furniture	Marine Goods
Candlesticks	Gifts	Model Boats
Chess Sets	Glass	Model Cannons
China	Glass Paintings	Oil Lamps
Coach Lamps	Hearth Accessories	Pewter
Coal Helmets	Horse Brasses	Pictures
Copperware	Hunting Horns	Pin Trays

Planters	Ships Lanterns	Trade Signs
Prints	Silver	Umbrella Stands
Pub Decorations	Small Furniture	Warming Pans
Pub Mirrors	Staffordshire China	Weapons
Roasters	Toby Jugs	Wooden Jugs

Bear in mind that all English shipments to this country are not in container-sized lots. Small packages weighing less than twenty-two pounds may be shipped via sea mail for about $8 each. Customs duty will be charged through your post office. Larger packages are frequently shipped via air freight with the Customs duty paid for you by the forwarder and collected upon delivery to you at the airport.

Wholesale Gift Centers—A State-by-State Listing

Call or write before traveling. Mart hours and days vary from area to area.

CALIFORNIA

Brack Shops Bldg.
527 West 7th Street
Los Angeles, CA 90014

Brack Shops East
649 South Olive Street
Los Angeles, CA 90014

Brack 520 Building
520 West 7th Street
Los Angeles, CA 90014

The Galleria Design Center
101 Kansas Street
San Francisco, CA 94103

The Icehouse
151 Union Street
San Francisco, CA 94111

Los Angeles Home Furnishings Mart
1933 South Broadway
Los Angeles, CA 90007

Los Angeles Merchandise Mart
712 South Olive Street
Los Angeles, CA 90014

Pacific Design Center
8687 Melrose Avenue
Los Angeles, CA 90069

The Showplace
No. 2 Kansas Street
San Francisco, CA 94103

Western Merchandise Mart
1355 Market Street
San Francisco, CA 94103

COLORADO

Denver Merchandise Mart
451 East 58th Avenue
Denver, CO 80216

The gift business has always been healthy. 1880s pen-and-ink sketch

FLORIDA

Miami Merchandise Mart
777 N.W. 72nd Avenue
Miami, FL 33126

GEORGIA

Atlanta Merchandise Mart
240 Peachtree Street N.W.
Atlanta, GA 30303

ILLINOIS

American Mart Corporation
666 Lake Shore Drive
Chicago, IL 60611

The Merchandise Mart
Merchandise Mart Plaza
Chicago, IL 60654

INDIANA

Indianapolis Gift Mart
25 West Maryland Street
Indianapolis, IN 46225

MASSACHUSETTS

The Center
59 Middlesex Turnpike
Bedford, MA 01730

Northeast Trade Center
Sylvan Road
Winburn, MA 01801

MICHIGAN

Gateway Center Building
1101 Washington Boulevard
Detroit, MI 48226

The Executive Plaza
1200 Sixth Street
Detroit, MI 48226

MINNESOTA

Midwest Merchandise Mart
800 N. Washington Avenue
Minneapolis, MN 55401

MISSOURI

The Corrigan Building
1828 Walnut Street
Kansas City, MO 63108

Davidson Building
1627 Main Street
Kansas City, MO 64108

NEW YORK CITY

11 East 26th Street
411 Fifth Avenue
New York, NY 10010

The Toy Center
(North and South Bldgs.)
200 Fifth Avenue
New York, NY 10010

212 Fifth Avenue Corporation
c/o F. M. Ring Associates
20 W. 47th Street
New York, NY 10036

225 Fifth Avenue
New York, NY 10010

230 Fifth Avenue
Lloyd S. Howard, Management
New York, NY 10010

New York Merchandise Mart
Madison Avenue and 26th Street
New York, NY 10010

NORTH CAROLINA

High Point Accessories Mart
114 S. Main Street
High Point, NC 27260

Southern Furniture Exposition Bldg.
209 S. Main Street
High Point, NC 27260

Charlotte Merchandise Mart
2500 E. Independence Boulevard
Charlotte, NC 28205

OHIO

Cleveland Merchandise Mart
420 Prospect Avenue
Cleveland, OH 44115

Columbus Gift Mart
106 North High Street
Columbus, OH 43215

Designers Building
2800 Superior Avenue
Cleveland, OH 44115

PENNSYLVANIA

Greater Pittsburgh Merchandise
  Mart
200 Mall Boulevard
Monroeville, PA 15146

TEXAS

Dallas Market Center
2100 Stemmons Freeway
Dallas, TX 75207

Oak Lawn Plaza
1444 Oak Lawn Avenue
Dallas, TX 75207

WASHINGTON

The 6100 Building
6100 Fourth Avenue, South
Seattle, WA 98108

Terminal Sales Building
1932 First Avenue
Seattle, WA 98109

Northwest Home Furnishings Mart
121 Boren Avenue, North
Seattle, WA 98109

Confirm current addresses
before traveling.

Chapter 24
STORE LAYOUT AND DISPLAY

Merchandising Techniques That Work

Even the most humble antique shop can employ modern merchandising and display methods to good advantage. Today's antique shopper is not the hardy soul of yesteryear who might spend half a day rummaging through piles of dusty junk in the poorly lit shed or basement of a secondhand dealer. More typically, the shopper is a worker on a lunch break or a housewife who just dropped the kids off at the Little League field. You will have the customer's attention for only a quarter of an hour or so at the most, so it is important that he or she be able to see most of your inventory in that brief period. Even tourists are in a hurry nowadays, rushing from one shop to the next in quest of their favorite collectibles. The only people who seem to ponder for a while are furniture shoppers.

How does one cater to a sophisticated clientele in any "luxury" business? By making shopping as easy and as pleasant as possible! Your first effort should be in the area of lighting. Take a look at the ceiling of your favorite supermarket or department store. Chances are that you will see quadruple eight-foot fluorescent fixtures, end to end, about ten feet apart, over the entire selling area. Don't settle for a couple of bare bulbs in your shop; invest in at least a few modern ceiling fixtures.

An effective store display can become a subtle buying suggestion to many potential customers. For years, furniture dealers have used creative environmental room settings to sell everything from oil paintings to sofas. Consider the possibility of arranging your shop's antique accessories as they might appear in a home setting. The general public still lacks confidence in its ability to pick the right piece for the right place.

Begin your sales campaign right on the sidewalk or in your front yard! Place a few attractive pieces outside your shop every day. If the weather is bad, put out waterproof items or primitives that won't be affected by rain. Don't cover your show windows with the backs of cupboards or drapery fabric. Create a clean, well-lighted display window that allows a look at the whole shop if possible. Your window display can sell antiques for you twenty-four hours a day! Take a good look at the show windows of a few successful furniture stores and gift shops in your area. Then step back and try to be more critical of your own display.

In high-traffic areas, it is important to change your window offerings every month. This creates added interest and eliminates damage from excessive sunlight. Be careful not to expose colored lithographs, textiles, or original artwork to direct sunshine.

Floor Plan. A square floor plan is more desirable than a long, narrow shop layout, and a high ceiling is preferable to the standard eight-foot variety. General-line antique shops smaller than six hundred square feet (twenty by thirty feet) tend to discourage serious shoppers. Prospective buyers often believe that the selection in tiny shops will be minimal (or that they might be intimidated by the close proximity of the proprietor). Most "mom and pop" shops average one thousand square feet of selling space and do well to gross $50 a foot per year.

If you have a choice, go for the largest number of square feet available (up to about twenty-five-hundred square feet for a furniture-oriented operation). Blind spots or multiple-room layouts encourage shoplifting. Arrange your taller furniture and china cabinets along the walls and keep center-of-the-room displays at a height of less than forty inches. Your customers will feel more comfortable; there will be less breakage, fewer injuries from falling objects, and a minimum of petty theft.

Anything smaller than a large handbag that is valuable enough to steal, and resell profitably, will eventually be stolen unless you keep it locked behind glass! You can't secure everything, but common sense tells us that anything made of silver, gold, ivory, or jade, and readily resalable items such as watches or firearms, should not be out where they may be handled (this includes your show window).

If you want to set up shop in an old house, you might try to get permission to knock out a few nonbearing walls and locate your counter in the center of the room or near the door. Other

Courtesy Country Antiques, Route 2, Pittsfield, New Hampshire

possibilities are to display only furniture and large antiques in the rooms that you cannot monitor from your cash register.

The low ceilings of many buildings can be ripped out to expose structural beams and rafters that will readily serve as additional hanging display areas. Many old store buildings have suspended acoustical tile ceilings that were installed thirty or forty years ago to give them a "modern" look. These are also easily removed to create hundreds of square feet of extra selling space. When you figure that a single square foot of floor space could produce up to $100 worth of sales a year, it is a powerful incentive to use every bit of available space to its very best advantage.

Many shopkeepers do not effectively utilize wall areas above eye level. A few good "wall fillers" are posters, paintings, advertising signs, sets of harness, wagon wheels, farm tools, chairs hung on pegs, lanterns, cigar and cookie molds, mirrors, kitchen primitives, printer's type boxes, trophy heads, quilts, textiles, and stained glass.

Frequent Rotation of Store Stock.   is an accepted axiom in almost any type of retail situation. Everyone from J. C. Penney to Neiman-Marcus has been doing it for years. Nothing succeeds like success, and regular stock rotation creates the illusion of constant buying and selling. The average retail antique shop inventory turns over only about one and a half times a year, and regular repeat business is discouraged by customers seeing the same old things in the same old setting month after month (and often year after year). Some antique dealers have accidentally learned the correlation between "shifting" and selling when a regular customer "discovers" a recently moved shop sitter that has been around for a year or more and buys it. Move something *every week;* change a complete display *every month;* and rearrange the whole selling floor at least *once a year!*

Emphasize the Positive, Not the Negative! A policy of "no refunds or exchanges" often means "no business." Avoid entirely the use of those cute little "lovely to look at, lovely to hold, but if you break me, to you I am sold" signs that one finds in the shops of negative people. If you don't want an item to be handled, put it where it cannot be reached without assistance.

Anticipate possible accidents before they happen! Display fine china and glassware in a thickly carpeted area well away from primitives (which are often handled). Don't lean things against walls or showcases where a wandering child may venture. Keep breakables well away from the edges of shelves and tabletops; purses and elbows often extend into these areas. Don't place very expensive objects on pedestals or lamp tables in traffic areas; they belong against walls or in roped-off displays. Check all corner cabinets, armoires, and china cupboards to see if they fall forward when both doors are open, which is frequently the case. This can be remedied by a few bricks or heavy sadirons placed against the back bottom shelf or a large screw eye wired to the wall.

After operating various retail stores for over twenty years, we have come to several conclusions: *"Anything that can fall . . . will*

Primitives displayed on a concrete-block wall. Courtesy Tom Warren

fall." "*Anything that can leak . . . will leak.*" "*Anything that is easily damaged . . . will be damaged.*" "*Anything that can be knocked over . . . will be knocked over,*" and "*Anything that looks easy to pilfer . . . will be pilfered.*" In spite of all the dire possibilities, common sense will triumph—if you give it a chance!

Decor.   In this day of theme restaurants, theme nightclubs, and theme amusement parks, it would seem timely to open a theme antique shop. In our city, there are several successful antique shops already employing a total-environment concept. Among them is a nautical antique specialist whose entire store interior is laid out exactly like the main deck of an old sailing vessel. To heighten the atmosphere, the proprietor has piped in waterfront sound effects complete with creaking masts, screaming seagulls, and foghorns.

Another remarkable shop is a re-creation of an early 1900s candy store and soda fountain. The inventory for sale is not edible; it consists entirely of sterling silver flatware and hollow-ware artfully displayed where the candy would be. Other specialty antique shops that we have seen of late are: a barber shop (mugs, razors, soap, and scents), an 1800s newspaper (type trays, wood type, prints, photos, and political memorabilia), and a unique "gallery" selling nothing but antique musical instruments, sheet music, books, autographs, phonograph records, and opera programs.

While we are on the subject of stimulating decor, let's touch on what constitutes good or bad taste in store design. First of all, money has only a little to do with creating an eye-pleasing, sales-stimulating shop interior. Let's start with the walls. They can account for half of your sales if utilized effectively. What can you do to them before the furniture, counters, and showcases are moved in? Make sure before you sign a lease or rental agreement that you can drive nails into the landlord's walls, or that you can cover them with a material that will accept hooks and nails. Many shopping centers require that fireproof materials be used as all wall coverings. For about $15 a gallon, you can buy a fire retardant that passes most building codes and can be used on bare or painted wood surfaces. Fabrics must pass a fire department inspection before they can be applied to wall surfaces in shopping centers.

As we have mentioned, old barnwood, moss-covered shingles, or any type of new or used lumber makes a practical backdrop for antiques. So do sandblasted bricks or plain old plaster, as long as the color is subdued (preferably not in pink and blue shades). White, yellow, tan, or earthy tones are much better choices than red, green, or blue. You want your antiques to stand out, not the walls! Pegboard wall treatment is very practical (but it certainly doesn't create the illusion of yesteryear). You can disguise existing pegboard walls by painting them a flat dark brown (it hides the holes) or covering them with natural burlap, which still allows the use of pegboard hooks.

Also, you can hang things on concrete block and brick walls by driving one-inch-long cement nails into the mortar between the bricks or blocks. Wear safety goggles when you do this; the nails often bounce back at lethal speed! A solid concrete wall can be attacked by contact gluing one-by-two-inch strips of lumber across the top, bottom, and middle to provide a support for nailing up wallboard or barnwood.

Courtesy Unicorn Antiques, San Diego, California

Floor display case, circa 1880. Courtesy Tom Warren

An important decision is whether to install wall-hung shelving, with an occasional break for pictures and mirrors. If your square footage is eight hundred feet or more, we would not recommend permanent shelving of any kind unless you are re-creating a country store. Antique furniture, old china cabinets, and bookcases will normally provide all the wall shelf space needed, while allowing you the luxury of complete flexibility in merchandise display. This method of shelving also allows you to sell your "fixtures" twice a year. Remember that your complete furniture inventory will be constantly coming in and going out, so you don't want to be stuck with large areas of fixed shelving that won't allow you to move any piece when the need arises.

If your shop is too small or too narrow for room settings, you can still make it easy for customers to see things by displaying them in related groups: tools with tools, china with china, chairs with tables, and so forth. Maybe a country store layout would work out best, with lots of bins, shelves, and barrels containing compatible merchandise.

Don't depreciate your antiques by displaying them among the inevitable junk and secondhand stuff that you acquire in complete house or garage lots. Send the substandard stuff off to auction or let the kids grow rich selling it at swap meets. If you have to sell it on the premises, put it all in a separate "junk room" and price it cheap; there's lots more where it came from.

Next would be your choice of showcases. Avoid anything in chrome or Formica. Look, instead, for secondhand oak or mahogany showcases that have a lot of mellow old wooden trim. If you can't find one, advertise for it. Vintage showcases are still in storage in garages and basements all over the country. As stated before, you shouldn't have to pay over $250 for a nice one, perhaps in need of a new glass top (order beveled glass for a stunning replacement).

Security.   Also to be taken into consideration during preopening planning is the important question of store security. The cost of all-inclusive insurance, covering theft, is too prohibitive for all but the most affluent operators. (You may find your fire and liability insurance alone running well over $500 a year.) The first security checkpoints are all the windows and doors. Hidden alley and side entrances are especially vulnerable. Inside bars on all back and side windows are a must if you plan to carry anything that a thief can resell. Both back and front doors should be equipped with deadbolt or mortise locks containing pickproof cylinders.

Some shopkeepers put an additional padlock on the front door in case a pry bar is used by a burglar to spread the door frame. The doors themselves should be reinforced with sheet iron or three-quarter-inch plywood screwed to the inside surface. Hollowcore, residential-type doors are easy to kick in or quickly saw through. If the hinges or hinge pins are on the outside, they must be modified so that they cannot be removed. Use an additional drop bar or manual deadbolt inside back doors in case a burglar pulls off your doorknob. Skylights and attic access doors must also be locked or barred from the inside. Trim away all hedges and shrubs from your back and side walls. Don't leave packing boxes or trash around for prowlers to hide behind.

Put yourself in the burglar's shoes. He's in need of a quick fix and looking for an easy, low-risk opportunity. The last thing he wants to do is be seen in, or near, your shop! For this reason, good night lighting is the most effective deterrent against any type of crime. Keep a tall outside light on all night and when you are away for weekends. Automatic, dusk-to-dawn, roof-mounted mercury vapor lamps are the best outdoor insurance policy. Inside your shop a pair of 150-watt bulbs in porcelain sockets should be on all night. Don't use a table lamp or an old ceiling-mounted fixture for a night light. They are apt to short circuit or become dangerously hot during twelve hours of continuous burning. (Make sure your night-lighting system is installed by an electrician and kept well away from flammable materials.)

Alarm systems are a nuisance—and expensive too. Your best insurance is a burglarproof safe, lots of night lighting, and double locks throughout.

Shoplifting.   Professional shoplifters employ a number of simple but effective methods other than just concealing merchandise on their person and walking out. Keep in mind that much of the stealing from antique stores is done in broad daylight with bad checks and phony identification. Limit the amount of an out-of-town check that your firm will accept. Sometimes you are better off to take major bank cards such as VISA or MasterCard because all such purchases over $50 require telephone authorization.

Never place more than one piece of expensive jewelry on top of the counter at a time; as each new piece is asked for by the customer, replace the previously shown item to its proper spot in the showcase. Better to lose a single ring than a $10,000 trayful. Never leave your store unattended or unlocked to look at merchandise being offered to you from a vehicle parked "just outside." (A confederate is often left inside to pocket valuables.) Some thieves enter a shop and stall around for an hour or so until "nature" calls you to the little room out back. They might even offer to "watch the shop" while you take your coffee break.

No matter how busy you are, take time to greet each person who enters your store, even if it's just a smile and a "hello there" from across the room. (Once you have acknowledged someone's presence, he or she is much less apt to steal from you!) A last note of caution: Keep anything well away from the front door that can be carried out easily. It's a good spot to display furniture and larger primitives. A friend of mine who is a veteran shopkeeper gets rid of his shoddy old lamps and hopeless vases by placing them on a table just inside the front entrance (which is out of his line of view). "Nothing ever stays there more than a day or two," he says with a grin.

Now that we have convinced you that all shoppers are potential thieves and bad-check writers, may we close this chapter by stating that collectors are really the finest kind of clientele! We have owned all kinds of businesses and have had only a fraction of the problems in our antique store that we have encountered elsewhere. One bad check in four years, and shoplifting has been confined, this season, to a ragged cookbook and a rusty sadiron. If you just exercise a little caution and keep your best stuff locked up in showcases, you won't have to worry about losing more than an occasional inexpensive item to a helpless kleptomaniac.

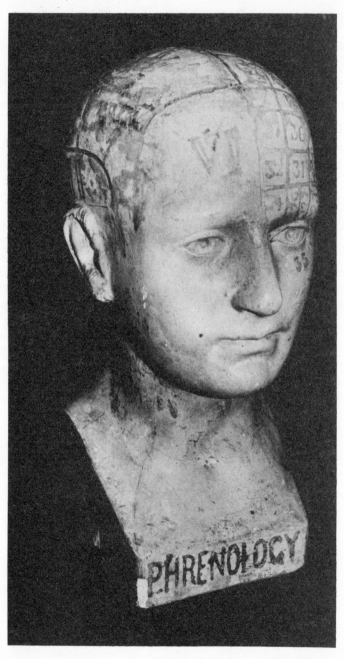

Courtesy Maine Antique Digest

Chapter 25

THE "COLLECTOR" MENTALITY

Are Freudian Impulses Involved?

To quote a quote from a recent article in *Maine Antique Digest:* "Everything is collected nowadays.... Almost everybody collects—the poor man as well as the rich, the man with taste and artistic instinct, and the man with neither. Any attempt, therefore, at grouping the various things which are collected, or at classifying the people who collect, *must inevitably fail!"*—William Roberts, 1896.

Modern psychologists are stumped by collectors. Freudian theories have been thrown out. Fetishism does not motivate the average collector. "Collecting" among youngsters has been recently related to a desire for higher learning and an early entry into the adult world. Grownups collect (or hoard) for numerous reasons. For some, accumulating certain material things provides a sense of security. Others are attracted to antiques as investments. Many of us sustain a link to the past through the ownership of items actually used by our forebears. Aesthetic considerations may also play a part in one's preference for tried and true designs. Vanity also accounts for a great number of collections; let's face it, we all enjoy the attention our hobbies bring us!

A whopping 20 percent of the population collects something! Everyone claims that his or her hobby is among the most popular, but statistics still rank stamps and coins as having the most devotees. Porcelain, glassware, dolls, firearms, antiques, and art follow in close pursuit. About a third of this 20 percent collect a diversified list of odd items that don't fall into any overall category (beer cans, comic books, baseball cards, and so forth). Most of these collectors are not interested in selling their treasures; however, they do like to trade duplicates with other enthusiasts. Perhaps this is why collector clubs flourish.

What can dealers learn from these findings? I would suggest that collectors are sensitive people who are proud of their accumulations. Dealers would be wise to avoid verbal scoffing at any field of collecting (including milk bottles); you never know whose feelings might be hurt. Secondly, it may pay to cater to the ego of any potential customer. Ask people what they collect. Never depreciate or apologize for any of your own merchandise (or that of others). If you don't like it, why should anyone else buy it? It's not necessary to close every sale with the words "that's a good buy you are making" or "these can't go anywhere but up in price." Collectors already know if they are making a good buy, and most of them resent the fact that things are going up. Last but not least, *be a good listener*. We all like people who actually listen to what we have to say!

No two dealers have exactly the same approch to selling antiques. I feel that good merchandise will sell itself, and so I don't normally do much more than smile and wave a casual greeting to customers entering our shop. I will answer questions cheerfully, but I don't conduct people around the store showing them particular pieces of merchandise. My outward appearance might be described as "courteous disinterest"; selling anything would seem to be the furthermost thought from my mind. This "technique" works for me. My wife, on the other hand, uses a different approach entirely. She talks constantly to her customers and uses a "show and tell" method until they either buy or leave the store. We both seem to sell something to one out of three "lookers," and other dealers report a similar ratio of customers to sales. Courses in salesmanship emphasize that the first step in selling anything is to sell yourself. People who like you will want to buy something from you. Selling your personality may not entail much more than expressing a genuine interest in others. Smile and give it a try!

If you are seeing a couple of dozen people a day, and not closing at least six sales, then something is wrong with your inventory. Maybe the price level of your goods is too high for impulse sales or casual gift giving. Perhaps there are too many "chip"-indales in your stock (remember that first quality sells first). Maybe you have all English stuff and homemakers in your area are looking for Country French. Ask questions; look at other retailers in your neighborhood. What is needed in the area?

Would the addition of apple cider, greeting cards, homemade baked goods, or garden seeds pay your rent? Maybe you should take up chair cane replacement, add price guides, lamp parts, or reproduction hardware to your stock in trade? If the inventory is all wrong, dump it at auction and start over with a more diversified selection. Play it by ear. Avoid preconceived notions about where the emphasis should be; local customers will determine to a great degree what you must carry to survive!

A "specialist dealer" will take longer to develop a sustaining trade but, once established, he or she is less subject to popular trends within collecting or decorating. Some oldtimers say, "Be yourself and stock what you like; you will develop your own following." This is true, but it takes a lot of exposure, to a lot of people, to gain a following that will support extremes in taste or personality. The middle of the road is where the big dollars are in America today. The upper end, the real carriage trade in the antique business, is supported by a comparative handful of museum curators and very wealthy collectors. Their absence, or presence, at an "important" auction can mean the difference between its failure and success. Their numbers are said to be in the low hundreds. We are speaking of people with unlimited funds—jet-setters who can buy anything they desire. This is why if you have something really important to sell it should have the worldwide exposure that only an international auction house can provide.

The larger auction firms are not difficult to approach. Send them a complete description and a good Polaroid photo or a 35-mm slide of your treasure. If you have had a local appraisal, include this information also. Figure on a 10 to 20 percent selling commission plus any repair or restoration that must be done.

The psychological makeup of auction buyers would perhaps merit a chapter of its own. The best prices seem to be realized when buyers are provided with strong reassurance that the goods for sale have intrinsic value or a ready resale potential. A history, documentation, pedigree, or "provenance," as it is termed in the trade, can double or triple the potential value of many items. Auctioneers often create the illusion of these credentials through the lavish use of illustrations, appraisals, and quotations in their catalogs. The psychological impact of an exceptionally large auction crowd can also create wild bidding, especially if a few "celebrities" are in attendance. Sometimes, it would seem that certain persons bid solely for the attention it brings them. More than a few dealers and collectors have succumbed at one time or another to a malady known as "auction fever." The only cure is to leave the common frailties of vanity and covetousness at home. One must adopt the demeanor of a professional gambler who knows the odds and never overplays his hand.

Chapter 26 DEALING WITH THE HAGGLERS

"Recorded" Dealer Conversations

For the edification of beginners, and the entertainment of established shopkeepers, we will "play back" a few tape-recorded dealer/customer conversations:

CUSTOMER: Isn't that an interesting table?
DEALER: Yes, you have excellent taste! We don't often find them in that condition. Notice the sturdy bottom stretcher; see how it is tenoned into each leg.

CUSTOMER: I wonder, though, how this red mahogany would fit in with my Danish Modern decor?
DEALER: Oh, mix and match is the latest decorating trend; you don't want your rooms to look like something out of a Sears catalog, do you?

CUSTOMER: I am supposed to buy a silver wedding anniversary gift, but I don't know if Harold and Maud would like this Hawaiian souvenir spoon.
DEALER: Everyone appreciates sterling silver these days, with inflation being what it is! The nice thing about spoons is that you can also use them to eat with.

A little reinforcement can go a long way toward closing a difficult sale. We always mention that anything purchased from our shop may be returned for exchange or a full refund. Most reputable dealers nowadays concur with this practice wholeheartedly. I mentioned before how we harbor second thoughts when we enter a shop where there is a large sign behind the cash register which proclaims "Absolutely No Refunds or Exchanges—All Sales Final." In these cases most intelligent people would assume the merchant is not sure enough of his goods to stand behind them! The inconvenience of an occasional exchange or refund is a drop in the bucket compared to the long-term customer goodwill it can create.

Some dealers, to the consternation of others, use the age-old technique of lowering the price by about 20 percent if a potential customer shows more than a passing interest in an object. This tried-and-true closing method involves overpricing everything in one's shop by at least 20 percent. (I wonder if it doesn't scare off as many sales as it produces?) Most of us won't come down much on our prices unless the rent is past due, or our truck tires are getting bald. Seriously, a price reduction of some sort is all it takes to sell an item to many "hard core" antiquers. If one offers to at least pay the sales tax for these diehards, many times a sale can be made that might otherwise have been lost. We try to follow a firm price policy; however, we will bend the rules if our tag code indicates an item has been in stock for a year or more. Our feeling is that the floor space should be given over to something that has a better probability of moving in six months or less. A twice yearly turnover does not happen by accident—you must work every possible angle to coax your inventory out the front door at a profitable pace!

Allow us to play a few more "tape-recorded" dealer/customer conversations:

CUSTOMER: I am a dealer. What's the best you can do on this $1.50 thimble? It has a dent in it.
DEALER: Look around and see what else you can use; we offer a 15 percent discount to dealers on a combined total of $150 or more.

CUSTOMER: I've only got $5 left from my grocery shopping. Would you take it for this $8 vase?
DEALER: That *is* a lovely vase and they sell for $10 elsewhere. Would you like to lay it away until next payday?

CUSTOMER: There isn't any price tag on this varnished tin coffeepot [worth $900]. Will you take a quick ten bucks for it? [The price tag is now in his pocket.]
DEALER'S HELPER: Sorry, sir, I can't sell any untagged items! I'll ask Mrs. B. to look it up as soon as she returns.

CUSTOMER: [after stacking up a heap of antiques on your counter] What's the best price you can make me on the whole shebang—if I take everything?
DEALER: Well, sir, you must have excellent taste! Those are the best decoys we've ever run across, and that fly rod is a signed Winchester! If you will pay my asking price, I won't charge you any sales tax. That's a 6 percent discount.

CUSTOMER: Are you sure this isn't a reproduction? I've handled a lot of them and it doesn't feel quite right—but it's worth five bucks to me to use as a pencil holder.
DEALER: Gosh, Doctor Larkin over at the museum thought it was pre-Columbian and quite a buy at $15. He may be interested, too! Could you check back in a month and, if it's still here, I'll see what I can do for you.

CUSTOMER: What is your best cash price on this $150 table?
DEALER: Well, the price on that table includes two days of hard labor, Sir. It had about three layers of buttermilk paint on it and my elbow still hurts!

CUSTOMER: A shop down the street is selling button hooks like this one for a quarter, but I like yours best. Would you take the same price?
DEALER: Oh? I haven't been down to Mary's for ages. Is she still in business?

CUSTOMER: Can you give me a better price on this four-piece tea set if I buy the whole group?
DEALER: Up in Wilksborough, they's gittin' what we are askin' for the set, jest on their teapots alone.

The byword in dealing in antiques is *flexibility!* Your kid may need braces next month. If an item has been in stock for eight months or more, make a quick guess as to what it would bring at auction (less the commission) and let the customer have it at a reduced price. Remember, the time to sell is when you have a willing buyer. Don't let pride prevent you from making a price adjustment when necessary—turning merchandise is the name of the game!

Chapter 27

THE NINETY-DAY LAYAWAY

And Other Forms of Risk-Free Credit

Traditionally, the antique business has been a "cash and carry" operation, but postwar dealers discovered that larger-ticket items could be sold if the customer was given enough time to pay. Since "possession is nine-tenths of the law" and "absence makes the heart grow fonder," a system evolved called *layaway*. Most layaway purchases are made with a minimum down payment to hold the item until the purchaser figures out a way to sneak the balance due out of the household budget. We encourage layaway shoppers because it keeps a steady cash flow coming in our shop all year round. (You can have a month when customer payments on layaways may even exceed net sales.) Habitual layaway buyers never seem to get out of hock to antique dealers! They are exposed to new merchandise every time they stop in to make a payment on an earlier purchase. Often customers will bring in friends to see the beautiful accessories which will eventually grace their homes. These friends become buyers too.

Most dealers feel that it is important to set a maximum time limit of sixty or ninety days on layaway purchases. The use of a printed form is the best procedure because it eliminates the possibility of any misunderstanding and allows for the return of merchandise to stock if it is not paid for within a given time period. (We personally would rather return the customer's money and retain his or her goodwill.)

Some dealers have found that the acceptance of credit cards, like VISA or MasterCard, can also increase sales, especially in tourist areas where impulse buying is more apt to occur. Sure, the issuing bank takes about 3 percent, but you get immediate cash from them and rarely does a credit card customer ask for a discount. Another benefit derived from accepting credit cards is eliminating the risk involved in accepting large checks from out-of-town customers. If they are solid citizens, they will defer to your desire to put their purchase on a credit card (and the bank guarantees the entire amount if you call in for verification). *You don't have to accept any form of credit.* My experience over the years has been that credit card purchases have actually account- ed for less than 10 percent of our gross sales. We keep our VISA sign on display as a tactful alternative to the revolving charge ac- counts with which many gift shops are saddled.

LAYAWAY FORM

I, _____ hereby agree to purchase
(please sign here)

the following merchandise: _____

_____

from _____ at the total price of

$ _____ Invoice No. _____

It is agreed that after the down payment, one-third of the balance remain- ing due shall be paid within 30 days from today, one-third within 60 days, and the final payment in full, within 90 days from date below. In the event of my failure to make payments as set out above, any previous payments shall be forfeited and said merchandise shall be returned to dealer's stock.

Invoice total $ _____ Name _____

less dwn. pym't. _____ Address _____

                                   _____
balance due
in 90 days _____   _____

Date _____ Telephone _____

A fundamental business practice many neophyte dealers inevitably learn the hard way is to obtain a signed receipt, or memo, for any item that leaves a shop without being paid for in full! This includes dealer-to-dealer trades, merchandise loans, and trial purchases. Place a stated dollar value on any item taken on approval—it may be lost or stolen while in the care of the borrower.

Chapter 28 SELLING AT AUCTION

A Quick Source of Ready Cash

The typical "Estate Auction" advertised in a local newspaper may actually be nothing more than half a dozen items left over from a legitimate estate. The bulk of the auction might consist of several hundred other consignments from local pickers and dealers who have found auction selling to be a profitable sideline. Many times the auctioneer himself is the major "consignor," in that he actually owns most of the inventory scheduled to go on the block. His sources may consist of regular container shipments from abroad or local purchases made through aggressive "Wanted" advertisements.

There are many different types of auction-house operations. Every auctioneer has different "standards" and modes of operation. Some own all of their inventory and accept few, if any, consignments, preferring not to be bothered by the complaints of disappointed consignors. Others handle estates only and will not accept any dealer consignments, preferring fresh merchandise or "untainted" goods. In the Midwest, there are many "free-lance" auctioneers (perhaps farmers by vocation), who will sell anything, anytime, anywhere—for a 6 to 15 percent commission. In the East, there are a few independent operators who hold only one or two important events a year, perhaps grossing $150,000 to $350,000 at each sale and netting up to 10 percent of the take after expenses.

An auction house conducting regular weekly events really has to hustle to come up with three hundred items every seven days. Such an operation might have two or three radio-equipped trucks on the road at one time—with a central dispatcher telling each driver where to make his next stop or what to pay for items he might not be familiar with. These driver/buyers may be either salaried or self-employed. A couple of thousand dollars is usually enough to "capitalize" each picker. This capital is returned to him each week following the auction. The house takes a fixed percentage of the gross or, in many cases, splits the profit down the middle.

A rule of thumb for buying used furniture, appliances, and antiques for the purpose of reselling through an auction is to pay no more than one-half of wholesale. (That's about 30 cents on the retail dollar.) To buy this "dearly" means passing up many nice pieces which are offered you at a figure just below retail, knowing that more desperate (or less aware) sellers will be found in the course of a normal week's buying. A dining table that might retail in a shop for $250 frequently sells at auction for $150. If you deduct the auctioneer's 20 percent commission, the driver or picker ends up with $120 for this $250 retailer— if he bought the table at one-half of its $150 wholesale value, he stands to make $45 on it before his hauling expenses.

Shop retail value	$250
Sold at auction for	$150
Less commission	− 30
Picker receives	$120
Picker bought at	− 75
Gross profit	$ 45
Less hauling	− 5
Picker's net profit	$ 40

As a professional auction picker gains experience from recording prices obtained by various auction houses, he can pay more for specific items. Figure it out. If you turn $1,000 weekly at just a 30 percent profit, you could be netting $300 per week before expenses. The name of the game is a quick turnover! You don't have time to restore or even refurbish your pickings, so you've got to pass up the broken stuff! If you are a specialist picker, who deals only in antiques, you won't usually be able to find enough good items to be a weekly consignor, but you can (from my own experience) hope to find about sixty potentially profitable objects a month. This changes the profit picture substantially from the potential of a picker who will accept anything from a refrigerator to a stereo set. Your frequency of finds will be a fraction of his, but you won't need a two-ton truck to transport them. Let's say that your $2,000 purchased 60 items with a retail shop value of $6,000, and that these 60 lots sold on a good night for $4,000 (averaging $66.67 each). After paying the 20 percent commission frequently charged for antiques, your check from the auction would be $3,200, leaving a gross profit of $1,200 on your thirty-day investment of $2,000. After deducting "Wanted" advertising costs, meals, lodging, maintenance, and gasoline, you would be lucky to net $800 per month. Obviously, the way to make more money as an antique consignor is to find more "sleepers" in the higher ticket brackets. (This would entail spending more on advertising and a much larger capitalization than $2,000.) Some professional auction consignors spend the major portion of a year accumulating enough underpriced, quality merchandise to conduct a well-blanced major auction sale of 300 to 600 items. Their working capital must include enough to live on during a year's "picking" plus adequate funds for purchasing.

Dealers who travel frequently are in a good position to supplement their regular incomes by consigning merchandise purchased in one region to an auction in a different market area. Generally speaking, an antique is valued higher near its point of manufactured origin than in other localities. Who would think of offering Shaker furniture for sale outside of the four- or five-state area where it is actively collected? How many California collectors would recognize, let alone appreciate, a good Pennsylvania Dutch Fractur, a set of slipware, or a piece of Zanesville glass?

A well-traveled dealer can also spot trends, or downright fads, before they really take off. Some collecting trends or craft fads take years to work their way across the United States. Indian jewelry was popular in California in the late 1960s and did not reach its zenith on the Eastern Seaboard until the middle 1970s. As of late, a few savvy auction consignors have discovered the abundance of both old and new Oriental artifacts available from California's antique shops or directly from West Coast wholesale giftware marts (at prices low enough to be profitably resold through midwestern and eastern auction houses). Likewise, some western auctioneers (and consignors) have been "salting" local sales with small bronzes of dubious age and attribution which are readily available from New York City's wholesale antique sources. You should visit New York's wholesale antiques area, just to stay abreast of the latest fine art reproductions being brought in from Europe.

On an international scale, the supply and demand phenomena can be worked to a sophisticated trader's advantage, buying antiques and art at auction in one country and selling through an auction house in another country—original works of art are duty-free.

An airline stewardess we met abroad has been doing well buying European oil paintings of a nautical motif at inland provincial auctions and reselling them through the better auction houses in seaport cities. French art dealers have recently been spotted in Rhode Island, buying all the European oil paintings they can lay their hands on. (It seems that American tourists in Paris have depleted the local supply.) Dutch, German, Japanese, and Middle Eastern dealers are also scouring the world in search of the ethnic art and antiques of their respective homelands. The war years saw the "liberation" of many works of art by enterprising officers of the allied forces; thus the United States remains a fertile source for many sophisticated European dealers. A rather vivid example of the wisdom in sending rare artifacts to salesrooms in their native lands was Christie's recent world-record price obtained for a single ceramic tile. This glazed stoneware square, which might have gone for less than $100 at a stateside auction, was sold in Christie's Amsterdam salesroom for $6,200!

The significance of the auction market for the average antique shop proprietor is that it represents a growing trend in local and international buying, away from traditional retail outlets. The days of opening a well-stocked antique shop and sitting back to garner the profits from walk-in traffic are all but over. Today's aggressive merchant of antiques has to seek out his customers at shows, via advertising in collector publications, and also by selling at auction.

Near the end of our first year in business as the owners of a small suburban antique shop, we had to admit that our opening inventory (of largely 1920s English furniture) was apparently not what the neighborhood clientele was after. We decided to take our chances on unloading all of our dead stock at auction for quick cash and a new start. Luckily, a good-sized crowd was on hand the evening of the event, and we managed to get our money back (as well as a small profit). From that time on we have been regular consignors of merchandise to local auction houses and, on occasion, to Sotheby Parke Bernet in Los Angeles or Butterfield & Butterfield in San Francisco. We know of one San Diego dealer who sends most of his locally purchased art glass all the way to Sloan's auction gallery in Washington, D.C., in hopes of making a consistent profit.

Making a consistent profit on merchandise sold through auction is an elusive goal indeed. For some, it comes as easily as a duck takes to water, while others never make a dime on anything they put on the auction block. What the latter fail to realize is that successful consignors don't leave much to lady luck. They size up a prospective auction thoroughly before they consider risking their hard-to-find merchandise. You don't consign an old car to a doll auction or a doll to a furniture specialist. Finding the right auction house is half of the game. Buying specifically for auction selling is the other half. Many items that sell well in shops do not do well at auction!

Flashy goods with a "story" seem to always bring a good price! There is a fellow in Beverly Hills who spends all his spare time attending the garage and estate sales of well-known movie stars. Wherever possible, he obtains some sort of written documentation to enhance his purchases of movieworld memorabilia. I doubt if this part-time picker has ever paid more than $25 for anything; but you should see the prices that midwestern auctiongoers are willing to pay for these "Hollywood" discards!

Some strong selling categories of auction goods on the West Coast are sterling silver items; figural ivory, porcelain, and bronze; cut crystal; Oriental antiques and rugs; Art Nouveau items; brass and copperware; unique lamps; vintage firearms; illustrated books; nude anything; and, of course, refinished golden oak. Late nineteenth- and early twentieth-century items are completely acceptable to most of the collecting community on the West Coast. (There is not an Early American auction house in California at the time of this writing.)

The Midwestern Auction Market Is Diversified. It would be impossible to begin to list the categories of collectibles that

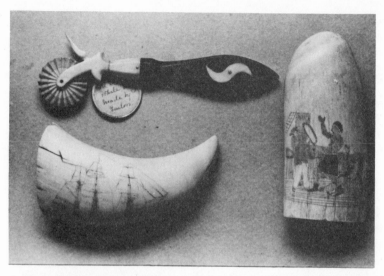

Scrimshaw pie crimper and whale's teeth went quickly at Julia's Auction in Maine. Courtesy *Maine Antique Digest*

bring premium prices when offered in this area of the country! Western and American Indian art is always in strong demand. Better quality nineteenth-century Victorian furniture and accessories are avidly sought after, and certain types of American pottery and glassware continue to command the highest prices at midwestern events.

The Eastern Market. The eastern auction scene is a different picture entirely. The purchasing power of museums, and second- or third-generation family money, is a potent force that almost guarantees newsmaking auction prices for important American art and antiques. Furniture buyers on the Eastern Seaboard prefer period pieces made before the 1850s, and preferably with the original old paint or finish intact and untouched. Nautical items, trade signs, folk art, and primitive paintings or textiles are also top performers at New England events. New York City alone accounts for at least $400 million in annual auction revenue. Sotheby Parke Bernet's Madison Avenue galleries accepted consignments from more than nine thousand individuals and institutions last year, and ten thousand eager buyers helped ring up sales exceeding $220 million!

If nothing else, you can use your auctioneer as a clearing-house for turning old stock into new. Nothing succeeds like "success," and regular customers will be amazed at how fast you seem to turn over your merchandise. Don't hesitate to send anything to auction that has been on the showroom floor for a year or more.

If you are consigning a particularly fine piece to an auctioneer, don't be afraid to place a minimum figure—slightly above wholesale—at which it can be sold. *Get this "reserve" agreement in writing* as part of the regular auction contract. Also include a limit on what you will pay for the photographic illustrations of your antiques which may appear in the auctioneer's catalog. A $40 photo fee amounts to an extra 10 percent commission if an item is sold for $400.

Many consignors insist that their better things be offered within the first two selling hours of an auction. The feeling is that many high-rolling "impulse buyers" may leave after the initial excitement of the event wears off. Don't be afraid to ask for a lower than normal commission percentage fee arrangement if your goods are the strongest or most numerous items in the auction. After all, you may be providing the "pulling power" for the auctioneer to unload many of his own purchases at a substantial profit! (All he can do is say no.) Commissions can run from 10 to 25 percent across the board.

Don't be timid about attending the auction preview early or helping "set up" the merchandise for presale viewing. You may save hundreds of dollars just by giving your own things preferential or thoughtful display. More than once I have rescued an important piece carelessly left in a box, or under a table, by an auction crew with too many things to set up.

Investigate your auctioneer's payment record. Ten days is plenty of time for him to balance his books and pay off all consignors. Some midwestern auction houses pay haulers off the night of the sale so that they don't have to lay over for another twenty-four hours. Customs vary from area to area, so it's best to get it all in writing.

Don't waste an auctioneer's time with items that may go for $20 or less. He can only sell 350 lots before the crowd is ready to go home and 350 times $20 (less 80 percent) isn't enough to justify his efforts. Try to consign at least $500 worth at a time (to get started). Then aim for, say, fifty lots—with a potential gross of $100 each. This is the only way that you can have any influence on the quality of the auction or become a regular "preferred" consignor.

If you, as a consignor, make a net profit of 20 percent on a $2,500 gross, you can be picking up an extra $500 a month profit outside of your regular retail antique shop operation. Add to this the "sleepers" you may acquire as a result of regular auction attendance and you'll wonder why you waited so long to try your luck!

Chapter 29
APPRAISING, OR COUNT THE WAYS

There Are No Licensed Antique Appraisers

At this writing there is no such thing as a "licensed" antique appraiser. Nowhere in the United States have I found a city or township that requires anything other than a regular business license for those who appraise personal property, fine art, and residential contents for private individuals. Even in the jewelry trade, where great sums are at stake, the price of a retail business license will grant you the power to make appraisals—whether you are qualified or not!

Appraisal Associations. The American Society of Appraisers, a six-thousand-member organization of appraisal practitioners (International Headquarters at Dulles International Airport, P. O. Box 17265, Washington, DC 20041), sponsors a degree program in general valuation sciences, which is currently being offered at several colleges and universities around the country. The society's goal is to end unfair and biased appraisal practices, and establish a formal, fully accredited academic degree in the discipline of valuation science. The ASA offers its membership a full range of services, which include bulletins, monographs, a trade journal, reference volumes, a tape cassette series on appraisal practices, and a continuing series of educational programs. The society's associate membership fee is approximately $70. Full membership requires two years' full-time appraisal experience, the passing of a written examination, a thorough background check, and an interview with the Board of Examiners.

The second-largest professional antique appraiser's association is a New York-based organization of about nine hundred members called the Appraisers Association of America. The AAA's membership requirements are: a minimum of five years' appraisal experience, completion of an application, submittal of several completed appraisals, and a fee of $150 to 541 Lexington Avenue, New York, NY 10022. In the mail we received an application form from the Mid-Am Antique Appraisers Association, Springfield, MI 65803. Among conditions stated for joining this group were: the payment of $70 and affiliation with the "Arts" for at least three years. Reading further, we find that "Membership is open to all qualified individuals in the Antique, Art, and Collectible field, on approval of the board of directors. Members agree to maintain a high standard of ethics, by appraising merchandise at the current fair market value, to the best of one's ability."

If you live on the West Coast and are looking for some "credentials," you might write to the Antique Appraisal Association of America, Inc., at 11361 Garden Grove Boulevard, Garden Grove, CA 92640. Its code of ethics includes "Honesty, integrity, and professional conduct." It provides all members with a list of "specialists" in the varied fields of antique appraising and a plastic-encased card, complete with passport photo and membership identification. This group's rules of conduct include a statement that the appraiser does *not* appraise for the purpose of future buying from a client and that members agree to keep a copy of all written appraisals for three years. You are required to fill out a simple application, enclose a photo along with a business card, copies of two recent appraisals, and $135 to be eligible for membership.

If you live in a remote area, you might eventually want to start your own appraisal association. You will be providing a service for your area, and the association itself might well make money for you. Why join any appraisal association? Because the uninformed public considers the appraisal business a profession and, as a professional person, you are expected to have some sort of diploma or credentials. The courts consider appraising a trade, an art—not a science. We would be inclined to agree. It is our own feeling that an active, well-read, long-established dealer, with an open shop and numerous trade connections, is an individual's best bet for a realistic appraisal.

It's Not a Science. Some of the finest talent in the country goes into making the presale estimates which appear in the catalogs of long-established auction houses, such as Christie's or Sotheby's, and yet wide discrepancies frequently appear between the presale estimates and the prices actually realized at auction ($600 items have gone for $6,000, and vice versa). Antique valuation can never be a science. At best, it is an educated guess based on the prices recorded from previous sales of similar goods. The variables are considerable. International monetary fluctuations, fads, publicity, supply, demand, intrinsic value, and so forth all play a part in the price that an antique might bring at any given time or place. A couple of prominent museums or collectors can run up the price of an item to an astronomically high figure. Record prices often flush identical items out of private collections, and the old highs are never achieved again.

We frankly inform our clients that it is not likely that any two appraisers would ever come up with the same individual valuations on a list of a dozen items—however, they should be within 25 percent of one another if they are both familiar with the current replacement cost of similar merchandise. We also explain that there are different types of appraisals—retail value to establish insurance coverage for replacement costs, estimated estate valuation for inheritance tax purposes, estimated valuation for immediate liquidation at auction, property settlement cases, and damage estimates.

We take the position of a consultant, not an absolute authority. The client has a preconceived notion of what each item is worth. The appraiser's job is to arrive at an estimate of fair market value (without alienating the client to the point of not getting paid). We ask a lot of questions during the examination of each significant piece: "How long has this been in your family? Where was this purchased? How much, may I ask, did you give for this hand-carved monkey? What sentimental value do you place on this portable potty?" Don't quote any figures until you have completed your off-the-premises research. Advise the client that not all your valuations are inflexible—that you are willing to discuss the matter if you are too far apart for comfort on a specific item. You can cover yourself in appraisal situations where you and the client don't agree by using the client's price but inserting a footnote after the inflated figure. The disclaimer might read something like this:

> Client values handcarved crucifix at $500 because of its great sentimental importance (having survived four wars and eight marriages; it belonged to a great-grandfather's mistress at the time of her beheading).

Some Helpful Tips. How does one get started in the great guessing game (after several years of dealing, studying, and auction going)? A Yellow Pages advertisement under the Appraiser heading will begin the telephone ringing right away. People shop for appraisers the same way they shop for antiques. A $25-an-hour quote should generate plenty of business because professionals frequently charge from two to four times this amount. Direct-mail announcements sent to all of your regular customers as well as local lawyers and insurance agents will start the ball rolling. A dealer friend of ours launched himself in the appraisal business by running a classified newspaper advertisement. In it he announced a weekend Appraisal Clinic at which he would verbally appraise any item for $2. The response was enough to fill up his appointment book for several months!

One of the first things a caller might ask is, "How much do you charge?" Put yourself in the customer's position and try to anticipate any other questions or doubts he might have. Explain at the onset that you don't mix buying with appraising but that you would be glad to make an offer if selling is his primary interest. Then go on to explain how a written appraisal will run so many dollars per hour, or item (avoid percentage fee schedules based on the value of the goods; they are simply not ethical). Note whether or not your fee includes travel time and research as well as typing and multiple copies for the client. Try to schedule your appointments in the daytime. It is twice as much work to examine antiques at night, especially in rooms where there are few, if any, electrical outlets. Find out the nature of the items to be appraised in advance of your trip. You may feel the need to take along a specialist or an advanced collector. Be enthusiastic. It's an ego trip for most people to have their collections examined by an "expert" like yourself.

What value would you place on this Queen Anne Spanish foot chair and bird cage tilt-top table? See footnote on page 183 for the correct answer. Courtesy **Maine Antique Digest**

Back at the office—you don't have to type up long, drawn-out descriptions, but it is important to describe the item by name, size, color, and period (also note any defects or repairs). Two or three typewritten lines will usually suffice for all but the most valuable antiques. If you are appraising for a client who plans to donate a very expensive item to an institution for the express purpose of a tax writeoff, it would be wise to also include the date of acquisition, where purchased, history, and perhaps some clues or proof of authenticity. Ask a fellow dealer or an appraiser in another area for a look at some typical appraisal sheets if you are not sure of how to proceed. We head the top of each appraisal with a preliminary statement, which reads something like this:

> Appraisal of art, antiques, and collectibles for Mr. and Mrs. Otto Dunwell, 1666 Prosperity Lane, Someplace, California. Valuations are at today's fair market value and reflect the approximate replacement cost of each item.

At the end of the last sheet, we type in our firm's name and affix the date and our signatures (and a notation of the total number of pages included in the appraisal).

Ironically, a dealer can learn more by appraising than from many other experiences. Where else can you closely examine an antique while discussing its merits with the owner? Who else will pay you $25 an hour to do your own homework? At our first appraisal were half a dozen hunting case pocket watches. I was so "green" that I didn't even know how to open the back of a case to read the maker's name, number of positions, number of jewels, karats of gold, or to copy down the model and serial number (all these elements are necessary to appraise a watch). I was able, however, to accurately assess my client's old book collection, and that display of knowledge somehow got me through the whole ordeal unscathed, with credentials apparently intact! (We took the watches to an antique clock repairman for evaluation and an hour-long lesson on timepiece pricing.)

After your first few appraisals, subsequent valuations will take less of your time. Many common items will be almost identical to previously researched antiques, and the description and current price will take less than a minute to type.

Never price an unfamiliar item on the basis of one or two brief entries found in a popular "price guide." Call up specialist dealers or experienced collectors in your area and inquire if they have a similar item in stock. Consult recent back issues of a number of trade tabloids for related wares. Look up prices realized at auction in individual catalogs or annual indexes. Trade favors or share fees with another appraiser in your association.

---

*The value of the Queen Anne Spanish foot chair and table is $1,200.

Last but not least, look it up in at least half a dozen price guides and average out the results.

Remember it's just a guessing game. Do your best to establish the immediate market value and don't take yourself or anyone else too seriously. The practical study of art and antiques encompasses just about everything produced on this planet over the past five hundred years. Nobody has all the answers!

Chapter 30
THE CARE AND FEEDING OF BOOKWORMS

How to Buy and Sell Old Books for Profit

Many seemingly sophisticated antique dealers are admittedly ignorant when it comes to buying, selling, or appraising old books. Most novice bookmen tend to overprice their wares, often using price guides that reflect only "fine condition" as a criterion for pricing foxed (yellowed), faded, stained, shaken, and otherwise less-than-desirable copies that book collectors would not want to own at any price. Age and original quantity produced are two factors that determine the value of many collectibles, including coins and stamps, but have little if any bearing on the price of antiquarian books. There are literally thousands of very rare books of which less than a dozen copies have survived that have no real market value. On the other hand, many modern editions, of several thousand copies each, are skyrocketing in value. Collector demand, more than any other factor, determines a book's true value. Only a very small percentage of the books you may encounter as an antique dealer are worth buying for resale. This small percentage could, however, amount to a hundred volumes a year and, if properly marketed, pay a substantial portion of your operating expenses.

As we mentioned earlier, subscribing to trade publications and dealer catalogs is the quickest way to learn the ins and outs of any specialist retail business. For starters, send a large, stamped, self-addressed envelope to the Antiquarian Booksellers' Association of America at 50 Rockefeller Plaza, New York, NY 10020, for a free copy of *Books and Values,* which is a large printed list of member dealers and their specialties. From this list you will find out, for instance, that Goodspeed's Book Shop is interested in buying genealogies and family histories, or that the Holmes Book Company is interested in California and Western Americana.

Most book scouts, booksellers, librarians, and serious collectors subscribe to the weekly trade journal of the hobby: *AB Bookman's Weekly* (the *Antiquarian Bookman*), at about $35 per year, from P. O. Box AB, Clifton, NJ 07015 (a sample copy is $3). This periodical features the active buy-and-sell lists of hundreds of book dealers, as well as trade advertising from publishers and news of interest to bookmen.

Almost every bookseller is an active wholesale buyer of those books, prints, autographs, catalogs, and manuscripts for which he feels a viable market exists. Some individuals spend almost all of their waking hours seeking out books to resell to antiquarian booksellers. These "pickers" are properly called *book scouts.* They frequent auctions, house sales, thrift shops, and secondhand book stores looking for single volumes or entire private libraries.

Offering one's wares "wholesale" to a dealer in out-of-print books is more or less a cut-and-dried proposition called "quoting." To quote best, you should put all the pertinent information on three-by-five cards which may be filed by the dealer for future reference (if he accepts someone else's quote before receiving yours). The standard or most widely used *quote card* format is author's name first, then title, size in inches, number of pages and illustrations, place, year, edition, publisher, condition, and your asking price (don't forget to include your name and address). If the bookseller feels that he can profitably sell your volume, he will either send you a check or will ask to see the book to examine it before purchasing. Books can be sent insured at a special parcel post book rate and will be returned prepaid by the same method if not purchased by the dealer. Write, in bold letters, across the front of all book mailings: **BOOKS, SPECIAL 4TH CLASS RATE, return postage guaranteed.**

Naturally, professional book buyers are very selective. If a book dealer has run an expensive "Wanted" ad, he is not going to accept any offering that does not measure up to the quality and price of other "quotes" submitted to him. Wise bookmen will wait at least two or three weeks to make a final comparison on the price and condition of all books quoted in response to an ad. You won't hear from the dealer unless your quote was among the best. (If your asking price was too far out of line, he might not even open any future letters from you.) If your quote was in the ball park, it might make it into his inventory file, where it will sit until another dealer, retail customer, or librarian requests the same title. In order to make a living, professional book scouts must quote as many as a hundred titles per week. Some of these scouts achieve a success ratio of one book sold out of three offered. If professional pickers average only one out of three, you must underquote their prices to win even token consideration! After all, you are an unknown quantity—a supplier who might not grade his finds accurately or ship them padded well enough to arrive with unbent corners and creaseless dust jackets.

The Secret of Pricing Anything Correctly at a Wholesale Level. Keep your hand on the very pulse of the market. After you have subscribed to *AB Weekly,* you should start ordering the retail sales catalogs of dealers who advertise therein. The next step in becoming "price-wise" is to subscribe to the mail-order auction catalogs of a few of the nation's more active book-auction firms. Auction "prices realized" are closer to wholesale than the dealer catalogs, which will be mostly retail offerings. To be successful on a regular basis, you should quote 10 or 20 percent *below* one-half of the going retail price. Dealers buying for shelf stock don't like to pay more than 25 cents on the retail dollar because most of their used-book inventory is carried over year after year. However, a dealer with a firm buyer's order in hand should be willing to pay from 40 to 60 percent of the going retail price.

You can order book auction catalogs from these firms:

Americana Mail Auction
4015 Kilmer Avenue
Allentown, PA 18104

Samuel T. Freeman & Co.
1808-10 Chestnut Street
Philadelphia, PA 19103

California Book Auction Galleries
358 Golden Gate Avenue
San Francisco, CA 94102

Charles Hamilton
25 East 77th Street
New York, NY 10021
(autographs, letters, documents)

Economy Books
1125 King Street
Alexandria, VA 22314

Harris Auction Galleries
873 North Howard Street
Baltimore, MD 21201

George H. LaBarre Galleries
111 Ferry Street
Hudson, NH 03051
(paper Americana and collectibles)

Swann Galleries, Inc.
104 East 25th Street
New York, NY 10010

Montreal Book Auctions Ltd.
1529 Sherbrooke Street W.
Montreal, H3G 1L7, P.Q. Canada

Always pay whatever token extra amount is specified for an end-of-sale list of *prices realized.* It is this list of the actual auction results that makes any catalog a working tool.

So far, we have discussed only the "wholesale" opportunities for part-time dealers and book scouts. If you have an established antique shop, you may have on hand at least a couple of hundred colorful old volumes on various subjects in addition to popular poets and the classics. At the general retail level, second and third editions sell well because they are in the $2 to $5 price range for spontaneous impulse purchasing. In addition to the volumes that you may be using to weight down china cabinets or fill up bookshelves, you should sprinkle a few dozen titles around your shop on tables and chairs where colorful old covers may be seen in their entirety. Most of your impulse sales will be made from these displays. Only confirmed bookworms will paw through row after row of volumes identified solely by faded spines.

The relatively few "price guides" published for the rare and out-of-print book trade are very sophisticated and expensive, especially when compared to the $8.95 annuals that cover the field of antique collecting. If you are going to appraise many books or purchase anything out of the ordinary, it will pay you to invest in at least one of these used-book price guides. Beware of any book guide that lists less than 25,000 titles! They are not large enough to be useful in pricing and identifying more than one out of ten volumes you may encounter. The following guides are among the most popular used in the trade today:

- *American Book Prices Current,* a five-year market index, records 150,000 auction prices. Recent volume priced at $76.50. Bancroft Parkman. 121 East 78th Street, New York, NY 10021

- *The Book Collector's Handbook of Values,* by Van Allen Bradley ($25.00). G. P. Putnam's Sons. 200 Madison Avenue, New York, NY 10016
- *Bookman's Price Index,* the most comprehensive price guide of its kind. Each volume prices over 40,000 books. Fifteen volumes available at $64 each from Gale Research Company. Book Tower, Detroit, MI 48226
- *The Used Book Price Guide,* by Mandeville (about $84 per set). Three volumes, 114,000 price entries. Price Guide Publishers. 525 Kenmore Street, Kenmore, WA 98028

Not all of your wholesale quotes need be made by mail. If you live in or near a good-sized city, chances are that there are half a dozen local dealers who might be interested in a nicely chosen wholesale selection of old books, prints, photos, or other paper Americana, including catalogs, magazines, comic books, sheet music, and scrapbooks. Don't waste any dealer's time looking for offers or free appraisals. Be prepared with a list of your books and the asking prices, or a wholesale quote on the entire lot. Do not include any stained, dirty, torn, shaken, or damaged copies, and do not offer any ex-library editions or common fare such as old newspapers, schoolbooks, bibles, encyclopedias, or obscure novels of the turn of the century. A quick look at the Wanted ads in the *Antiquarian Bookman* will tell you what is currently in demand.

A few categories of popular subject matter:

Advertising (cards and catalogs)
Aeronautics (of World War I and World War II)
Africa
American Indians
Americana (from any state or county)
Architecture
Fine Art
Autographs
Books about Books
Botany
Boy Scouts
Children's Books
Cookbooks

Popular Fiction
Genealogies
Illustrated Books of Merit
Japanese Titles
Older Magazines
Early Maps and Atlases
Medicine (pre-1900)
Military Books and Prints
Natural History
Occult
Opera
Oriental Subjects
Vintage Photography Books and Journals
Poetry
Postcards (pre-1920)
Posters (pre-World War II)
Science Fiction
Sea and Ships
Sheet Music
Sporting Subjects
Victoriana
Western History
Winemaking
Zoology

Contrary to popular opinion, specialized titles such as *Golfing in Guatemala* or *Sailing up the Suwannee River,* and regional works, such as county or town histories, are more valuable than most first-edition novels!

Generally speaking, first editions are more valuable than re-prints, and the first published work of an author is usually the most valuable. Novices are quick to claim that they have the first edition if the date on the title page and the copyright date seem in agreement. Actually, first editions are very difficult to identify without the help of outside information unless the words "First Printing," or their equivalent, appear somewhere on the title page. You can look for all sorts of clues to eliminate a book's chance at first-edition status. Somewhere on the title page, or in the introduction, may appear the words new, amended, correct-ed, or enlarged edition. Authors who refer to the fact that they "enjoyed preparing this revised edition," or were "called upon to update my earlier work," may also provide the telltale clues of a later edition. If you feel you have a very valuable first edition, it will pay you to go to a library and consult author bibliographies and other books about books, such as H. Boutell's *First Editions of Today and How to Tell Them,* or *U.S. Ianna* by R. R. Bowker.

Some price guides and catalogs will indicate "points" (technical clues regarding printing errors, copy changes, cover material, size and illustrations, and so forth) in their descriptions. You must qualify your books on the basis of these small "points," which can spell the difference between first, second, and third state printings—often all produced within the first few months of a popular publication's birth.

There are more than two thousand antique and collector titles currently in print, with new ones coming off the presses daily. Mail-order book dealers, specializing in this area, have little competition from regular bookstores because of the limited number of titles retailers have room to stock. Many antique shop owners have discovered the resale potential of new books on antiques and collectibles; but a large percentage of these dealers don't buy directly from the publishers, and sacrifice 10 to 20 percent of their profits by not doing so. We're not saying that wholesale book distributors don't have a place in the economic chain, but any time you order five assorted titles or more you should receive a full 40 percent discount from retail. Two leading distributors of antique and collectible titles are Green Gate Books, P. O. Box 934, Lima, OH 45802, and Collector Books, P. O. Box 3009, Paducah, KY 42001.

The best books to begin carrying are the popular price guides selling from $8.95 to $10.95 each. (Every time a customer asks for a free appraisal, you can sell a price guide.) Sometimes publishers do not include their mailing addresses inside the book. This is done to protect retail bookstores, and also to avoid processing single copy orders, which are not always profitable. Your librarian can give you the mailing address of any publisher in the world in about two minutes.

Book publishers are easy to deal with on a wholesale level. Just write to them on your letterhead, or a purchase order form, and ask for a copy of their latest *trade catalog and dealer discount schedule.* Indicate that you are willing to pay in advance for any books ordered, but you are enclosing bank and credit references in case they would rather bill you. (Normal terms are thirty to sixty days from date of invoice.) A good list of firms to start with would be the publishing houses listed in the chapter "Selected Reading Material." You will find lots more when you start subscribing to the antique trade tabloids (also listed herein). P.S.: Running a paperback bookstore is a tough, thankless task at best. Don't jump in without knowing what you're biting off. It's a paperwork mill and a human relations clinic, all rolled into one—talk to a bookstore owner.

In closing this chapter, we dare to commit a sacrilege and mention the enormous profit margin possible in "butchering" books! Many old illustrated volumes can be sold for several times their "unbroken" retail value, by framing the best prints and discarding the remainder of the pictures and text. We have gotten up to $15 per plate for 1930s Shirley Temple books and from $50 to $100 for better quality antique lithographs, sporting prints, firefighting scenes, children with toys, birds, butterflies, military battles, animals, and advertising pictures. The obvious markets for tastefully framed prints are interior decorators, gift boutiques, furniture stores, consignment shops, flea markets, and local auction houses. Who knows? You might end up in the picture-framing business. (See the trade journal *Decor*, the magazine of pictures, prints, and frames, 408 Olive Street, St. Louis, MO 63102.)

Weights of Round, Brilliant-Cut Diamonds

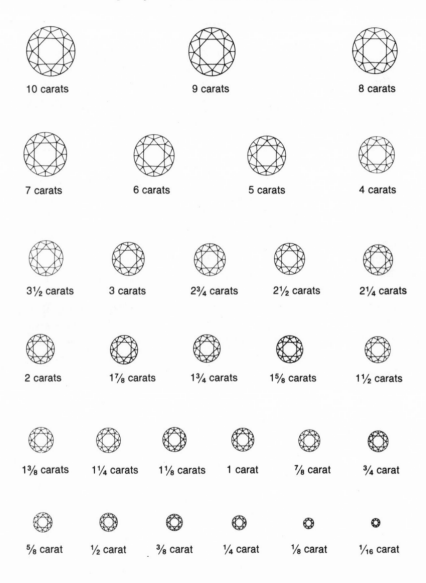

10 carats   9 carats   8 carats

7 carats   6 carats   5 carats   4 carats

3½ carats   3 carats   2¾ carats   2½ carats   2¼ carats

2 carats   1⅞ carats   1¾ carats   1⅝ carats   1½ carats

1⅜ carats   1¼ carats   1⅛ carats   1 carat   ⅞ carat   ¾ carat

⅝ carat   ½ carat   ⅜ carat   ¼ carat   ⅛ carat   1/16 carat

Courtesy Gemological Institute of America

Chapter 31
ALL THAT GLITTERS IS NOT GOLD

An Introduction to the Jewelry Business

On the surface, every deal in the gem game appears to be a cool, calculated transaction based on the grade, weight, workmanship, and comparative rarity of the goods. DeBeers Mining Company has a virtual monopoly in the diamond market (they regulate the supply and quality that reaches wholesalers). Likewise, small groups of London brokers gather round tables to determine the world price of gold every weekday afternoon. Maybe it's this seemingly unromantic "science" of dealing in gemstones and precious metals that turns most of us antique dealers off before we ever get started.

Our eyes were opened when a couple of local dealers who specialize in antique jewelry bought 75 percent of the stuff that we had in our showcase, paid our retail price, and left the shop with smug smiles on their faces. Would we have continued to wear blinders if a fellow antique dealer had come in and bought most of our furniture, for resale, at the asking price? No sir! We would have tailed him across the state line, if necessary, to find out where he was unloading our merchandise at a double markup!

"Show" dealers discovered a long time ago that vintage jewelry, sterling silver items, and pocket watches were the most consistently profitable items that they could stock on the road. One weekend a couple of dealer friends of ours grossed $4,500 from a tabletop display of such merchandise at a shopping mall show. Nothing exotic was sold, just a lot of $50 to $100 pieces of collectible old jewelry picked up from garage sales and nonspecialist dealers.

When measured against the odds of turning up a spectacularly undervalued find in the antique, philatelic, or numismatic fields, gemology offers a much greater chance of frequent discovery. Just about anyone with a little training, a jeweler's loupe, a bottle of acid, and spare time to hound flea markets and garage sales can score with amazing frequency.

The average general-line antique dealer passes up a potential gold mine when he or she refers walk-in offerings of old gold, silver, and gemstones to the jewelry store or pawnbroker up the street. Ignorance is, as always, no excuse. Did you know that you can learn to identify and appraise jewelry and gemstones through a mail-order correspondence course offered by the *Gemological Institute of America*? This nonprofit institution, with headquarters located at 1660 Stewart Street, Santa Monica, CA 90404, graduates hundreds of students annually with G.I.A. certificates in gemstone identification and appraisal. The G.I.A. also has classrooms in Chicago and New York City, and offers lab services, gem-testing instruments, and several publications for sale in addition to its mail-order courses. The three most popular (and accredited) classes offered by mail are "Diamonds," "Colored Stones," and "Gem Identification." "Diamonds" is a separate course because diamonds differ widely from other gemstones in value, hardness, and clarity. (I understand that there are from sixty to one hundred distinct grades of diamonds.) Either course takes about twenty-four months to complete on a part-time basis if a certificate is desired. Incidentally, G.I.A. certificates have been granted to men and women who have not even graduated from high school. If a part-time course of study does not seem practical, you might avail yourself of some of the excellent books marketed by the G.I.A., all written by "insiders" in the jewelry trade. One in particular is *The Jeweler's Manual* by Liddicoat and Copeland. It covers, in 360 pages, gem testing, diamond grading, precious metals, silverware, watches, clocks, jewelry mountings, settings, and marketing—almost everything a jeweler should know, in one $12 volume.

While we are pushing books, we might mention a good identification and price guide for determining the value of most Victorian, Art Deco, and Art Nouveau pieces. It is *100 Years of Collectible Jewelry* by Lillian Baker (Collector Books, Paducah, KY 42001). A complete list of additional jewelry titles appears in Selected Reading Material.

Oddly enough, only a few of the antiquarian jewelry dealers whom we interviewed had received any specialized training. Not many owned any lab equipment other than a ten-power magnifying glass and perhaps a bottle of acid for gold and silver testing. In answer to my oft-asked question, "How do you identify the gemstone you are looking at?" they quickly reply, "I just know by looking"! This casual appraisal method had always puzzled me; what were they looking for through that tiny loupe held so very closely to the object in question? Bubbles, carbon inclusions, chips, scratches, telltale mold marks, color, clarity, quality of mounting, hallmarks, carat stamps, and a host of other visual clues which a ten-power magnifying glass and a strong light source can provide. After reading *The Jeweler's Manual*, I found that positive identification of gemstones and pearls requires further testing by several methods, including hardness, heat reaction, specific gravity, X ray, acid reaction, light refraction, and other instrumental readings. The only reason we mention all of these tests is to emphasize how no one can really make a positive stone identification without a well-equipped laboratory. A lot of so-called experts can't tell the difference between a diamond and a dozen other bright colorless stones! Among current diamond substitutes are glass, beryl, corundum, quartz, spinel, topaz, zircon, and a host of synthetics, with new and better ones hitting the market monthly. As we mentioned earlier, the G.I.A. is also a manufacturer and distributor of gemological lab equipment. It currently markets a small box that, when properly used, can help to identify most natural gemstones. It is called a "port-a-lab," sells for $650, and consists of a refractometer, polariscope, and a leveridge gage along with other tools of the trade. Don't rush out and buy one—proper use of this kit requires extensive gemological training.

In the beginning, you should never pay much more than the value of the gold or silver mounting for an uncertified stone (unless you like to gamble). Of course, you don't tell the vendor of auntie's costume jewelry this bit of information! You simply eyeball the best pieces, look for good quality open-backed mountings, signs of wear through plating to base metals, sniff or taste for the smell of copper or brass, and perhaps rub any pearls against your teeth for the telltale sandpaper feeling of the real thing. On a cursory examination, your offering price should not exceed one-third of what you feel you can get for the most important items alone. Even at a 30-cent-on-the-dollar buying price, you are not ripping off the vendor. Diamond brokers in

Los Angeles today rarely pay more than one-third of low retail for fine-quality certified gems, ready to resell. Who says diamonds are a "good investment"?

Once you have gotten your feet wet by buying a few pieces over the counter (and later paying a gemologist for an accurate appraisal), you will wonder how many thousands of dollars you have lost by ignoring this "extra" opportunity for those who deal in antiques. At a local estate sale, my wife asked if any costume jewelry was available for purchase. The young bachelor who was conducting this garage sale disbursement (of a deceased aunt's household) went inside and returned with a small box of vintage costume jewelry, which he offered to my wife for $75. After digging through its contents for a minute or two, she spotted a small fourteen-karat gold diamond wedding ring that would hopefully justify the price he was asking, and hurried home with her "box lot" purchase to have a closer look. The retail value of this windfall worked out to exactly $1,200! It contained several sleepers; among them was an English signet seal in sapphire and gold and two signed silver pieces, black with tarnish from half a century of neglect. The lesson is that no matter what you see at a garage or house sale, always ask about the unseen!

No one can keep up with the current value of every antique and collectible! Even dealers who specialize in conducting estate sales have gaps in their knowledge of antiques. We have purchased valuable Oriental items (for a pittance) from specialists in American furniture, and we have also hauled away a vanload of pre-1850 Pennsylvania furniture from an "Oriental" estate in Southern California. (Who knows what "finds" other dealers have made from our own stock?) Trade publications that may improve your chances of striking it rich are: *Lapidary Journal*, Box 80937, San Diego, CA 92138, and *Jeweler's Circular Keystone*, Chilton Company, Radnor, PA 19089.

Antique jewelry sells itself. Once you have plainly priced an item, determined its gold or silver content, and identified the stone, nothing more needs to be done other than a quick dip in detergent and a little buffing with a jeweler's cloth. *Ninety-five percent of all heirloom jewelry sales are spontaneous purchases.* People don't drive for miles looking for a particular piece of adornment as they might when shopping for a kitchen table and chairs. Inflation breeds spending just as deflation encourages thrift. If a browsing shopper tries on a becoming gold ring and it fits, chances are fifty-fifty that she will buy it. After all, it's a better investment than the stock market and will probably appreciate more than a 6 percent savings account. Europeans have stashed their savings in jewels for years, and Americans are just now waking up to the fact that handcrafted antique jewelry is priced far below the modern mass-produced product.

Many general-line antique shop owners also have a blind spot in regard to the true value of their old gold and silver scrap. Most antique dealers toss this scrap into a shoe box under the counter and wait for an itinerant precious-metal buyer to come along and pay them the "melt-down" price. Let us say right here that one man's "melt down" is not necessarily another man's "melt down." The key to what you should expect to receive for scrap silver and gold is the daily spot metals quote that appears on the stock market page of the newspaper (don't confuse this with the "futures" market).

Many free-lance metal buyers and about twenty nationwide converting firms make a substantial profit buying scrap silver and gold at several dollars below this daily "spot" quote and re-selling the metal to large industrial users and fabricators that actually make the market. Handy and Harman, in New York City and El Monte, California, is probably the best known refiner; other smaller firms base their retail asking and wholesale offering prices on those of Handy and Harman. You may have a local market for accumulated scrap sterling or gold. Check with the art departments of local college and adult schools. Jewelry-making students are happy to pay $1 per troy ounce under the daily spot silver price.

At the time of this writing, Handy and Harman was paying 98 percent of the New York spot silver price for *the refined metal* and 99.6 percent of the London P.M. quote for *fine gold.* A flat fee is charged for smelting out impurities. Smaller refineries pay 5 or 10 percent less, but will process smaller quantities.

If you have a very accurate postal scale, you can use it to buy metal by converting each avoirdupois ounce to 18 pennyweight. A method used by coin dealers who have a gram scale is to multiply the gram weight by .67 to find the approximate dwt (pennyweight).

Example: 3 grams × .67 = 2.01, or approximately 2 dwt. Better yet, buy a good pennyweight scale and forget the math!

TABLE OF WEIGHTS

ABBREV.	NAME	U.S.A.	METRIC
cg	Centigram	0.154 grains	0.01 grams
dkg	Decagram	0.352 ounces	10.00 grams
dg	Decigram	1.543 grains	0.10 grams
gr	Grain	1/7000th pound	0.06 grams
g or gm	Gram	15.432 grains	1.00 grams
hg	Hectogram	3.527 ounces	100.00 grams
kg	Kilogram	2.204 pounds	1000.00 grams
mg	Milligram	0.015 grains	0.001 grams
oz	Ounce, avoirdupois	1/16 avpd. pound	28.35 grams
lb	Pound, avoirdupois	16 avpd. ounces	453.59 grams
dwt	Pennyweight	1/20 Troy ounce	1.555 grams
oz	Ounce, Troy	1/12 Troy pound	31.103 grams
lb	Pound, Troy	12 Troy ounces	373.25 grams

NOTE: There are a little more than 14 Troy ounces in an avoirdupois pound (a Troy ounce weighs 3 grams more than an avoirdupois ounce).

Gold has a hardness factor of about two and is the most malleable of all metals. The hardness factor is based on a scale of one to ten; a diamond has a hardness factor of ten, for instance, while soapstone has a factor of one. One grain of pure gold can be drawn into a weblike wire over a mile long or pounded into an ultra-thin leaf measuring two by three feet. Since gold, in its pure state, is too soft to be practical for jewelry, it must be alloyed with a harder metal, such as copper or silver. One karat is $\frac{1}{24}$ pure gold and $\frac{23}{24}$ alloy content. Twenty-four karat is 100 percent fine gold, while twelve karat is 50 percent, or one-half pure gold and one-half alloy. Therefore, when you are selling twelve-karat gold to a refiner, you will receive only half as much as you would for twenty-four-karat scrap.

The same principle applies to silver. Sterling silver is not less than 925 parts per one thousand, pure fine silver. "Coin silver" is a little more alloyed, or less pure, and contains at least 900 parts fine silver per one thousand (the alloy is copper). Many European, South American, and Oriental silver pieces are even less pure, and are usually marked with the number of parts silver per thousand (.800 silver is 800 parts silver and 200 parts copper). Many of the watch cases, flatware, hollowware, and jewelry items that you encounter will not be of high gold or silver content. During my youth I was employed as a metal electroplater and, as best as I can remember, we never left anything in the gold tank for more than thirty seconds.

Karat markings can be deceiving; for example, "$\frac{1}{10}$ 14k gold filled" means that the gold content of the very thin surface alloy alone is less than 10 percent—while the heavy base metal to which it is adhered has no intrinsic value at all. My wife's method for making a preliminary check for plated or filled items is to clean them first with a strong liquid detergent, using an old toothbrush, and then examine the items with a ten-power magnifying glass and a powerful light. She looks for the telltale dark spots in areas that are subject to normal wear. These indicate a base metal—not gold! "Duragold," "Mirigold," "Monarch 14K," "Nickel silver," "Silveroid," "Brazilian silver," "Alpacca," and "German silver" are a few of the misleading markings found on lightly filled, plated, or alloyed base metals of nickel, copper, and zinc. EPNS, EPBM, EPWM, and EPC are markings that signify electroplated items.

The two ultimate determining factors in what scrap silver or gold are worth are their *weight* and *purity.* You should invest $20 in a pennyweight scale and another couple of bucks for an ounce of pure nitric acid. You might also have a local pharmacy or chemical supply house mix you up a small bottle of "aqua regia" for high-karat gold testing. It is composed of three parts nitric and one part hydrochloric acids.

Once you have determined that an article is worth testing for its gold content, you must scratch through any gold-filled surface to make an accurate assay. On a watch, the area inside the back cover near the hinge is an unobtrusive spot to file for testing. A single link, or the underside of a catch, should be filed on chains and bracelets.

GOLD TESTING

STEP 1—Using a glass rod as a dropper, drip some pure nitric acid on the scratch. If you get green bubbles, you have plated gold on brass, or a base metal between layers of filled gold.

STEP 2—If there is a slower reaction, observe the color change—little or no action means better than ten-karat gold;

eighteen karat will actually repel the solution; fourteen karat will turn the drop brown in a minute or so; and nine karat will turn brown at once. A creamy pink may indicate gold plate on silver. Again, *green indicates the presence of a lot of brass or copper, not gold!*

Gold of over ten karat is soluble in a solution of aqua regia. To determine the exact karat content, rub a touchstone with an exposed portion of the test item. Beside this mark on the stone, make other marks with karat-testing needles or objects of known gold content (you can buy a set of karat needles at a jeweler's supply house or gem wholesaler). Using the aqua regia for higher than ten karats, apply an acid covering over all the marks at once. *The two marks that disappear at the same time are the same karat.* If the needle mark disappears first, leaving the object mark, the item is of a higher karat content than the testing needle. Testing kits are manufactured by J.N.T. Company of· Stormville, NY 12582. (We paid $30 for ours, bought locally.)

SILVER TESTING

There are two or three tests for silver content. In Britain, sample scrapings are weighed and then dissolved in nitric acid. The resulting solution is titrated with a solution of sodium chloride, and its flocculence indicates the degree of base metals in the alloy, if any. A simple nitric acid test for silver is that a single drop, on a filed-edge surface, will turn *plated silver* green and *coin silver* black. Pure nitric acid on .925, or sterling silver, leaves a cloudy spot on the object; while on silver of .750 or lower, the stain shows greener with progressively less pure silver content. Again, a touchstone test with another silver item of known purity will give a more accurate reading.

CAUTION: Nitric acid is a powerful compound. If the test object is not of high gold or silver content, you may well end up with a deeply pitted blemish that must be buffed out. Store all testing solutions in labeled glass containers with nonmetallic lids. Use a glass rod to transfer acid from bottle to work surface. Never pour water into acid. Add the stronger to the weaker solution. If spilled, flush with water and neutralize with baking soda.

Chapter 32

COSMETIC FURNITURE REFINISHING

A Little Bit Is Better than a Lot

There really is no need to become a slave to furniture refinishing. Resolve before you start refinishing to purchase only pieces that can be cosmetically restored. *Avoid the frequent mistake* made by neophyte dealers who rush out and buy the first barnful of "bargain" furniture they find. Some of these bargains will take years to make shop-ready. If you've already made this mistake, my advice to you is to take everything to an auctioneer and put your money back to work buying quality pieces with most of the original finish intact.

If you enjoy refinishing furniture and restoring bric-a-brac, fine! You can make a pile of money, if you employ your talents on upper-end merchandise. It takes the same amount of man hours to refinish a $45, 1920s kitchen chair as it does to reglue a fine old Windsor that could bring up to $800 in its original paint. It takes only a little bit longer to refinish a $1,500 rolltop desk than it does a "plain Jane" sideboard perhaps worth only $150, and difficult to sell at any price.

You must use your own workshop time to its very best advantage, or you may end up working as a hired hand in someone else's back room. Don't feel that you have to "skin" every piece of scratched, dented, and water-stained furniture you acquire for resale. Depending upon the age of the piece and the region that you are selling in, you could be destroying 90 percent of its retail value *the minute you sand away the original finish!* Here on the West Coast, a lot of dealers use a liquid chemical blend appropriately called Howard Restor-A-Finish (Howard must be rich by now, my own consumption being about a pint a day). Nicks, scratches, and faded areas disappear instantly when you rub a little of this "snake oil" into most neglected wooden surfaces. Howard's is available from Howard Finish Restorers, Inc., 411

A note found in a drawer of this wonderful highboy stated that it had been bought in 1894 and was to remain unfinished. Courtesy Maine Antique Digest

West Maple, Monrovia, CA 91016. It comes in seven shades and is applied with a pad of #0000 steel wool and wiped off a few moments later with a soft cloth. The only drawback to this product is that (although it is not sticky) it takes forever to dry to the point where it won't leach onto wallpaper, textiles, or books (the lingering oil stains will not endear you to a customer who has to rewallpaper a living room). We have resolved this problem by following the application of Restor-A-Finish a day later with several coats of clear lacquer or semigloss Deft (both available in throwaway spray cans).

Some enterprising dealers have concocted their own finish "restoring" formulas, employing various volatile liquids such as denatured alcohol, lacquer thinner, shoe polish, linseed oil, olive oil, turpentine, and diluted oil stains. If you hit on the right combination you could sell a million cans of the stuff. Try a little fine steel wool (#0000) and some type of oil or polish on all but the roughest furniture before you commit yourself to the time and trouble involved in a complete refinishing job! The most popular "quickie" finish (after chemically stripping off old varnish and paint) is a fifty-fifty mixture of turpentine and boiled linseed oil (you can also tint this mixture with artist's oils or a little oil-base wood stain). Just slop it on liberally with a large old paint brush and let it stand and soak in for an hour or so before wiping it off. The results will amaze you.

Avoid the Use of Water on Any Cleanup Chore. Mineral spirits will usually get the job done. Water is the natural enemy of wooden furniture. It raises the grain, warps the boards, and undermines the holding power of the old finish by swelling the fibers near the surface. If you have to apply it, use a damp cloth and dry immediately. Water, if not wiped quickly from a finely finished wood surface, will soon penetrate all but the thickest varnish and create objectionable light spots. Sometimes this can be remedied by the application of a little paste wax with #0000 fine steel wool to the damaged area. Another effective technique is to press through a clean thick blotter with a warm (not hot) electric iron until the spots disappear.

Water- and Alcohol-Caused Rings. On newer furniture, these can almost always be removed with the rottenstone and oil method. Rottenstone is available at most paint or hardware stores. Put a few drops of salad oil on the damaged area and sprinkle on enough rottenstone to make a fine paste. Using a soft cloth, rub briskly in the direction of the grain of the wood. Clean it off often to check the restoration with the undamaged finish. Try to achieve the same degree of gloss before a final waxing and polish. If you can't find any rottenstone, try silver polish, wet cigar ashes, linseed oil, or toothpaste and then rewax.

Deep Scratches. In most finishes you can camouflage scratches by using the thick residue at the bottom of a can of oil-based stain or by the careful application of artist's oil colors. First, clean off all of the wax so that the color will sink in (use paint thinner or naptha). Take a #00 pointed red sable artist's brush and apply the lightest shade of opaque stain or oil colors first (add a drop of japan, or cobalt, drier to speed drying). When the first color coat is dry, take the same pointed brush and drop in the secondary colors which appear on the original finish but are interrupted by the scratch. Let your artwork dry overnight and coat it with a clear lacquer, varnish, or shellac that will not bubble the original finish or the touched-up area. (You will have to experiment on a hidden sample area that you created at the same time you touched up the exposed scratch.) It sounds difficult, but once you have accumulated a few baby food jars full of various shades and mixes of opaque stains or oil pigments (with dried samples on their lids), the whole touchup game is quite simple. Remember, work from light to dark; it's impossible to cover dark colors with lighter transparent shades! Other "quickie" scratch fillers are colored putty sticks, paste shoe polish, melted crayons, and model airplane cement.

Burns and Deep Gouges. These will require scraping and filling before you can practice your retouching artistry. You can't just sand away burn marks. Professional furniture touchup men use *colored shellac sticks* that are melted and applied with a heated spatula (use a clean heat source, such as an alcohol burner or a hot plate, not a sooty candle flame). Press the melted shellac off the stick and into the hole with the spatula. Level the patch with a final swipe of the clean, hot blade, and then sand down the area with the finest emery paper and tint with stain powders. If no more retouching is needed, buff the patch and the sur-rounding area with #0000 steel wool and rewax or apply a thinned-down clear finish that doesn't react with the old one. A final buffing may be needed later to match the two surface sheens. Stick Shellac is available in twelve colors from: *Constantine's Catalog/Yearbook* (send $1.50 postage), 2050 Eastchester Road, Bronx, NY 10461.

Refinishing. Refinishing secondhand furniture is probably one of the most popular American pastimes. Everybody tries it soon-er or later (although reactions can be mixed). Millions of dollars are spent annually on strippers, stains, varnishes, lacquers, and abrasive compounds, and new products are constantly being developed.

The amount of refinishing that you do depends upon just how much you value your time and your health. After half a century as the key ingredient in most paint-removing products, *benzene* has been removed because of its link to blood and bone cancer. Many of the strippers and solvents remaining on the market to-day can still be quite harmful if used indoors or ingested through the skin by prolonged direct contact. If you are working in a garage or indoors, *all doors and windows must be open* and *a powerful exhaust fan kept running at all times!* Aprons, goggles, and gloves are also a must. CAUTION: Water heaters, furnaces, pilot lights, and other heat sources with open flames have been known to blow careless refinishers into the next world!

Such are the hazards of making a living with one's hands; may-be you had best hire out the stripping and concern yourself only with the finishing fun! *Hot dips, cold tanks, foam on, flow on,* and *hand stripping* are a few of the choices you have among commer-cial finish removers. The latter two are the mildest, and some-times you even get chairs back in one piece (tank strippers are hard on glued joints). Rates vary from area to area, but the fol-lowing chart will give you a ballpark figure to add to the cost of any piece you might purchase which is in need of stripping. These prices do not include sanding to prepare for stain appli-cation. The broad price range includes latitude for the size and intricacy of each piece and for whether varnish or paint finishes are being removed.

Some dealers find that local teenagers are eager to strip furniture at inexpensive hourly rates. Or social service agencies might be able to put you in touch with handicapped people who have had experience working with the trade.

RECENT RATES FOR FURNITURE STRIPPING

Chairs . . . .$ to $14	House Doors . . . . 14 to $ 40	
Rockers . . . .$10 to $25	Wardrobes . . . . $ 50 to $100	
Tables . . . .$20 to $45	Desks . . . . $ 30 to $ 65	
Dressers . . . .$15 to $45	Rolltops . . . . $ 50 to $150	
Beds . . . .$14 to $50	Secretary/Bookcase $ 40 to $120	
Sewing Machines . . . . .$10 to $16	Pianos . . . .$125 and Up	
China Cabinets . . . .$35 to $65	Stool or Bench . . . . $ 15 to $ 20	
Pie Safes . . . .$35 to $65	Washstand . . . . $ 20 to $ 30	
Hoosier Cupboards . . .$50 to $75	Bookcases—per section . . . .$ 15	
Iceboxes . . . .$30 to $60	Hall Trees . . . . $ 25 to $ 75	

There are two basic types of stripper/remover. One is watery and good for varnish removal without disturbing the stain too much. The other is a creamy paste that clings and works on the surface longer; it is good for painted items. Both are best rinsed with lacquer thinner rather than water.

If you are going to strip it yourself, work outside, in the shade, on a sixty- to eighty-degree day, for best results. If it's too hot, the gunk dries up too fast to penetrate the surface coating. And if it's too cold, little or no amalgamation takes place.

Start by pouring a little (well shaken) remover into a coffee can. Apply liberally with an old pig bristle brush, flowing it on without any pressure on the first couple of coats. Allow the remover to stand for at least twenty minutes before you try to scrape it off with a round-cornered putty knife (file off the points). If it doesn't act like soft butter against the flat edge of the knife, then slop on some more remover and take a lunchbreak. If it still does not yield easily after an hour of repeated application, then you have a casein-based, or buttermilk, paint, which must be sanded off or waxed, and sold as is.

Let the chemicals do most of the hard work for you. After you have gently removed the bulk of the old finish with a putty knife, apply a fresh coat of remover and approach the piece with a bowl of lacquer thinner and a pad of #2 or #3 steel wool. Saturate the pad with thinner and rub the remaining gunk off. On dainty surfaces, or on the final cleanup, use a finer grade steel wool, like #0, also dunked in lacquer thinner. Before the piece has dried, wipe it clean with a soft lint-free rag. Now is the time to do any detailed cleanup of crevices or turnings that require added attention. Use a toothbrush, or a brass wire brush, dipped in lacquer thinner to scrub out the still-soft muck in these recesses. Don't wait until the next day to do this or you will have to apply the stripper all over again!

After an overnight drying, you can make a decision as to what degree of "skinning" needs to be done, if any. If the original stain is still there, minus its gloss, no sanding may be necessary. All you have to do is apply a tinted finish restorer, like Howard's, or a fifty-fifty linseed oil and turpentine mix (or perhaps a Tung Oil finish). Again, if you use Howard's, be sure to seal it with several light coats of spray lacquer or Deft the next day.

Remember that after stripping, you must allow at least an overnight drying before sanding or staining. Sand with grain only. Cross-grain sanding will produce scratches that will show after spray finishing. Use the lightest grade of sandpaper possible to do the job. Don't try to remove every minute scratch in the piece or it will no longer look like an antique! Work on a table at chest level; don't spend the day bent over in a tiring position. After a light machine sanding using nothing coarser than #120 carbide paper, finish up by hand with extremely fine grades of paper from #150 to #320, and dust off thoroughly before applying the stain. (Flint sandpaper is no good. Garnet is better. Aluminum oxide is okay. Carbide is best.)

We prefer opaque stain vs. oil stain because these lacquer-thinner or alcohol-based stains dry immediately and have a better penetrating, coloring, and covering quality than oil stains. We don't normally use water-based stains because they raise the grain. However, they are noted for resisting sun fade because they are pigmented rather than dye based. If you want to try an oil-based stain (good for softer woods), be careful about spray coating too soon after application; it may run. We add cobalt or japan driers to oil stains rather than waiting days for a "dry-to-touch" surface.

There are a hundred and one different possible finish combinations (and new ones come out every day). Entire books have been written on furniture staining techniques. We only attempt to lay down some ground rules. Besides, it's something you have to learn from experience.

Just as in stripping, work in a ventilated area on a nice day. Never do staining or finish spraying in direct sunlight, unless you want to do the whole process over again. Sunshine leaches little drops of stain out of the wood pores for a dimpled effect. Do all repairing and regluing *before* final sanding and staining. Make sure that you wipe off all the excess glue with a damp cloth immediately, or it will dry in the pores and later resist the stain (if it does, you can still touch it up later using opaque stains or artist's oil colors).

Regluing and Repairing. Regluing is not just a matter of squirting "Willhold" into every loose joint. It won't stick because of the dirt, oil, and wax always present. You must knock some furniture completely apart with a rubber mallet, after softening the old glue joints with warm water or vinegar. Sometimes you can get away with scraping inside, still-assembled, loose joints with a fine pointed X-acto knife and rinsing with a stiff brush dipped in alcohol or lacquer thinner. Allow the cleaned areas to bone dry and then apply a little glue and force sharpened match sticks (carved to fit) into any slack areas like chair rung joints. Wrap up the whole thing with lots of rope and let it stand overnight before proceeding with a final sanding and staining. Use a glue gun or a fine-pointed brush to get into hard-to-reach areas. Constantine sells a glue syringe needle for this purpose. We have been told of a highly regarded liquid wood "penetrator/expander" called Chair-Loc, which eliminates the need to reglue loose chair rungs.

If glue won't hold it—and the piece isn't an heirloom—use woodscrews, or dowels, across stubborn cracks (or into loose joints at an angle) when you reglue. Be sure to bore a slightly smaller hole than the screw threads, and also countersink the screw head so that it can be plugged or patched. Never use nails (except in predrilled holes) to hold loose joints or otherwise repair antique furniture. One hammer blow can destroy a week's work or shatter a century of care! We use nails only to replace original nails or to apply some types of molding on very soft woods. If in doubt, it's best to predrill nail holes with a tiny drill bit or a Moto-Tool. Predrilling all screw holes is a common practice to avoid splitting.

Deep gouges, broken corners, and broad cracks in unfinished furniture require attention before the final sanding and staining. You can carve a wooden plug to fill some recesses or you can fill them with one-eighth-inch layers of artist's acrylic modeling paste, or regular old plastic wood. The advantage of modeling paste is that it provides a white ground which will accept artist's oil, opaque watercolor, or acrylic colors with equal ease. The advantage of plastic wood is that you probably have some in the garage right now. Add a tad of lacquer thinner if it has started to harden in its can.

Plastic wood (the fiber type) is a miracle worker if you use it correctly! The secret is to provide this cellulose with a clean, recessed surface and lots of extra supports to cling to. You don't feather the edge of a hole to be repaired with plastic wood. You undercut its edges so that at least a one-sixteenth-inch patch thickness is assured. On deep holes, broad cracks, and broken corners, the trick is to insert several little nails or screws as structural supports (much like reinforced concrete construction rods), and drill some shallow holes to give the patch a much expanded surface to adhere to. Fill the area with firmly pressed-in layers of moist plastic wood, no more than one-eighth-inch thick at a time. Allow one full hour drying time between one-eighth-inch coats so the plug will not sag. Sand down the slightly overfilled patch a day later, stopping just short of the original surface to switch to a very fine grade of carbide emery paper (#180 to #320). The patch should almost glisten with smoothness.

After staining the whole surface, the patch will have to be matched to the original surrounding grain and coloration *before* a final finish spray is applied. Purchase a few tiny tubes of artist's oil and a two-ounce bottle of japan, or cobalt, drier at an art supply store. The most often used colors will be yellow ochre, burnt sienna, burnt umber, raw sienna, raw umber, and ivory black. Add one drop of drier and a drop or two of rectified turpentine to a blob of color and mix well with a palette knife. It's wise to prepare several tints of premixed color on a scrap of cardboard that you can lay near the wood patch to see which color mixtures blend best with the two or three predominant colors in the surrounding wood. Brush on the *lightest* basic color that you have observed in the adjacent wood, then move to a #00 fine-pointed sable brush and paint in the secondary stripes that also appear in the surrounding wood. After the two or three basic shades are laid down and are dry, take a final close look at the *grain pattern* of the area to be matched. Then apply those final delicate darker lines or flecks which make your miniature oil painting look like a piece of natural wood. If there are lighter line variations that you can't paint in, try scratching through to the nut brown tone of the plastic wood with a pin or X-acto knife. Allow to dry overnight and spray finish the whole piece with Krylon Clear Finish, spray lacquer, or Deft. Use extremely light spray coats or your patch will run together into a solid puddle of muddy color.

"Brushed-on" finishes are a lot of hassle and never come out as nicely as a $1.95 spray can job. Be sure to try the finish spray on a sample before you attempt to coat a freshly stained object. A "tac" coat (an extremely light, fogged on spray) will help seal the stain and keep it from running. Don't rush a spray job; take several coffee breaks before applying the final coat. Four light coats are better than two medium ones! Most shops that do more than one or two finishing jobs a week use an air compressor and a spray gun. Deft can be left in a spray gun for days at a time without skinning over. You can also use the air supply to dust pieces after sanding or to flatten out runs in a clear coat before they dry.

Supplies.   A craftsman is no better than his tools, and your local hardware store may not carry all the refinishing supplies that you need to do a professional job. In addition to half a dozen shades of lacquer-based wood stains, shellac sticks, and powdered stains, you will need some sable artist's brushes, tubes of oil paint, acrylic colors, opaque water colors, turpentine, linseed oil, paint thinner, denatured alcohol, lacquer thinner, plastic wood, white glue, and contact cement. These are all everyday ingredients in the furniture refinishing trade. Catalogs of the mail-order houses catering to furniture craftsmen are real eye openers. They not only show pictures and prices of odd tools, finishing compounds, veneers, and hardwoods but also give detailed instructions on how to use them. A few firms offering catalogs are:

- *Constantine's Woodworkers Catalog,* 2050 Eastchester Road, Bronx, NY 10461 ($1.50)
- *Craftsman Wood Service Catalog,* 2729 South Mary Street, Chicago, IL 60608
- *Garrett Wade Hand Tool Catalog,* 302 Fifth Avenue, New York, NY 10001 ($1)
- *Sears Craftsman Power and Hand Tool Catalog* (free from any Sears Roebuck store)

Confirmed woodworking buffs, as well as those in need of more instruction, will also enjoy the monthly magazine *Fine Wood Working,* $12 a year from the Taunton Press, 52 Church Hill Road, P. O. Box 355, Newton, CT 06470. It's written and illustrated by a group of master craftsmen in an easy-to-understand style that covers everything from furniture finishing to carving ball-and-claw feet.

If you have a lot of patience, you can learn to restore glass, china, paper, oil paintings, sculpture, silver, lamps, frames, rugs, furniture, and so forth from three books:

- *The Antique Restorer's Handbook,* by George Grotz. Doubleday and Company, Garden City, NY 11530
- *How to Restore China, Bric-a-Brac and Small Antiques,* by Raymond F. Yates. Gramercy Division of Crown Publishers, Inc., One Park Avenue South, New York, NY 10016

- *Restoring and Preserving Antiques,* by Frederic Taubes. Watson-Guptill Publications, New York, NY 10036

You should own these books, anyway. They will remove much of the mystery and folklore surrounding the repair of antiques, and you will be surprised at how elementary many restorations can be!

Chapter 33 METAL PROCESSING TECHNIQUES

Effortless Brass Polishing and Other Secrets

The average antique dealer doesn't have the slightest idea what to do with dirty, rusty, corroded, or peeling metal objects. You will be surprised at how many of these hopeless-looking finds can also be "cosmetically" upgraded.

As in cleaning an oil painting, it is best to use the weakest solvent that will get the job done. Who knows what delicate Victorian stencil or pinstriping may be beneath the grime on a piece of cast iron! Cleaning naphtha, mineral spirits, and kerosene are common degreasers. More powerful solvents are lacquer thinner, methyl ethyl ketone (MEK), plain old paint remover, and household oven cleaner (which is a lye compound). Regular cleaning naphtha can be used over and over again, simply by letting the sediment settle to the bottom of the bucket you are using and pouring the lighter (cleaner) liquid back into an airtight container. Using a solvent-saturated bristle brush, scrub the oil and dirt off and allow the piece to drain dry on some old newspapers. A sealer coat of matte spray lacquer may be the only further treatment necessary. A rusty patina is not ugly to look at if it is brushed and oiled, or given a sealer coat of clear spray lacquer. We routinely spray every sadiron, single tree, spur, branding iron, wood plane, or broad axe that we find. This simple step makes most ranch primitives into highly prized decorator items.

Before you seal the rust, remove any loose particles with steel wool, brush, or buffing wheel. If you don't have an electric grinder to mount your wire wheel on, simply clamp, or strap, your drill motor in a bench vise and use it with a wire brush attachment (leaving both of your hands free to manipulate the piece being cleaned). There are two grades of wire wheels and several diameters in each grade. Buy both fine and coarse wheels in two-inch, four-inch, and six-inch sizes and several wheel arbors to fit the chuck in your drill motor. Be sure to place an old carpet scrap under the wheel and wear thick leather gloves and apron when buffing! Even the most skilled buffers often lose their grip on the work in process.

P.S.: *Don't ever use a power tool without putting on safety goggles or full face shield. Ear plugs are also a must!*

Dainty (but dull and faded) painted surfaces, such as those found on old toys, scale faces, japanned tinware, and so forth, are easily brightened up with the application of a thin coat of household oil or paste wax.

Brass and copperware seem to sell better in most areas if they are highly polished. We are talking about tea kettles, wash boilers, andirons, blowtorches, and nautical hardware, not ancient bronzes or fine Oriental pieces, which should have their original patina left intact (or chemically reapplied if removed by a previous owner).

Most people are so brainwashed by trade-name advertising that they don't ever consider alternatives to prepackaged household cleaners (including brass and copper polishes). Half a lemon or a cup of vinegar, fine steel wool (#00), and a few tablespoons of salt make an excellent brass cleaner. Rinse under hot water and dry with a cloth. A final buffing should be done a day later to remove the haze caused by the acid eating away a layer of metal and grime. A goldlike effect can be obtained by using a hard commercial buffing wheel with a series of jeweler's rouges applied to it. Also known as buffing compound sticks, these are available from Sears Roebuck. Purchase several *industrial-grade* cloth buffing wheels, two to six inches in diameter, and arbors to adapt them to your drill chuck or bench grinder. Again, it's best to clamp your drill down to a stand or bench and leave both hands free to manipulate the work in progress. It takes a high-speed motor—1,200 to 1,500 R.P.M.—to achieve a mirrorlike finish.

Many novices have trouble cleaning copper and brass because they forget that it is often protected with several coats of clear lacquer. This factory sealer must be removed before any of the previously described buffing or cleaning techniques will work effectively. Simply remove accumulated lacquer and corrosion with conventional paste paint remover and steel wool, followed by a brief immersion in Lysol liquid toilet bowl cleaner (wear

Vintage photo from the author's collection

rubber gloves and a plastic face shield).* The liquid bowl cleaner is so powerful that it eliminates the need for lemon juice or
weaker acid cleaners. Wipe off the bowl cleaner with #00 steel
wool and rinse with water very thoroughly. Hand buff with
#000 steel wool the next day.

Nickel-plated items may be accumulated and sent to a metal
plating shop to be electrically stripped down to the underlying
copper or brass. Or, if you are impatient and want to do your
own thing, you can remove most of the nickel with an orbital vi-
brator sander and #180 silicon carbide emery paper or cloth.
The resulting crazed surface can be easily buffed to a high luster
with coarse black emery cake buffing compound applied to a
hard cloth wheel.

How many times have you passed up a scratched or dented
antique because you felt that the cost of removing the dent
would triple the price of your acquisition? Metal working is no

---

*People who don't know much about chemistry or cleaning can cook up some
very deadly chemical compounds in their homes without realizing it. Mixing
bleaches with an acid compound such as bowl cleaner will produce deadly chlo-
rine gas! Mixing bleaching agents with rust removers and oven cleaners can also
create other poisonous gases! Adding water to acid instead of acid to water can
also produce violent results!

more difficult than furniture refinishing; it just takes a different set of tools.

Have you ever watched an auto body-and-fender man at work? He basically just beats the metal until it more or less conforms to its original curvature. His tools are shaped like jeweler's tools, only much larger. After reshaping the metal, using a curved steel block on the inside and a smooth flat-faced hammer on the outside, he is left with a very scratched and dimpled surface. A few swipes with a file and a disk sander, and most of these irregularities disappear.

Jewelers use somewhat the same technique, but finish up with finer files and buffing compounds. Pick up a book on basic jewelry making and try your hand at straightening up some of that scrap sterling or those dented pocket watch cases. Gold and silver are the most malleable and easiest of metals to work with.

Never strip or repaint an antique metal item. Collectors prefer tools, toys, advertising signs, and tins with as much of the original finish as possible. This includes the rusty patina, which

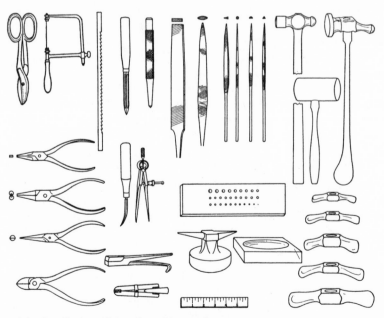

A basic selection of metal-working tools

should never be sanded or scratched with coarse abrasives. Repainted metal objects are almost impossible to sell. If you have purchased a painted piece and want to give it an "antique" finish, brush on some warm bacon grease and put your find in the kitchen oven at 400 degrees. Items too large to "grease and bake" can be "antiqued" by throwing them into a bonfire and leaving them outdoors for a month or two. Another "quickie patina" for painted surfaces is to apply a sloppy coat of walnut stain, drip dry, and leave in direct sunlight for two weeks. Shiny bare metal may be aged quickly by using a blowtorch, salt bath, acid treatment, or manure-pile burial. All of the above antiquing methods are commonly used to duplicate the ravages of time. A recently applied patina or quickie rust treatment usually can be detected by rubbing, or scratching with a fingernail—the pigment will come off.

Chapter 34 CONCLUSION

From Rags to Riches?

We are optimistic about the future of the antique business because it has always flourished in the civilized world. As people develop an excess of education, income, and leisure, they tend to seek out the fine and unusual in both home furnishings and personal adornment. History continually repeats this cycle. The supply of antiques is self-perpetuating. In 1845, upon attending an estate auction in New England, Henry Thoreau wrote, "After lying half a century in his garret and other dust holes these things were not burned. Instead of a bonfire, there was an auction, an increasing of them! The neighbors eagerly collected to view these items, bought them all, and carefully transported them home to their garrets and dust holes to lie until their estates are settled, when they will start again." And so it is today. As each generation passes on, their collections are ultimately dispersed on the open market. Each succeeding generation of collectors appreciates items of twenty years or so less vintage than those esteemed by their parents, and, as Thoreau observed, the cycle repeats, and feeds itself, ad infinitum.

Can one make a fortune in the antique business today? Yes, but you can make it faster and easier in almost any other type of retail endeavor! To grow rich in any small business you must multiply yourself, and your successful operation, with competent employees at additional promising locations. The very nature of the antique business does not lend itself to the idea of a help-run branch with an absentee owner. If you cannot contain a burning ambition to become rich, attempt to get there slowly by expanding a profitable operation at one giant location.

Most full-time antique shop operators feel they must gross at least $35,000 a year to stay in business (at a commercial location). From this figure upward to an annual sales volume of $250,000 is where the bulk of the business takes place in the antique trade today. At the other end of the spectrum are literally thousands and thousands of part-time dealers who are thrilled to achieve sales of even $50 a day. Many of the dealers we interviewed described their business ventures as profitable hobbies or tax writeoffs. In other words, a great number of those who seem to be very active in the trade aren't really making any money! Most of these "dealers" simply enjoy handling beautiful things or traveling and dealing with interesting people.

If you are still thinking seriously about making the move into full-time antique dealing, now is the time to begin putting your financial house in order. Antique dealers don't buy furniture, clothes, or automobiles on the installment plan. Cash and carry is the rule rather than the exception. Paychecks will no longer arrive with computer-programmed regularity, and it is impossible to predict gross sales from one month to the next. The oft-quoted saying to the effect that it takes three years to break even in a new business is very true. If you have a growing family to support and cannot capitalize your venture at the ideal $15,000 to $25,000 figure, we suggest you get started as a weekend entrepreneur. A few hundred dollars can launch you as a picker, auction consignor, show dealer, flea market vendor, or yard sale operator. When you have gained enough confidence and experience at one of these levels, you can seek a business loan.

Again, we stress the fact that *broad knowledge is essential to survival and success in a field where most deals are made on the basis of one party knowing appreciably more than the other!* You can gain this knowledge the hard way, from experience, or in a much shorter time by subscribing to at least half a dozen of the collector publications listed on the following pages. As a self-employed capitalist, literally living by your wits, you must be in a position to fathom and exploit every buying or selling opportunity that comes your way. Trade periodicals provide constant exposure to the facts, trends, prices, and markets necessary for survival in an extremely competitive game. The more you read, the luckier you will become!

The real riches to be gained from participation in the business of antiques are intangible. What value can be placed on the sense of adventure, independence, and fulfillment that comes with succeeding in any self-started enterprise? If you are willing to put up a substantial amount of cash, work long hours at home as well as in the shop, remain flexible, cheerful, and optimistic during the days when no customers darken your door, then the antique business may be for you!

SELECTED READING MATERIAL

There are currently more than two thousand different antique and collectible titles in print, and new titles are being brought out at a rate of more than five hundred a year. Less than a third of the new books offered may be of any real value to the antique dealer, and book reviews in trade publications are often inconsistent. It would be wise, at first, to order only those titles currently held in favor by advanced collectors or recommended by fellow dealers. Our purpose in presenting this exhaustive list is to illustrate the fact that instant antique knowledge is readily available today. Those who buy, or sell, in ignorance are really without excuse.

TRADE AND COLLECTOR PUBLICATIONS
(Featuring Material of Value to Dealers)

AB Bookman's Weekly. P. O. Box AB, Clifton, NJ 07015 ($3 for sample copy)

American Collector. Drawer C, Kermit, TX 79745 ($1 for sample copy)

Antique & Collectors Mart. 15100 West Kellogg Street, Wichita, KS 67235

Antique Dealer. Ebel-Doctorow Publications, 1115 Clifton Avenue, Clifton, NJ 07013 ($1 for sample copy)

Antique Monthly. P. O. Box 2274, Birmingham, AL 35201 ($1 for sample copy)

Antique Trader Weekly. P. O. Box 1050, Dubuque, IA 52001 (75 cents for sample copy)

Antiques & Art Weekly. Independent Magazines Ltd., Bridge House, 181 Queen Victoria Street, London EC4V 4DD, England ($1.50 for sample copy)

Antiques and the Arts Weekly. Bee Publishing Co., Newtown, CT 06470 (35 cents for sample copy)

Antiques Trade Gazette (weekly). Metropress Ltd., Langley House, 116 Long Acre, London WC2E 9PA, England ($1 for sample)

Antiques World. 122 East 42nd Street, New York, NY 10017 ($3)

Art & Antiques. 1515 Broadway, New York, NY 10036 ($3.50)

Art & Auction. 250 West 57th Street, New York, NY 10019 ($3.50)

Collectors News. 606 Eighth Avenue, Grundy City, IA 50638 ($1 for sample copy)

Hobbies. 1006 South Michigan Avenue, Chicago, IL 60605 ($1.50 for sample copy)

Magazine Antiques. 551 Fifth Avenue, New York, NY 10017 ($4)

Maine Antique Digest, "The Marketplace for Americana." Box 358, Waldoboro, ME 04572 ($1 postage for sample)

The Ohio Antique Review. P. O. Box 538, Worthington, OH 43085

Additional Trade and Collector Periodicals.   Newspapers, magazines, and club publications are listed in both *Ayer Directory* and *Ulrich's Periodical Directory* (both available at the public library).

POPULAR REFERENCE BOOKS AND PRICE GUIDES
Books and guides that are priced and illustrated are marked (P & I). Those without prices are marked (N P).

Advertising—Signs, Tins
American Beer Can Encyclopedia. Thomas Toepfer. Gas City, Ind.: L-W Promotions (P & I)

Antique Advertising Encyclopedia. Ray Klug. Gas City, Ind.: L-W Promotions (price guide available)

The Beer Book: An Illustrated Guide to American Breweriana. Will Anderson. Des Moines: Wallace-Homestead Books (N P)

The Illustrated Guide to Collectibles of Coca-Cola. Cecil Munsey. New York: Hawthorn Books (N P)

Official Coca-Cola Collectibles Price Book. Cecil Munsey and Allan Petretti. 21 South Lake Drive, Hackensack, N.J. 07601: The Nostalgia Publishing Co. (P & I)

Old Advertising, Food, Beer, Tobacco, etc. Jim Cope. 5513 Hwy. 290W., Austin, Tex.: Great American Publishing Co. (P & I)

Antiques—General Price Guides

American Country Antiques. Don and Carol Raycraft. Des Moines: Wallace-Homestead Books (P & I)

Americana at Auction. S. Pennington, T. Voss, and L. Solis-Cohen. New York: E. P. Dutton (P & I)

The Antique Trader Quarterly Price Guide. Dubuque, Iowa: Babka Publishing (P & I)

Antiques and Their Prices. E. G. Warman. Uniontown, Pa.: Warman Publishing (P & I)

Collector's Identification and Value Guide to Antiques. Lar Hothem. Florence, Ala.: Books Americana (P & I)

Collector's Identification and Value Guide to North American Indian Artifacts. Lar Hothem. Florence, Ala.: Books Americana (P & I)

Know Your Antiques. Ralph and Terry Kovel. New York: Crown Publishers (N P)

Kovels' Complete Antiques Price List. Ralph and Terry Kovel. New York: Crown Publishers (P & I)

Lyle's Antiques and Their Values. Galashiels, Scotland: Lyle Publications. Distributed in the U.S. by Apollo Books, Poughkeepsie, N.Y. (P & I)

Lyle's Official Antiques Review. Galashiels, Scotland: Lyle Publications. Distributed in the U.S. by Apollo Books, Poughkeepsie, N.Y. (P & I)

Official Price Guide to Antiques and Collectibles. Grace McFarland. Orlando, Fla.: House of Collectibles (P & I)

Pictorial Price Guide to American Antiques. Dorothy Hammond. New York: E. P. Dutton (P & I)

Primitives and Folk Art, Our Handmade Heritage. Catherine Thuro. Paducah, Ky.: Collector Books (P & I)

Primitives, Our American Heritage. Katherin McNerney. Paducah, Ky.: Collector Books (P & I)

Wallace-Homestead's Price Guide to Antiques. Des Moines: Wallace-Homestead Books (P & I)

Art—Paintings, Prints, Drawings, Sculpture

Art Deco and Other Figures. Bryan Catley. Poughkeepsie, N.Y.: Apollo Books (N P)

Art Sales Index. Richard Hislop. Weybridge, Surrey, Great Britain: Art Sales Independent Ltd. Distributed in the U.S. by Apollo Books, Poughkeepsie, N.Y. (P & I)

Auction Prices of American Artists. Richard Hislop. Weybridge, Surrey, Great Britain: Art Sales Independent Ltd. Distributed in the U.S. by Apollo Books, Poughkeepsie, N.Y. (P & I)

Benezit Dictionary of Artists (10-vol. set). Paris:Librairie Gründ(P&I)

A Biographical Index of American Artists. R. C. Smith. Poughkeepsie, N.Y.: Apollo Books (N P)

Bronze and Sculpture at Auction Around the World. William Edwin Day. Paducah, Ky.: Collector Books (P & I)

Bronze Sculpture of Les Animaliers. Jane Horswell. Poughkeepsie, N.Y.: Apollo Books (P & I)

Christie's Review of the Season (auction results). New York: Christie's (P & I)

Classified Directory of Artists Signatures. H. H. Caplan. Poughkeepsie, N.Y.: Apollo Books (N P)

Currier and Ives Prints. Frederic Conningham. New York: Crown Publishers (P & I)

Dictionary of American Painters, Sculptors, Engravers. Mantle Fielding. P. O. Box 38, Green Farms, Conn. 06436: Modern Books and Crafts (N P)

Dictionary of Artists (British 1760–1893). A. Graves. Poughkeepsie, N.Y.: Apollo Books (N P)

Dictionary of British Artists 1880–1940. J. Johnson and A. Greutzner. Poughkeepsie, N.Y.: Apollo Books (P & I)

Dictionary of British Steel Engravers of the 19th Century. Basil Hunnisett. Poughkeepsie, N.Y.: Apollo Books (N P)

Dictionary of Victorian Painters (British 1837–1901). Christopher Wood. Poughkeepsie, N.Y.: Apollo Books (N P)

Dictionary of Western Sculptors in Bronze (1700–1960). J. Mackay. Poughkeepsie, N.Y.: Apollo Books (N P)

Folk Art in America, Painting and Sculpture. J. T. Ericson. New York: Mayflower Books (N P)

Gordon's Print Price Annual (18,000 auction prices). Poughkeepsie, N.Y.: Apollo Books (P & I)

International Auction Records (26,000 listings). E. Mayer. Poughkeepsie, N.Y.: Apollo Books (P & I)

Lyle Official Arts Review. Galashiels, Scotland: Lyle Publications. Distributed in the U.S. by Apollo Books, Poughkeepsie, N.Y. (P & I)

Mallet's Index of Artists: International-Biographical. Poughkeepsie, N.Y.: Apollo Books (N P)

National Academy of Design Exhibition Records (1861–1900).
Poughkeepsie, N.Y.: Apollo Books (N P)
*New-York Historical Society Dictionary of Artists in America Before
1861.* New York: New-York Historical Society (N P)
Sotheby Parke Bernet, Art At Auction. New York: Sotheby Parke
Bernet (P & I)

Autographs

Autographs and Manuscripts: A Collector's Manual. E. Berkeley. New
York: Charles Scribner's Sons (N P)
The Book of Autographs. Charles Hamilton. New York: Simon and
Schuster (P & I)
Collecting Autographs and Manuscripts. Charles Hamilton. Norman,
Okla.: University of Oklahoma Press (N P)

Baskets and Boxes

American Basketry and Woodenware. William C. Ketchum. Wood-
ridge, Ill.: McMillan Publications (N P)
Antique Baskets and Basketry, A Collector's Guide. Frances Thomp-
son. Cranbury, N.J.: A. S. Barnes Co. (N P)
Baskets of Rural America. Roth Teleki. New York: E. P. Dutton (N
P)
Collecting Traditional American Basketry. Roth Teleki. New York:
E. P. Dutton (N P)
Neat and Tidy: Boxes Used in Early American Households. Nina F. Lit-
tle. New York: E. P. Dutton (N P)
Seat Weaving: A Manual for Furniture Fixers. L. Day Perry. New
York: Charles Scribner's Sons (N P)

Books

American Authors and Books, 1640–1970. W. J. Burke and W. D.
Howe. New York: Crown Publishers (N P)
American Book Prices Current (85 vols., international auction
prices). New York: Bancroft Parkman (P & I)
The Book Collector's Handbook of Values. V. A. Bradley. New York:
G. P. Putnam (P & I)
Bookman's Price Index (15 vols. price 600,000 books). Detroit:
Gale Research (P & I)
Bookman's Weekly (weekly trade publication). P. O. Box AB, Clif-
ton, N.J. 07015 (P & I)

Children's Books of the 19th Century. L. McCullough. Des Moines: Wallace-Homestead Books (P & I)

Comic and Science Fiction Books. Orlando, Fla.: House of Collectibles (P & I)

How to Identify and Collect American First Editions. Jack Tannen. New York: Arco Publishing (N P)

The Used Book Price Guide (3 vols.). Mildred S. Mandeville. 525 Kenmore Station, Kenmore, Wash. 98028 (P & I)

Bottles, Jars, Insulators

American Bottles and Flasks and Their Ancestry. H. McKearin and K. M. Wilson. New York: Crown Publishers (N P)

800 Insulators. B. Schroeder. Paducah, Ky.: Collector Books (P&I)

Kovels' Official Bottle Price List. Ralph and Terry Kovel. New York: Crown Publishers (P & I)

Official Price Guide to Bottles: Old and New. Dot and Carlo Sellari. Orlando, Fla.: House of Collectibles (P & I)

1,000 Fruit Jars. B. Schroeder. Paducah, Ky.: Collector Books (P & I)

Red Book of Fruit Jars. Alice M. Creswick. Paducah, Ky.: Collector Books (P & I)

The Illustrated Guide to Collecting Bottles. Cecil Munsey. New York: Hawthorn Books (N P)

Clocks and Watches

American Pocket Watch Indicator. Roy Ehrhardt. Kansas City, Mo.: Heart of America Press (P & I)

American Pocket Watches, Book 2. Roy Ehrhardt. Kansas City, Mo.: Heart of America Press (P & I)

Clock Guide: Identification with Prices. Robert W. Miller. Des Moines: Wallace-Homestead Books (P & I)

Clock Identification and Price Guide. Roy Ehrhardt. Kansas City, Mo.: Heart of America Press (P & I)

Collector's Price Guide to American Pocket Watches. David Criss. 330 Capac Road, Imlay, Mich. 48444 (P & I)

Foreign and American Pocket Watches. Roy Ehrhardt. Kansas City, Mo.: Heart of America Press (P & I)

The Price Guide to Clocks (British) 1840–1940. Alan and Rita Shenton. Poughkeepsie, N.Y.: Apollo Books (P & I)

Repairing Antique Clocks. Eric P. Smith. New York: Arco Publishing (N P)

Coins

Coin World (newspaper). P. O. Box 150, Sidney, Ohio 45365 (P & I)

Coinage (magazine). 17337 Ventura Blvd., Encino, Calif. 91316 (P & I)

A Guide Book of United States Coins, "Redbook." R. S. Yeoman. New York: Western Publishing Company (P & I)

Numismatic News (newspaper). Krause, Iola, Wis. 54945 (P & I)

Official Blackbook Price Guide of U.S. Coins. Orlando, Fla.: House of Collectibles (P & I)

Official Blackbook Price Guide of U.S. Paper Money. Orlando, Fla.: House of Collectibles (P & I)

Photograde, A Pictorial Guide to Grading. Q. David Bowers and James F. Ruddy. Bowers and Ruddy Galleries, 6922 Hollywood Boulevard, Los Angeles, Calif. 90028 (N P)

Dolls—Antique, Modern

Antique Collector's Dolls, I and II. Pat Smith. Paducah, Ky.: Collector Books (P & I)

Blue Book of Doll Values (4 vols.). Jan Foulke. Riverdale, Md.: Hobby House Press (P & I)

Collectible Black Dolls. John Axe. Riverdale, Md.: Hobby House Press (N P)

Collectible Patsy Dolls and Patsy Types. John Axe. Riverdale, Md.: Hobby House Press (P & I)

Collector's Encyclopedia of Dolls. Elizabeth and Evelyn Coleman. New York: Crown Publishers (N P)

Collector's Encyclopedia of Half-Dolls (pincushion). Frieda Marion and Norma Werner. New York: Crown Publishers (N P)

Dollspart (catalog of parts and reproductions). Dollspart Supply Co., 5–15 49th Avenue, Long Island City, N.Y. 11101 (P & I)

Doll Values—Antique to Modern. Pat Smith. Paducah, Ky.: Collector Books (P & I)

Focusing on Effanbee Composition Dolls. Jan Foulke. Riverdale, Md.: Hobby House Press (N P)

4th Antique Doll Price Guide. Marlene Leuzzi. P. O. Box 587, Corte
Madera, Calif. 94925 (P & I)
The Handbook of Doll Repair and Restoration. Marty Westfall. New
York: Crown Publishers (N P)
Kestner and Simon and Halbig Dolls. Pat Smith. Paducah, Ky.: Col-
lector Books (P & I)
Madame Alexander Dolls. Pat Smith. Paducah, Ky.: Collector
Books (P & I)
Modern Collector's Dolls, I, II, III, IV. Pat Smith. Paducah, Ky.:
Collector Books (P & I)
Schoenhut Dolls and Toys. Susan Manos. Paducah, Ky.: Collector
Books (P & I)

Flea Market Guides

The Antique Traveler's France. R. Long. 634 Bellmore, East Mead-
ow, N.Y. 11554
Europe's Hidden Flea Markets. R. Long. 634 Bellmore, East Mead-
ow, N.Y. 11554
Fleamarket U.S.A. (quarterly directory). Rt. 1, #470, Canton-
ment, Fla. 32533
Guide to the Antique Shops in Britain (annual). Poughkeepsie, N.Y.:
Apollo Books
Swap Meet U.S.A. (semiannual directory). P. O. Box 272, Sagi-
naw, Mich. 48606

Furniture

American Antique Furniture, Vols. I and II. E. Miller, Jr. New York:
Dover Publications (N P)
American Country Furniture, 1780–1875. Ralph and Terry Kovel.
New York: Crown Publishers (N P)
Antique American Country Furniture—A Field Guide. Thomas M.
Voss. Philadelphia and New York: J. B. Lippincott Co. (N P)
Antique Oak Furniture. Conover Hill. Paducah, Ky.: Collector
Books (P & I)
The Current Antique Furniture Style and Price Guide. George Grotz.
Garden City, N.Y.: Doubleday and Co. (P & I)
The Easy Expert in Collecting and Restoring American Antiques. More-
ton Marsh. Philadelphia and New York: J. B. Lippincott Co.
(N P)

Field Guide to American Victorian Furniture. Thomas H. Ormsbee. Sparks, N.Y.: Bonanza (N P)
Fine Points of Furniture. Albert Sack. New York: Crown Publishers (N P)
Furniture Treasury, Volumes I, II, and III (reprint). Wallace Nutting. Woodridge, Ill.: McMillan Publications (N P)
An Illustrated Guide to Shaker Furniture. Robert Meader. New York: Dover Publications (N P)
The Marketplace Guide to Oak Furniture Styles and Values. Peter S. Blundell. Paducah, Ky.: Collector Books (P & I)
Stickley Craftsman Furniture Catalogs (reprint). New York: Dover Publications (N P)

Glass

American Glass. George and Helen McKearin. New York: Crown Publishers (N P)
Art Glass Nouveau. Ray and Lee Grover. Rutland, Vt.: Tuttle Co. (N P)
The Cambridge Glass Book. Harold and Judy Bennett. Des Moines: Wallace-Homestead Books (N P)
Cambridge Glass I and II (reprinted manufacturer's catalogs). Paducah, Ky.: Collector Books (P & I)
Carnival Glass Price Guide. Sherman Hand. Paducah, Ky.: Collector Books (P & I)
Carved and Decorated European Art Glass. Ray and Lee Grover. Rutland, Vt.: Tuttle Co. (P & I)
Collector's Encyclopedia of Depression Glass. Gene Florence. Paducah, Ky.: Collector Books (P & I)
Colored Glassware of the Depression. Hazel Marie Weatherman. Springfield, Mo.: Weatherman Books (priced supplement available)
Early American Pattern Glass, I and II. Alice Metz. Paducah, Ky: Collector Books (P & I)
Emile Galle. Phillip Garner. New York: Rizzoli International Publications (N P)
Encyclopedia of Victorian Colored Pattern Glass (4 vols.). William Heacock. Des Moines: Wallace-Homestead Books (P & I)
English Cameo Glass. Ray and Lee Grover. New York: Crown Publishers (P & I)

French Cameo Glass. Henry and Berniece Blount. Des Moines: Wallace-Homestead Books (N P)

Heisey's Glassware: Pressed Ware Catalogue. Harold E. Wiley. Des Moines: Wallace-Homestead Books (price guide available)

Heisey's Lead Blown Glassware. Des Moines: Wallace-Homestead Books (price guide available)

Kovels' Illustrated Price Guide to Depression Glass and American Dinnerware. Ralph and Terry Kovel. New York: Crown Publishers (P & I)

Lalique for Collectors. Katharine McClinton. New York: Charles Scribner's Sons (N P)

Libbey Glass Since 1818. Carl U. Fauster. P. O. Box 7269, Toledo, Ohio 43615: Len Beach Press (N P)

Milk Glass. E. M. Belknap. New York: Crown Publishers (N P)

Pairpoint Glass. Leonard Padgett. Des Moines: Wallace-Homestead Books (N P)

Pocket Guide to Depression Glass. Gene Florence. Paducah, Ky.: Collector Books (P & I)

The Standard Cut Glass Value Guide. Joe Evers. Paducah, Ky.: Collector Books (P & I)

Wallace-Homestead Guide to Antiques and Pattern Glass. Robert W. Miller. Des Moines: Wallace-Homestead Books (P & I)

Jewelry—Antique, Modern

Creative Gold and Silversmithing. Sharr Chote and Bonnie C. De May. New York: Crown Publishers (N P)

Gem Testing. B. W. Anderson, Buchanan, N.Y.: Emerson Books (N P)

Handbook of Gemstone Identification. R. Liddicoat. Santa Monica, Calif.: Gemological Institute of America (N P)

Jeweler's Circular-Keystone (retailer's trade publication). Radnor, Pa.: Chilton Co. (P & I)

The Jeweler's Manual. R. Liddicoat and L. Copeland. Santa Monica, Calif.: Gemological Institute of America (N P)

Jewelry Repair Manual. R. Allen Hardy and John J. Bowman. New York: Van Nostrand Reinhold (N P)

Official Guide to Antique Jewelry. Arthur G. Kaplan. Orlando, Fla.: House of Collectibles (P & I)

Old Costume Jewelry, 1870–1945. Lynn Sallee. Florence, Ala.: Books Americana (P & I)

100 Years of Collectible Jewelry. Lillian Baker. Paducah, Ky.: Collector Books (P & I)

Price Guide to Jewelry 3,000 B.C.–*1950* A.D. Michael Poynder. Poughkeepsie, N.Y.: Apollo Books (P & I)

Van Nostrand's Standard Catalog of Gems. John Sinkankas. New York: Van Nostrand Reinhold (N P)

Kitchen Items

American Kitchen Collectibles. Mary Lou Matthews. Gas City, Ind.: L-W Promotions (P & I)

Butter Molds, An Illustrated Value Guide. Jim Trice. Paducah, Ky.: Collector Books (P & I)

Early American Kitchen Antiques. Don and Carol Raycraft. Des Moines: Wallace-Homestead Books (N P)

From Hearth to Cookstove: Kitchen Collectibles 1700–1930. Linda C. Franklin. Orlando, Fla.: House of Collectibles (P & I)

Graniteware. Fred and Rose Booher. Paducah, Ky.: Collector Books (P & I)

Lamps

Aladdin, The Magic Name In Lamps. J. W. Courter. Des Moines: Wallace-Homestead Books (P & I)

Art Nouveau and Art Deco Lighting. A. Duncan. New York: Simon and Schuster (P & I)

Bradley and Hubbard Lamps (catalog reprint). Drawer Y, Washington Mills, N.Y. 13479: Gilded Age Press (P & I)

Early 20th Century Lighting Fixtures (current values). Paducah, Ky.: Collector Books (P & I)

Evolution of the Night Lamp. Ann G. McDonald. Des Moines: Wallace-Homestead Books (price guide available)

Handel Lamps and Fixtures (catalog reprint). Drawer Y, Washington Mills, N.Y. 13479: Gilded Age Press (P & I)

Jefferson and Pittsburgh Lamps (catalog reprint). Drawer Y, Washington Mills, N.Y. 13479: Gilded Age Press (P & I)

Lamps: A Collector's Guide. James Paton. New York: Charles Scribner's Sons (N P)

Louis C. Tiffany's Glass, Bronzes and Lamps. Robert Koch. New York: Crown Publishers (N P)

Oil Lamps: Kerosene Era in North America. Catherine Thuro. Des Moines: Wallace-Homestead Books (P & I)

Pairpoint Lamps, St. Aubin (catalog reprint). Drawer Y, Washington Mills, N.Y. 13479: Gilded Age Press (P & I)

Military—Firearms and Edged Weapons

The Collector's Pictorial Book of Bayonets. Frederick J. Stephens. New York: Hippocrene Books (N P)

The Firearms Price Guide. David Byron. New York: Crown Publishers (P & I)

Flayderman's Antique Firearms Guide. Norm Flayderman. New Milford, Conn. 06776 (P & I)

Lyle's Official Arms and Armour Review. Galashiels, Scotland: Lyle Publications. Distributed in the U.S. by Apollo Books, Poughkeepsie, N.Y. (P & I)

Military Collectibles. R. H. Rankin. Orlando, Fla.: House of Collectibles (P & I)

The Price Guide to Antique Guns and Pistols. Peter Hawkins. Poughkeepsie, N.Y.: Apollo Books (P & I)

Robert Abels Inc. (retail catalog of antique weapons). Hopewell Junction, N.Y. 12533 (P & I)

Shotgun News (newspaper of the firearms trade). P. O. Box 669, Hastings, Nebr. 68091 (P & I)

Swords and Other Edged Weapons. Robert Wilkinson-Latham. New York: Arco Publishing (N P)

World War II German Collectibles. J. Kaduck. Des Moines: Wallace-Homestead Books (P & I)

Music—Records, Instruments

American Premium Record Guide. Less Docks. Des Moines: Wallace-Homestead Books (P & I)

Catalog of Books and Repair Manuals (antique pianos, music boxes, gambling machines, jukeboxes, organs, radios, and phonographs). Vestal, N.Y.: Vestal Press (P & I)

Collectible Rock Records. R. C. Hill. Orlando, Fla.: House of Collectibles (P & I)

Encyclopedia of Automatic Musical Instruments. Q. David Bowers. Vestal, N.Y.: Vestal Press (N P)

Music Collectibles. S. Gould and R. Fredericks. Orlando, Fla.: House of Collectibles (P & I)

Olde Records Price Guide: 1900–1947. Peter A. Soderbergh. Des Moines: Wallace-Homestead Books (P & I)

Player Pianos and Music Boxes. Harvey N. Roehl. Vestal, N.Y.: Vestal Press (N P)

78 RPM Records and Price Guides. Peter A. Soderbergh. Des Moines: Wallace-Homestead Books (P & I)

Violin Identification and Price Guide. Roy Ehrhardt. Kansas City, Mo.: Heart of America Press (P & I)

Oriental Art and Rugs

The Collector's Book of Jade. Arthur and Grace Chu. New York: Crown Publishers (N P)

Oriental Antiques and Collectibles. Arthur and Grace Chu. New York: Crown Publishers (N P)

Oriental Art (*Lyle's Antiques and Their Values* series). Poughkeepsie, N.Y.: Apollo Books (P & I)

Oriental Carpets. U. Schurman. Poughkeepsie, N.Y.: Apollo Books (P & I)

Oriental Cloisonné and Other Enamels. Arthur and Grace Chu. New York: Crown Publishers (N P)

Oriental Rugs (*Lyle's Antiques and Their Values* series). Poughkeepsie, N.Y.: Apollo Books (P & I)

Oriental Rugs, An Updated Guide. Charles Jacobsen. 401 South Salina Street, Syracuse, N.Y. 13201 (P & I)

Price Guide to Oriental Antiques. Sandra Andacht. Des Moines: Wallace-Homestead Books (P & I)

The Wonderful World of Netsuke. Raymond Bushell. Rutland, Vt.: Tuttle Co. (N P)

Paper Americana—Printed Ephemera, Political Items, Song Sheets, Sports Memorabilia

American Sheet Music, 1775–1975. Daniel Priest. Des Moines: Wallace-Homestead Books (P & I)

The Buyer's Guide for Comics (newspaper). 15800 Rt. 84, North East Molina, Ill. 61244 (P & I)

Collecting Political Americana. Edmund B. Sullivan. New York: Crown Publishers (includes some general price guidelines)

Comic Book Price Guide. Robert Overstreet. New York: Crown Publishers (P & I)

Currier and Ives Prints. Frederic Conningham. New York: Crown Publishers (P & I)

The Democratic Art, Pictures for 19th Century America, Chromo Lithography. Peter Marzio. Boston: Godine (N P)

Encyclopedia of Political Buttons (3 vols.). Theodore L. Hake. P. O. Box 1444, York, Pa. 17405: Americana and Collectibles Press (P & I)

Louis Prang: Victorian Color Lithographer. Larry Freeman. Watkins Glen, N.Y.: Century House (N P)

Official Guide to Paper Collectibles. William Rodger. Orlando, Fla.: House of Collectibles (P & I)

Paper Collectibles. Robert D. Connally. Florence, Ala.: Books Americana (P & I)

The Sport American Baseball Card Price Guide. James Beckett and Dennis Eckes. Cleveland: William Collins Publishers (P & I)

The Sports Collector's Bible. Bert R. Sugar. Indianapolis: Bobbs-Merrill (P & I)

Photographs—Cameras

Cameras, from Daguerreotypes to Instant Pictures. Brian Coe. New York: Crown Publishers (N P, 600 drawings)

Collecting Old Photographs. Margaret Haller. New York: Arco Press (N P)

Collecting Photographica. George Gilbert. New York: Hawthorn Books (P & I)

Collecting Photographs: A Guide to the New Art Boom. Landt and Lisl Dennis. New York: E. P. Dutton (P & I)

The Photograph Collector's Guide. L. Witkin and B. London. New York: New York Graphic Society (N P, the definitive reference, 437 pages)

The Photographica Collector's Price Guide. George Gilbert. New York: Hawthorn Books (P & I)

Photographs: A Collector's Guide. Richard Blodgett. New York: Ballantine (P & I)

Price Guide to Antique and Classic Cameras. James M. McKeown. P. O. Box 36, Grantsburg, Wis. 54840: Centennial Photo Service (P & I)

Vintage Cameras and Images: An Identification and Value Guide. John Maloney. Florence, Ala.: Books Americana (P & I)

Postage Stamps

Harris Catalog of Postage Stamp Prices, U.S. and Canada (retail dealer catalog). H. E. Harris and Co., Box O, Boston, Mass. 02117 (P & I)

How to Detect Damaged, Altered and Repaired Stamps. Paul W. Schmid. P. O. Box 373, Huntington, New York 11743: Palm Press (N P)

Linn's Stamp News (newspaper). P. O. Box 150, Sidney, Ohio 45365 (P & I)

Scott Specialized Catalog of U.S. Stamps. New York: Scott Publishing Co. (P & I)

Scott Standard Postage Stamp Catalog. New York: Scott Publishing Co. (P & I)

Postcards

The American Postcard Guide to Tuck. Sally S. Carver. 179 South Street, Chestnut Hill, Mass. 02167 (P & I)

Collectors Guide to Postcards. Forrest Lyons. Gas City, Ind.: L-W Promotions (P & I)

International Postcard Market Yearbook. J. H. D. Smith. 30 Shirley Avenue, Old Coulsdon, Surrey CR31 1QW, England: IPM Promotions (P & I)

Rare and Expensive Postcards: Book I. John M. Kaduck. Des Moines: Wallace-Homestead Books (P & I)

Rare and Expensive Postcards: Book II. John M. Kaduck. Des Moines: Wallace-Homestead Books (P & I)

Pottery and Porcelain—Dinnerware, Figurines

American Pottery and Porcelain. D. Robinson and B. Feeny. Orlando, Fla.: House of Collectibles (P & I)

The Book of Pottery and Porcelain (rev. edition). Warren E. Cox. New York: Crown Publishers (N P)

China For America: Export Porcelain 18th and 19th Centuries. Herbert and Peter Schiffer. Exton, Pa.: Schiffer Publishing (N P)

Chinese Export Porcelain: Standard Patterns and Forms. Peter, Herbert, and Nancy Schiffer. Exton, Pa.: Schiffer Publishing (N P)

Collector's Encyclopedia of Fiesta. Sharon and Bob Huxford. Paducah, Ky.: Collector Books (P & I)

Collector's Encyclopedia of Limoges Porcelain. Mary F. Gaston. Paducah, Ky.: Collector Books (P & I)

Collector's Encyclopedia of Nippon Porcelain. Joan Van Patten. Paducah, Ky.: Collector Books (P & I)

Collector's Encyclopedia of Weller Pottery. Sharon and Box Huxford.
Paducah, Ky.: Collector Books (P & I)
Collector's Handbook of Marks on Porcelain and Pottery. A. Peterson
and E. Paul, eds. Des Moines: Wallace-Homestead Books (N P)
Dictionary of Marks. Ralph and Terry Kovel. New York: Crown
Publishers (N P)
A Dictionary of Marks: Ceramic, Metal, Furniture. Margaret McDon-
ald-Taylor. New York: Hawthorn Books (N P)
Encyclopedia of Roseville Pottery. Sharon and Bob Huxford. Padu-
cah, Ky.: Collector Books (P & I)
European Pottery and Porcelain. P. J. Atterbury. New York: May-
flower Books (N P)
Guide to American Art Pottery. Ralph and Terry Kovel. New York:
Crown Publishers (N P)
Haviland China, Volumes I and II. Gertrude T. Jacobson. Des
Moines: Wallace-Homestead Books (N P)
Hummel Art. John F. Hotchkiss. Des Moines: Wallace-Homestead
Books (P & I, annual price supplement available)
The Kovels' Illustrated Price Guide to Royal Doulton (all items).
Ralph and Terry Kovel. New York: Crown Publishers (P & I)
Noritake Collectibles. Lou A. Donahue. Des Moines: Wallace-
Homestead Books (N P, price guide available)
Occupied Japan Collectibles, I and II. Gene Florence. Paducah, Ky.:
Collector Books (P & I)
Porcelain Marks of the World. Emanuel Poche. New York: Arco
Press (P & I)
The Price Guide to 19th and 20th Century British Porcelain. D. Battie
and M. Turner. Poughkeepsie, N.Y.: Apollo Books (P & I)
Royal Doulton Figurine Price Guide. Mary Lou Yeager. Box 1042,
Williamsburg, Va. 23185 (P & I)

Primitives and Folk Art
American Bird Decoy. William F. Mackey. Exton, Pa.: Schiffer Pub-
lishing (N P)
American Folk Art in Wood, Metal and Stone. Jean Lipman. New
York: Dover Publications (N P)
American Folk Painters of Three Centuries. Jean Lipman. New York:
Whitney Museum (N P)
American Primitive Painting. Jean Lipman. New York: Dover Pub-
lications (N P)

East Coast Decoys of the Mid-Atlantic Region. Henry A. Flecken-
stein. Exton, Pa.: Schiffer Publishing (N P)
Folk Art in America: Painting and Sculpture. Jack T. Erickson. New
York: Mayflower Books (N P)
Folk Painters of America. Robert Bishop. New York: E. P. Dutton
(N P)
Pennsylvania Dutch American Folk Art. Henry J. Kauffman. New
York: Dover Publications (N P)
Primitives and Folk Art, Our Handmade Heritage. Catherine Thuro.
Paducah, Ky.: Collector Books (N P)
Wild Fowl Decoys. Joel Barber. New York: Dover Publications
(N P)

Reproductions—Limited Editions
Collector Prints (modern limited editions). Ruth Pollard. Orlando,
Fla.: House of Collectibles (P & I)
Confusing Collectibles (vols. I and II). Dorothy Hammond. Des
Moines: Wallace-Homestead Books (N P)
Gifts & Decorative Accessories (trade publication). 51 Madison Ave-
nue, N.Y. 10010: Geyer McAllister Publications (P & I)
Giftware Business (trade publication). 1515 Broadway, New York,
N.Y. 10036 (P & I)
*Kovels' Price Guide for Collector Plates, Figurines, Paperweights, and
Other Limited Edition Items.* Ralph and Terry Kovel. New York:
Crown Publishers (P & I)

Restoration, Repair, Refinishing
The Antique Restorers Handbook. George Grotz. Garden City, N.Y.:
Doubleday and Co. (N P)
The Artist's Handbook of Materials and Techniques. Ralph Mayer.
New York: Viking Press (N P)
The Care and Repair of Antiques. J. Ridley. New York: Sterling Pub-
lishing Co. (N P)
The Furniture Doctor. George Grotz. Garden City, N.Y.: Double-
day and Co. (N P)
How to Restore China, Bric-a-Brac. Raymond F. Yates. New York:
Gramercy Press (distributed by Crown Publishers) (N P)
Restoring and Preserving Antiques. Frederic Taubes. New York:
Watson-Guptill Publications (N P)
Woodworker's Catalog (all refinishing supplies). 2050 Eastchester

Road, Bronx, N.Y. 10461: Albert Constantine and Son, Inc.
(P & I)

Sewing—Tools, Textiles, Needlework

Antique and Unusual Thimbles. JoAnne Rath. Cranbury, N.J.: A. S.
Barnes Co. (N P)

Book of a Thousand Thimbles. Myrtle Lundquist. Des Moines: Wallace-Homestead Books (N P)

Button Parade. Dorothy F. Brown. Des Moines: Wallace-Homestead Books (N P)

A Gallery of American Samplers. Glee F. Krueger. New York: E. P.
Dutton (N P)

A Gallery of Amish Quilts. Robert Bishop and Elizabeth Safanda.
New York: E. P. Dutton (N P)

Old Time Tools and Toys of Needlework. Gertrude Whiting. New
York: Dover Publications (N P)

101 Patchwork Patterns. Ruby S. McKim. New York: Dover Publications (N P)

The Standard Book of Quilt Making and Collecting. Marguerite Ickis.
New York: Dover Publications (N P)

Traditional Patchwork Patterns. Carol B. Grafton. New York: Dover Publications (N P)

Silver—Flatware, Hollowware, Plate, Pewter

American Silver Flatware, 1837–1910. Noel D. Turner. Cranbury,
N.J.: A. S. Barnes Co. (N P)

American Silver and Silver Plate. Dorothy N. Robinson. Orlando,
Fla.: House of Collectibles (P & I)

American Silverplate. Ivan and Dorothy Rainwater. Des Moines:
Wallace-Homestead Books (N P)

Book of Old Silver. Seymour B. Wyler. New York: Crown Publishers (N P)

Directory of American Silver, Pewter, and Silverplate. Ralph and Terry Kovel. New York: Crown Publishers (N P)

Encyclopedia of American Silver Manufacturers. Dorothy T. Rainwater. New York: Crown Publishers (N P)

A History of American Pewter. C. F. Montgomery. Winterthur, Del.:
Winterthur Museum (N P)

The Magazine Silver (bimonthly publication). P. O. Box 22217,
Milwaukie, Oregon 97222 (P & I)

The Price Guide to Victorian Silver. Ian Harris. Poughkeepsie, N.Y.: Apollo Books (P & I)

Silver Auction Records (Teaspoons to Wine Coolers). Baile De La Perrierre. Poughkeepsie, N.Y.: Apollo Books (P & I)

Sterling Silver, Silverplate, and Souvenir Spoons. Gas City, Ind.: L-W Promotions (P & I)

Tools—Farm, Woodworking

American Woodworking Tools. Paul B. Kebabian. New York: New York Graphic Society (N P)

Ancient Carpenters' Tools. Henry C. Mercer. New York: Horizon (N P)

Antique Tools, Our American Heritage. K. McNerney. Paducah, Ky.: Collector Books (P & I)

The Chronicle (quarterly publication of the Early American Industries Association). c/o Mrs. P. B. Kebabian, 11 Scottsdale Road., South Burlington, Vt. 05401 (P & I)

Dealer Catalog: B. Steere. 110 Glenwood Drive, N. Kingstown, R.I. 02852 (P & I)

Dealer's Catalog: The Mechanick's Workbench. P. O. Box 544, Marion, Mass. 02738 (P & I)

A Museum of Early American Tools. Eric Sloane. New York: Ballantine (N P)

Toys—Cast Iron, Tin, Lead

Antique Toy World (magazine). 3941 Bell Plaine, Chicago, Ill. 60618 (P & I)

Art of the Tin Toy. David Pressland. New York: Crown Publishers (P & I)

Cast Iron and Tin Toys of Yesteryear. Don Cranmer. Gas City, Ind.: L-W Promotions (P & I)

Collecting Antique Marbles. Paul Baumann. Des Moines: Wallace-Homestead Books (P & I)

Collecting Model Farm Toys. Raymond E. Crilley and Charles E. Burkholder. New York: E. P. Dutton (includes price range)

Collecting Toys. Richard O'Brien. Florence, Ala.: Books Americana (P & I)

Dictionary of Toys Sold in America, I and II. Earnest A. Long. P. O. Box 272, Mokelumne Hill, Calif. 95245 (P & I)

Disneyana, Walt Disney Collectibles. Cecil Munsey. New York: Hawthorn Books (N P)

Encyclopedia of Toys and Banks. Don Cranmer. Gas City, Ind.: L-W Promotions (P & I)

Greenberg's Price Guide to Lionel Trains, 1901–1942. Bruce C. Greenberg. New York: Crown Publishers (P & I)

Illustrated Mechanical Bank Book. Kenneth Griffith. P. O. Box 323, Sea Girt, N.J. 08750 (P & I)

Illustrated Radio Premium Catalog and Price Guide. Tom Tumbusch. Des Moines: Wallace-Homestead Books (P & I)

INDEX

Illustrations are noted in *italics*.